LITERARY PRIMITIVISM

LITERARY PRIMITIVISM

Ben Etherington

STANFORD UNIVERSITY PRESS
STANFORD, CALIFORNIA

Stanford University Press
Stanford, California

Printed in the United States of America on acid-free, archival-quality paper

Library of Congress Cataloging-in-Publication Data

Names: Etherington, Ben, author.
Title: Literary primitivism / Ben Etherington.
Description: Stanford, California : Stanford University Press, 2017. |
Includes bibliographical references and index. |
Identifiers: LCCN 2017028665 (print) | LCCN 2017031111 (ebook) |
ISBN 9781503604094 (electronic) | ISBN 9781503602366 (cloth : alk. paper)
Subjects: LCSH: Primitivism in literature. | Literature—History and criticism—Theory, etc. | Literature, Modern—20th century—History and criticism.
Classification: LCC PN56.P7 (ebook) | LCC PN56.P7 E86 2017 (print) |
DDC 809/.9145—dc23
LC record available at https://lccn.loc.gov/2017028665

Typeset by Bruce Lundquist in 10/14 Minion

For Norman

The Earth has become one place, instead of a romantic tribal patchwork of places.

Wyndham Lewis

Thought remains faithful to the idea of immediacy only in and through what is mediated; conversely, it falls prey to the mediated as soon as it tries to grasp the unmediated directly.

Theodor Adorno

Rediscovering tradition, living it as a defence mechanism, as a symbol of purity, of salvation, the decultured individual leaves the impression that the mediation takes vengeance by substantializing itself.

Frantz Fanon

CONTENTS

PREFACE

Primitivism was an aesthetic project formed in reaction to the zenith of imperialist expansion at the start of the twentieth century. As those spaces in which
"primitive" modes of existence were imagined to be possible either were directly colonized or otherwise forcibly integrated into a geographically totalized capitalist system, so dissenting spirits responded by trying to rekindle the
primitive by means of their art. As such, primitivism was a project specific to
this world-historical situation: an undertaking to become primitive in a world
where, it seemed, such a possibility had been voided.

The "primitive" condition toward which primitivist works aspire thus is constitutively speculative. Where once archaeology, history, travel reportage (including artistic impressions), and later ethnology had seemed to bring to those
residing in "civilization" knowledge about those leading supposedly "primitive"
forms of life, the global saturation of that form of "civilization," modern capitalism, meant that the "primitive" had either been lost or become irredeemably
mediated (that is, no longer primitive). If the idealization of the primitive, what
this study calls philo-primitivism, previously had tended to take the form of a
fixed representation, with the onset of the conditions that gave rise to primitivism, it fell to the transformative capacity of art to make possible the incarnation
of the primitive and the restoration of immediate experience.

The primitivist project was not restricted to Western artists, which is to
say, those situated in or near the metropolitan centers of the capitalist world-
system. It was an aesthetic mode taken up across its span. Indeed, artists from

colonized peripheral societies were the ones who most keenly felt the loss of unalienated social worlds, and it was they who most energetically pursued an aesthetics of immediacy. The most intensively primitivist works were written by the Martinican Aimé Césaire.

▮ ▮ ▮

Such is the understanding of primitivism advanced in the following study. Those familiar with the term and its usage in humanistic scholarship will recognize immediately that this understanding is at odds with the conventional view. Primitivism usually is considered as "the idealization of the idea of the primitive," and, in theory, it is a mode of idealization that can take hold in any given "civilized" society. In practice, though, it is thought to be a peculiarity of the modern "West," whatever that civilizational entity is reckoned to be. Scholarly effort thus has been directed at trying to work out why the advent of modern Western civilization should have prompted this kind of idealization. In recent years these questions have been posed almost exclusively in terms of ideology and discourse. Primitivism has been regarded as a unidirectional ideological projection from the colonizer onto the colonized: a racial and imperialistic "discourse" according to which Western artists and thinkers idealize those non-Western peoples whom they suppose to be "primitive." There were good reasons for this turn to discourse and ideology, especially in view of the undeniably racial character of the phenomenon. Naive assumptions about primitivism's good intentions were banished and its appropriative impulse exposed. It was cast from its once heroic place in the narrative of aesthetic modernism, especially in the visual arts, and the primitivist work of revered artists like Pablo Picasso and D. H. Lawrence came to be regarded with suspicion if not contempt. Lawrence's reputation, for one, has not recovered.

The purpose of this study is not to revisit primitivism thought of in such terms. It is, rather, to *change the object*. The assumptions that underpin the now conventional understanding of primitivism need to be interrogated in the light of methodological developments in literary studies and its significance reappraised. Most significantly, recent efforts to understand the systemic integration of literary cultures can help to open our eyes to the global nature of this aesthetic mode and to perceive that it was an aspiration in both the "West" and "non-West" (categories that this study will treat with a high degree of skepticism). A pariah term in recent scholarship, the idea that primitivism was only an ideological projection of those from the center of empire has meant that its most powerful expressions in the peripheries either have been overlooked or miscast as second-order appropriations. However vexed, primitivism holds an important place in the utopian memory of attempts to negate the social logic of globalizing capital. To recover primitivism's aesthetic force and political horizon, this study dismantles the reigning assumptions surrounding the concept before exploring the theoretical and interpretative possibilities made available by doing so.

Accordingly, the book is arranged into two parts. In the first part I revisit the scholarly debates concerning primitivism that have lain dormant for some years and set out the theoretical claims and historical argument that will enable us to reconceive of primitivism as an aesthetic phenomenon specific to the period of finance-driven imperialism. In the second part I undertake three detailed studies of literary primitivism, centered on the work of Aimé Césaire, D. H. Lawrence, and Claude McKay, respectively. This book does not chart a "rise and decline" chronological story, nor does it attempt a survey of literary works that might be regarded as primitivist. My central purpose is to make primitivism as present to readers as possible, working outward from its epicenter. It is only after we appreciate what Césaire achieved that we can get a firm hold on what was going on in the earlier primitivist efforts of Lawrence and McKay (and thence other primitivist works). The book's conclusion reflects on the politics of primitivism, especially what I will call its decolonial horizon, and asks in what respects we might consider this global aesthetic phenomenon to be a manifestation of world literature.

The intellectual mood that has given rise to the recent resurgence of the concept of "world literature" has also given impetus to my revisionist thesis. This is not, though, a study of primitivism and/as world literature. Rather, it is motivated by the return of what György Lukács called the "point of view of totality" to literary scholarship; more especially, it participates in the attempt to understand the purpose of literature in a capitalist world-system marked by the uneven and combined development of its constituent parts.[1] To think in terms of totality is to approach social phenomena as interrelated parts of a dialectically evolving whole. This is crucial for our understanding of both terms in the compound *literary primitivism*. It could not have manifested itself across the breadth of the world-system had there not been (1) a general sense that the space of the "primitive" had been colonized once and for all and (2) a pervasive belief in the transformative agency of aesthetic practice. The latter is what gave the primitivist project its method. Primitivists turned to the illusory and speculative capacity of artworks to reanimate the primitive remnant and reawaken the possibility of a social reconciliation with nature.

This study focuses on literary works, but its basic thesis pertains to primitivism across aesthetic media. Where postmodern critics interrogated primitivist discourse with little regard for the kinds of texts and objects in which it appeared, I am concerned with the specific potentialities of aesthetic materials. Owing to its inherently speculative nature, the wish for the primitive could only be realized in the kinesis of aesthetic making—by which I am referring to that manipulation of language that animates an image or notion and gives shape to literary form, or that activation of the enabling limits of genre so that an illusion might achieve presence. Primitivism, in short, does not call on literature to supply a representational medium but a material that can make manifest the primitive.

By way of illustration, and to raise the curtain on the kinds of literary expression with which this study will be concerned, we can look at the cutting up and rearranging of language in the following excerpt from a poem by Césaire:

> Barbare
> du langage sommaire
> et nos faces belles comme le vrai pouvoir opératoire
> de la négation
>
> (Barbarity
> of rudimentary language
> and our faces beautiful as the true operative power
> of negation)[2]

The enjambment that separates "operative power" from "of negation" has a peculiar effect on the syntax of these lines. If grammatical habit at first pushes us to read lines 3 and 4 as a single clause, the break emphasizes the syntactical parallelism of lines two and four ("of rudimentary language" and "of negation"). This might cause us to wonder whether the third line is paratactical, with the stanza reading as the beginning of a list of barbarities interrupted by a longer and incomplete statement about "our faces." The pull of the conjunctions is perhaps too strong, but the hesitation allows "barbarity" to attach itself to the final line as well as the second, an impression strengthened by further such parallelism in the next stanza. It puts into play a crisscross of equivalences that can be paraphrased: our faces are as beautiful as negation; negation is barbarous; ergo barbarity is beautiful.

There is nothing rudimentary, though, about the word *rudimentary* (sommaire). We might even detect the air of condescension that emanates from the sort of person who makes judgments about "barbarity," especially when, in the French, the half-rhyme with *barbare* gives it the tone of an adult playing with words for the pleasure of a child. The tinge of sarcasm is at odds with that which it proclaims. "This [i.e., barbarity] is the word that sustains me," the voice declares at the poem's outset, and when the voice later occupies the position of barbarity in the first person ("barbarity I the spitting cobra"), it arises from the incantatory wish to *become* barbarous. The aesthetic logic of these lines crystallizes the paradoxes of negritude, which, so goes the argument of this book, is the same as saying that it is a quintessential utterance of literary primitivism.

Négritude: a cultural movement of the black francophone middle class, which saw itself from two irreconcilable perspectives—as the civilized subject and barbarous object of European civilization—and which resolved to negate that civilization by giving itself over to its objectification as "Negro." If the "Negro" is barbarity, and barbarity negates civilization, negritude will become barbarous, says this poem. Reading on, we see that this is not purely a negation: barbarity sustains the speaker because it holds the promise of reincarnating "the dead circulating in the veins of the earth" who "smash their heads against the walls of our ears" with "screams of revolt never heard."[3] Primitivism seeks out the remnants of the extinguished primitive, but its orientation is to the undeclared future. Such are primitivism's contradictions and vectors of force.

The title and subject of Césaire's poem raise the question of conceptual boundaries for a study of primitivism. Do not the terms *primitive* and *barbarity* have quite different etymologies and semantic resonances? Is this not *barbarism*? Throughout this book we will encounter a series of terms whose family resemblances overlap but that also have quite distinct meanings, both in our time and the period in question: *primitive/primitiveness/primitivity, savage/savagery, barbarian/barbarous/barbaric, brute, primeval, archaic, primordial,* even *uncivilized, uncultured, native,* and *aboriginal*. If it appears at times that I am playing loose with important linguistic distinctions and nuances, I must emphasize that this study seeks to identify the *morphology* (or formal structure) of the primitivist mode. As Sinéad Garrigan Mattar has commented, primitivism "is not a thing, but a process."[4] The morphology of this process centers on the relationship between what I will call, after Ernst Bloch, the nonsynchronous primitive *remnant* and the literary means by which this is activated. It is a dialectical relation in which the remnant is transformed by the process of its activation, and its trajectory within the work undergoes modification accordingly. It is therefore not especially important which of the terms listed above might be in play (if any of them are explicitly called on at all). The task is to seize on the dynamic presence of the primitivist process in the work and to understand its historic character. I retain the term *primitivism* partly to accord with scholarly convention, partly because it was the term used most frequently in the period on which I will focus,[5] and partly because it has for some time had the widest semantic purchase.

To look squarely at primitivism's utopianism is not easy, traversing as one must the racial mediations endemic to the colonial world. It has thus become habitual simply to dismiss any artistic attempt to affirm the primitive as an act of essentialism. This may be true of many aspects of the works discussed, but we must keep in mind that utopianism aims for the nonexistent. We will see that racial representations and ideas are rarely fixed in primitivist works but tend to get discarded or transcended in the course of trying to renew the possibility of primitive experience. The coherence of the concept of primitivism rests on the structural unity of the imperial world, but this was an emphatically uneven system. I do not claim an equivalence between the modalities of primitivism that arose at different locations, within different literary spheres, and from different social positions within this totality, but I am asking why it is that the primitivist morphology articulates across the imperial totality at this time.

This study also reconsiders the politics of primitivism. If we cease to regard primitivism as a fantasy of the "Western" subject, we can no longer confine our attention to the political viewpoints of Europe and North America. There is no single answer to the question of primitivism's political valence; historical connections can be found with communism, fascism, white and black nationalism, communitarianism, and anarchism, all of which refract in unpredictable ways through the prism of aesthetic form. Across primitivist works, though, there is a common desire for a determinate negation of the world order that culminated in imperialist capitalism. This is what I will refer to as primitivism's *decolonial horizon*, a term to be distinguished from historical decolonization. Quite evidently, primitivism was just one form of the proliferation of radical utopianisms in the early to mid-twentieth century, though perhaps unique in its gravitation toward the perimeter of the imperial totality. I will identify primitivism's "epoch of possibility," to borrow a phrase from Rory Dufficy, which opens at the moment of finance-driven "Imperialism" (as defined contemporaneously by J. A. Hobson, Rosa Luxemburg, and others) and closes with decolonization and the hope that Third World internationalism could inaugurate an alternative social world.[6]

This book is a conceptual reappraisal of the notion of literary primitivism, and it focuses on those authorships and works that sit at its heart. Just as a study of the modernist novel will be drawn to a work of the magnitude of *Ulysses* or one of romanticism to *The Prelude*, so is there an inherent pull toward Césaire's negritude and the debates surrounding it. If the intention were to attempt a survey, I might have covered a range of less intensively primitivist works, such as we find in the primitivist strain of European surrealism or the Haitian writers who anticipated negritude. I might even have looked at a group like the self-proclaimed "Jindyworobaks," who emerged in the 1930s in Australia and for whom the injunction was to "make / music for the / dead tribes' sake."[7] In any case a truly encompassing study would need to look at primitivism across aesthetic media. As primitivism was neither a genre nor a school but a historically contingent aesthetic mode, its articulations do not sit within firm boundaries. There are many works in which we can perceive the primitivist impulse but that do not carry this impulse through, something that is evident in the discussion of Langston Hughes in Chapter 4. This book presents the beginnings of a new reckoning with primitivism, not its circumference.

The task of rethinking primitivism from the point of view of totality recommends itself at a time when the conditions that gave rise to it over a century ago are, in many respects, being repeated. The new realities of Imperialism produced a disconcerting claustrophobia at the start of the twentieth century. A world that hitherto had been perceived as a patchwork of incommensurate social realities suddenly appeared as a single lit-up social space, and consciousness had to cope with this absolute immanence. Our new "one world" consciousness, for which nature itself now appears subsumed into a world refitted for capitalist humans (the so-called Anthropocene), is forming at a time when the Internet is consolidating itself as humanity's sole communicative medium and commodity markets the sole means of acquiring necessary goods. We are experiencing a new, ever more extreme claustrophobia of immanence. The withering of faith in the human subject and the concomitant rise of the ideology of "posthumanism" and attendant postcreative notions of aesthetic production appear as the wishful thinking of those who feel helpless before these processes. From the perspective of capitalism's global maturation, literary primitivism reads as a prophetic scream. In meditating on its truth content we might gain perspective on the philosophical, aesthetic, and political blockages of our day.

❙ ❙ ❙

This project did not begin life as a general study of literary primitivism, and it was only reluctantly that I came to address such a large subject. It was not a matter of setting out to reevaluate primitivism so much as the necessity of doing so revealing itself to me as I tried to confine the study to manageable proportions. Chapter 7, which concerns the primitivist novels of Claude McKay, bears traces of an abandoned project on imperialism and literary representations of music. This morphed into a study of primitivism in the Anglophone and Francophone Caribbean when I first read Jean-Paul Sartre's "Orphée Noir," and for several years I tried to restrict the focus to this region. When I tried to explain the relation of Caribbean primitivism to primitivist writing elsewhere, however, I finally had to admit to myself that what I had thought was a Caribbean strain of the phenomenon was the thing itself and that literary primitivism in general would need to be recast.

The journey has been long, and the book is the result of critical discussions with many scholars. Priyamvada Gopal has been with the project from the start, and I hear her voice probing at the ideas as I write this tribute. Her enthusiasm and encouragement did not falter. In the other ear is the more calming voice of Adrian Poole, who nevertheless pulled the rug from under a number of certainties in the early stages. Timothy Brennan invited me to present an early draft of Part I at the University of Minnesota, and his responses gave me the confidence to take the broad view. Later, he closely scrutinized much of the manuscript, identifying significant areas that had been overlooked. Jarad Zimbler has been a stalwart friend throughout, smiling and nodding quizzically while I contradicted and then corrected myself, and doing much the same with respect to prose, which he had a great hand in sorting out. Neil Lazarus, David Trotter, Nick Nesbitt, and Nicholas Brown gave incisive critiques of the manuscript at various stages, and I have referred to their comments often even as the book moved beyond the material they critiqued. David Nowell Smith, Sean Pryor, Victor Li, Keya Ganguly, Rachel Malkin, and Georgina Born were all readers of great care. Anthony Uhlmann and Ivor Indyk have given me a welcoming home at the Writing and Society Research Centre at Western Sydney University, where this book largely has been written. I would also like to thank the following for their intellectual friendship and specific contributions that are too numerous to list: Anna Bernard, Jocelyn Betts, Rachel Bower, Leila Bright, Rory Dufficy, Kate Fagan, Damien Freeman, Josie Gill, Holly High, Simon Jarvis, Megan Jones, Sarah Milne, Warren Montag, Sascha Morrell, Desha Osborne, Elizabeth Pender, Gautam Premnath, Kate Prentice, Jeremy

Prynne, Catherine Rashid, Joshua Robinson, Catherine Trundle, Chris Warnes, Daniel Wilson, Christopher Wortham, and Mi Zhou. Emily-Jane Cohen and her editorial team at Stanford University Press have been buoyant in communication and rigorous in their work with the manuscript.

The kinship of Robbie Wood has pervaded this project, as has the love of Maddie Kelly. To my family, Nathan Etherington, Peggy Brock, and Norman Etherington, do I owe the most—for their help and support at every stage and, above all, for cultivating the instinct to take the opposing view.

LITERARY PRIMITIVISM

PART I

Primitivism Regained

Chapter 1

PRIMITIVISM AFTER
ITS POSTSTRUCTURAL ECLIPSE

A Conceptual Reappraisal

The title of this book might be taken to indicate an intention to survey its subject—a work similar in scope to the monographs, catalogues, and anthologies on primitivism in the visual arts that go back to Robert Goldwater's *Primitivism in Modern Painting*.[1] In literary studies it is a surprise to find only one monograph that addresses literary primitivism in general: Michael Bell's slim 1972 volume *Primitivism*. Even here the author refuses to be drawn into attempting a survey, choosing instead to concentrate on "critical problems raised by the literature to which this term is commonly used."[2] This reticence is connected, no doubt, with his sense that the term refers to a "dauntingly ancient and universal human characteristic with a correspondingly wide range of manifestations."[3]

If a survey of literary primitivism were to set its scope according to received usage, a rigorous account would indeed present challenges that could take a career to surmount. *Primitivism* typically refers to the act of idealizing people, or entities of any sort, deemed "primitive." It can be used even more broadly to refer to any activity that in some way pertains to the primitive. In both cases the term *primitive* is conceptually prior to "primitivism": it is the primitivity of the entity that determines the nature of the primitivist idealization. I will come to the difficult question of what the term *primitive* might signify shortly. For the moment it is enough to note that its resonances are specific to the material circumstances in which it is used and that it tends to point to a condition in which humans are united with nature. Michel de Montaigne's famous statement "On Cannibals" contains a comment that is broadly representative: "that blessed state of desiring nothing beyond what is ordained by their natural necessities."[4] Its conceptualization thus is dialectical, emerging where humans are aware of themselves in contradistinction to nature.

Given the conceptual priority usually assigned to historical notions of the "primitive" in discussions of primitivism, it seems only logical that a competent account, whether in literature, art, music, intellectual discourse, or culture more broadly defined, will need to begin by outlining a history of ideas of the "primitive" before moving to consider the forms of primitivism that correlate to those ideas. When we sketch the expanse that a survey study would reach if it undertook to cover the history of primitivism approached in this way, we can see why Bell found the prospect daunting, especially if it also attempted to synthesize the existing scholarship.

Such a study would encompass the work of an array of eminent thinkers, the most prominent of whom are the focus of scholarly fields in their own right (the likes of Montaigne, Thomas Hobbes, Jean-Jacques Rousseau, Charles Darwin, Karl Marx, and Sigmund Freud), not to mention the history of an entire discipline, anthropology, which was founded on the civilized/primitive distinction.[5] Current standards of historical research would not admit such an account unless it established the circumstances in which these theorists came to be concerned with the notion. At the very least this would entail a consideration of the history of European colonial expansion that brought those who considered themselves to be civilized into contact with the peoples and objects that they contraposed as primitive.[6] There are also the related scholarly discussions concerned with the country-city relationship and the question of the origins of humanity.[7]

Before turning to the literature, we would want to note that primitivism flourished in a variety of artistic media,[8] flagging multidisciplinary aesthetic movements like German expressionism, French surrealism, Italian futurism, and the Soviet avant-garde,[9] and the work of figures long associated with primitivism, such as Paul Gauguin, Pablo Picasso, Wassily Kandinsky, and Igor Stravinsky.[10] Maintaining a rigorous historicism, we would need to keep in frame the historical processes that brought into their paths the objects and texts that catalyzed their primitivism, such as the "discovery" of African masks in prewar Paris.[11]

Moving to literary texts, the relevant writers and works would need to be demarcated. This is easiest where writers have engaged demonstrably with the history of ideas or representations of the primitive—D. H. Lawrence, certainly.[12] T. S. Eliot's anthropological interests would require attention,[13] and, with him, surely W. B. Yeats, taking us to other Irish revivalists and modernists like J. M. Synge, Lady Gregory, and James Joyce.[14] Gertrude Stein's *Melanctha* has received attention as a primitivist work,[15] leading us to scholarship on the primitivism of other North American writers such as Sherwood Anderson, Ernest Hemingway, and William Faulkner.[16]

Thus enlarged, the scope still includes only canonical white Irish, British, and American modernists. There is the question of primitivism in Europe's "peripheries" such as Poland,[17] and scholarship of the last thirty years has shown repeatedly that the work of Europeans by no means exhausts modernism, leading us to writers whose work displays primitivist tendencies, even if their modes of intention are shaped by vastly different social circumstances and cultural projects.[18] The Jamaican Claude McKay cannot be ignored.[19] Nor can the New Negro movement with which he is conventionally associated, drawing in the likes of Jean Toomer, Countee Cullen, Zora Neale Hurston, and Langston Hughes: "I've known rivers ancient as the world and older than the / flow of human blood in human veins."[20] McKay's quest for a primal African self was important for the Caribbean and African writers who would form the Négritude movement in Paris in the 1930s, bringing us to the work of Aimé Césaire, Léopold Senghor, Léon Damas, and their peers.[21]

If the currents of influence move back and forth across the Black Atlantic, so, too, do they flow down the Seine.[22] We could hardly overlook the primitivist work of Guillaume Apollinaire, André Breton, Georges Bataille, Michel Leiris, and other literary surrealists with whom we might have started had our investigation been bilingual.[23] And it would be hard to maintain a bilingual focus. German expressionist writing is often considered literary primitivism's fulcrum.[24] Worse, we would soon discover that the attempt to limit ourselves to the domain of modernism is futile.[25] If we accept the claims of Erik Camayd-Freixas, we could not disregard hispanophone primitivism, especially in Latin America; so our study swells to encompass the writers he discusses, such as Alejo Carpentier, Miguel Angel Asturius, Juan Rulfo, and even Gabriel Garcia Marquez.[26] What of the primitivism of an indigenizing movement like the Jindyworobaks in 1930s Australia?[27] Likewise, it would be hard to keep the reins on chronology. Moving forward in time, the word has been used to discuss a number of postwar countercultural figures,[28] taking us in the direction of present-day anarcho-primitivism and Deep Ecology.[29] Moving backward, Michael Bell considers *Moby-Dick* to be archetypally primitivist, and there is James Baird's oft-cited study of Melville's work in terms of primitivism.[30] We would want to understand Robert Louis Stevenson's attempts to create literary forms that could synthesize Scottish and Polynesian legend.[31] If we were to follow Frances Connelly in tracing the lineage of primitivizing styles to the moment at which, she argues, the "primitive" comes to designate the binary opposite of Enlightenment Europe,[32] we would need to turn the clock back to the early eighteenth century, raising the painful possibility that we would be obliged to discuss the writers of the romantic movement, or at least spend time distinguishing primitivism from romanticism,[33] and perhaps naturalism too.[34] Then there is the huge body of scholarship on the "noble savage," a subject on which debates are hardly settled.[35] Diligent historicism would require that we now have in view European colonialism in the *longue durée*, not just its late-Victorian apotheosis.

How far back, exactly, would we need to go? Nagging at us would be the study that did the most to shift the discussion of primitivism from race to culture and that has remained current in scholarship for eighty years: George Boas and Arthur Lovejoy's *Primitivism and Related Ideas in Antiquity* (1935). It was the first installment of a projected multivolume work that aimed to index the entire history of primitivism up to their time. Not surprisingly, it remained unfinished.[36] Boas and Lovejoy do not consider primitivism a phenomenon solely of the modern era but a constant feature of Western civilization, if not all civilizations. Perhaps the template for our hypothetical survey will not be the authorcentric literary history that we set out with but something more along the lines of Edward Said's *Orientalism*. We might be tempted to speculate that primitivism is a transepochal binarizing "discourse" according to which the Civilized, in the very act of constituting themselves, *necessarily* define themselves against that which they are not, the Primitive, only, in despair at their alienation, to then idealize this Other. Primitivism would not be something confined to a particular civilization but more like a structure of desire inherent to civilized life. Literary primitivism might thus be understood as one kind of manifestation of this broader primitivist "discourse."[37]

As useful as such a metacritique of literary primitivism might sound, the present study will not be taking this path. I will argue that the prevailing assumptions that would lead to the ever-widening scope just outlined need to be reassessed and the phenomenon, if there is such a thing as "literary primitivism," brought newly into the open. My intention is to change the object of primitivism. The title *Literary Primitivism* thus indicates a conceptual reappraisal rather than a survey of primitivist writing as determined by received usage.

Four Theses

What I hope to establish in this first part of *Literary Primitivism* is that if we were to embark on the hypothetical study just outlined, we would lose sight of literary primitivism at the first turn—that is, the moment that we accepted that notions of the "primitive" are conceptually prior to primitivism—and that it would therefore be necessary to ground our study in ideas of the "primitive" before moving to consider their various historical idealizations. If we assume that ideas (or representations or discourses or ideologies) of the primitive prefigure primitivizing idealization, we have put the cart before the horse, though this metaphor should not be stretched too far: the surging primitivist yearning that seeks out particular notions of the primitive comes to know that it cannot realize itself through an external vehicle. To reach its destination it must itself *become* primitive and so break free of any prior primitive concept or representation. It will emerge that it is constitutive of primitivism to be always in the mode of transcending any determinate notion of the primitive.

This is not to say that primitivism has no representational (or ideological) content. As it attempts to make itself primitive, primitivism gropes for concrete evidence that such a condition is or has been possible, and it is through such reaching that primitivism makes itself apparent to us. That which is yearned for, however, is inherently unstable for historical reasons that I will discuss in detail. As such, the aesthetic phenomenon of primitivism is historically specific, coming at a moment when what I will call the primitive remnant was yet believed to be enchanted with an alternate world. To be clear, I am not suggesting that we should disregard historical conceptions of the primitive. Rather, the task is first to identify the circumstances in which the desire to *become* primitive through the agency of aesthetic experience took hold, before looking to any determinate notions of the primitive that might then have been in circulation. We will discover that "the primitive" is more like a dialectical principle of aesthetic exploration than something that can be nailed to any particular conception.

This may strike some as counterintuitive. In her learned study *Primitivism, Science, and the Irish Revival* Sinéad Garrigan Mattar astutely comments that "primitivism cannot be so easily pinned down because it is not a thing, but a process: a process of self-referential idealization that can constitute an ideology, a poetic mode, a form of satire, a social contract, a religious instinct, an intrusive element in a 'scientific' discourse, or an instrument of tyranny."[38] Pursuing this insight, she demonstrates that W. B. Yeats, J. M. Synge, and Lady Gregory shifted from a romantic into a modernist mode following their encounter with the new discipline of cultural anthropology. Effectively, she divides the process of primitivization into separate moments. First there are the fields of inquiry that produce ideas of the primitive and, subsequently, the thinkers and artists who pursue their idealization.

If it seems self-evident that primitivism must idealize ideas of the primitive, the grammar of such a definition already starts to obscure the idealizing motion at hand. Literary primitivism does not start with the mold of a notional primitive entity into which is poured its idealizing zeal. Primitivism is the shape of the idealization in question. Its source is not an idea or representation but the anguished yearning of discontent that seeks self-transformation toward the primitive. It is not an idea lurking somewhere in the work that the literary critic must excavate. It is the work's aspiration and potentiality. It is thus somewhat misleading to speak of primitivism "in" literature (or music or sculpture or other artistic media). When it is appreciated that primitivism is the activity of coming into the primitive, we realize that its literariness is essential to it.

This is not to say that we should pass over any ideological untruth discerned in particular acts of reaching for the primitive. But the untruth of reaching for *this* specific thing—say, Parisian painters for masks from West Africa—should not cast the idealization as only a false consciousness to be unmasked as another colonial habit of mind. While always keeping in view primitivism's deep entanglement in colonial reality, the task here will be to recover its longing. It is important, therefore, to be able to distinguish between primitivist longing and that which is longed for. For this we can adapt Ernst Bloch's concept of *nonsynchronicity*, a term he devised to characterize the ways in which the remnants of a society's past persist in shaping social expectations and practices when their immediate utility has lapsed.

Particularly useful is Bloch's distinction between "subjective" and "objective" nonsynchronicity. He develops these concepts when considering the conditions that enabled the success of Nazism. The experience of continually being overwhelmed by capitalism's creative destructions, of not being able to *keep up*, had caused a buildup of subjective anger among Germans; a curmudgeonly "not wanting of the Now."[39] At the same time, the *remnants*—and this is a crucial concept for my study—of technologies, social relations and practices from the past served as objective reminders of previous social realities. Gothic churches, for instance, stand for a once common theology, and the exigencies of their upkeep require the otherwise redundant skills of the stonemason. The fascists, he argues, successfully had steered nonsynchronous discontent with the current capitalist crisis toward an irrational affirmation of the remnants of the surpassed social reality.

We will return to Bloch in Chapter 3 when adapting the chronological notion of nonsynchronicity from a German to a broader imperialist context. For the moment he helps us to distinguish between the subjective *discontent* that prompts primitivism and the objective *remnant* to which it appeals when trying to imagine its ends and thus to reorient our discussion so that the former no longer is understood as only an ideological reflex symptomized by an appeal to the latter. Rather than speculate about ideas or discourses of the primitive that might have informed literary works, it will be better to look for the actual remnants that get drawn into and set into motion by primitivist works themselves. Jean-Claude Blachère puts it well in his study of André Breton's primitivism: "Primitivist writing . . . does not speak *about*, it speaks *like*; it does not have a subject but a project, that of the simultaneous metamorphosis of the writer in enunciating the primitive tribe and of the savage mask in the poem."[40] This does not align exactly with my conception of literary primitivism, but Blachère is unusual for having grasped the difference between a weak primitivism that merely concerns a "primitive" object or notion and an emphatic one that projects itself toward the social world perceived to be latent in it.[41]

The understanding of literary primitivism that proceeds from this conceptual reorientation can be distilled into the following theses:

1. Literary primitivism was a *project*. It strived to realize a primitive condition that was perceived to be at the point of obsolescence. As such, its destination was ultimately speculative and could not be reached by mimetic means only.

2. Literary primitivism was an *aesthetic* project. It sought transformation toward the primitive condition in and through the artwork, which served as the vehicle of its negation.

3. Literary primitivism was a project most energetically pursued at the height of European imperialist expansion, when the belief that there could be an actually existing and autonomous primitive way of life *somewhere else* was at its vanishing point.

4. Literary primitivism was a mode of aesthetic negation immanent to the capitalist world-system. It did not stand against "civilization" or "the West" but rather this new and all-pervasive form of social domination.

These claims are intended only to prepare the way for the readings that follow. They are not hypotheses to be tested analytically in sequence. We can only bring literary primitivism into the open through the interpretation of literary works.

Also, I am not suggesting that all usages and considerations of "primitivism" need be confined to these claims. The term rightly will continue to be used to refer to practices founded on ideas of the primitive or to that which has perceived primitive characteristics, and scholars in cultural studies and the history of ideas will inquire into and critique such phenomena as such usages dictate. Perhaps the most straightforward way of distinguishing what I will be calling *emphatic* primitivism is to consider in what way the *-ism* modifies the stem. Previous scholarship has tended to take the suffix as denoting either "the name of a system of theory or practice . . . founded on the name of its subject or object" or "forming a term denoting a peculiarity or characteristic" ("-ism," *OED*, 2a and 3). The gloss closest to the view of primitivism that is taken here is: "Forming a simple noun of action (usually accompanying a vb. in -IZE suffix) naming the process, or the completed action" (*OED*, 1a).[42] Literary primitivism is to be found where a process of transformation toward the primitive is being undertaken. It involves what we could call "primitivizing" acts of writing.[43] For this reason any attempt to circumscribe the subject by drawing up an itinerary of primitivist techniques would be pointless. The primitivism of a work can only be perceived in its aspiration and desire, qualities to be identified by attending to the dynamic relationship of its artistic elements.

Instead of considering primitivism as a cover concept for any idealization of a form of life reconciled with nature, the studies in this book seek to illuminate an emphatic primitivism. (The term *primitivism* henceforth will refer to "emphatic primitivism" unless otherwise indicated.) This can be contrasted with what I will call *philo-primitivism*, something that has a broader historical purchase, and whose tenets have been well articulated in a recent study of postwar French primitivism: "an expressed affinity for people or peoples believed to be living simpler, more natural lives than those of people in the modern West."[44] I will argue that emphatic primitivism was manifested within a much more specific historical zeitgeist during which it attained the illusion of artistic necessity.

It might well be asked: if you mean to foreground the action, the "-ism," of primitivism, why retain the stem? Are we dealing with *primitiv*ism or any activity that seeks an absolute break from modernity and aspires to the condition of "nature"? Certainly the way to address this is not to fall back into the habit of identifying conceptions of the "primitive" that are common to all primitivizations. This study is concerned with a morphology of process, not of ends, and the end in question is highly variable because the project is so tenuous. Here the historical dimension is crucial. Primitivism emerged when a window of opportunity opened between a relatively unselfconscious globalization of capitalism through various specific colonial acts and the moment when late capitalism appeared irrevocably to have subsumed all human communities— a sudden and vertiginous realization that all humans were about to be drawn irretrievably into this world-system but when the remnants of alternate realities yet appeared to have life. The *remnant*, thus, is essential, not because it supplies a complete image of the objective but because it contains within it the sense of a lost whole.

Primitivism's Poststructural Eclipse

To break with the intuition that sets ideas of the primitive in advance of any consideration of primitivism is to bring into question a cluster of world-framing assumptions that have produced and been produced by prevalent methodologies in literary and cultural studies, particularly those that have persistently steered criticism toward questions of representation and identity.

The apparent tendency of works typically identified as primitivist to idealize those peoples who, speaking broadly, Europeans once regarded as "primitive," "savage," or "barbaric" had been regarded with suspicion well before primitivism's deconstruction in the 1980s. Yet, given the inversion that valorized the "primitive" over the "civilized," scholars had not quite been able to put their fingers on what was wrong. In 1984 William Rubin could still claim that the notion that *primitivism* is pejorative "can only result from a misunderstanding of the origin and use of the term, whose implications have been entirely affirmative."[45] This comment comes in his introductory remarks to the catalogue of the widely discussed Museum of Modern Art exhibition *"Primitivism" in 20th Century Art: Affinity of the Tribal and the Modern*. If one were not so biddable, one might have spoken of infantilizing "stereotypes." Yet such criticisms seemed to require uncomfortable counterclaims regarding the actual realities of the falsely accused "primitive" peoples. The situation changed when scholars across the humanities began to focus concertedly on the ways in which representations are mediated by power. It could now be argued that representations that appeared to idealize outsiders, foreigners, or strangers of any kind might nevertheless unconsciously manifest a will-to-power over them. As there was no need to credit any truth claims outside the domain of representation, one did not need to justify one's critique by resorting to empirical evidence concerning these outsiders. The phenomenological category of "the Other" was mobilized to critique representations of "primitive" peoples from non-European societies in the circumstances of colonial expansion, and, henceforth, any consideration of primitivism would be obliged to pass through this concept.

Armed with the procedures of discourse analysis and deconstruction, scholars in the humanities were poised to dispatch primitivism with the same demystifying force that had just been applied to representations of the "Orient" by Edward Said. The galvanizing moment was the MoMA exhibition. Rubin, the head curator, had hoped to sidestep any need to consider in depth the historical relationship between European modernists and the cultures of the African and Oceanic objects they drew on by claiming that "primitivism" had to do with "the history of modern art" (*PT*, 319) and that the relation was a matter of aesthetic "affinity." Critics seized on this: how could the curators pretend that there was a benign relationship between Western artists and the colonized cultures from which were drawn the objects that excited them? They argued that Rubin's approach unconsciously repeated the pseudocolonial appropriation inherent in primitivism.[46] Kurt Varnedoe, another of the curators, pointed out that the "focus of the exhibition was not on the Primitive . . . but on primitivism" (*PT*, 379), but this was precisely the move the critics sought to delegitimize. Appropriative primitivism stood revealed. So, too, the polemicizing ego of the deconstructive critic: Hal Foster boasted that the " 'eclipsed' or sublated primitive reemerges in Western culture as its scandal—where it links up genealogically with poststructuralist deconstruction and politically with feminist theory and practice" (*PT*, 389). Varnedoe wryly countered: "Art thus approaches correctness as it aspires to the condition of criticism" (*PT*, 377).

Such protestations were futile. A broad moral and methodological consensus had formed, which determined that all primitivist idealizations were an ideological reflex. To understand this phenomenon one would need to deconstruct its practices of representation. This constituted a basic reorientation of the thinking on primitivism that had been established by Lovejoy and Boas in the 1930s. They argued that there was no inherently primitive entity and that "primitivism" was a perceptual frame. With poststructuralism the historical and ideological character of this frame becomes the object of critique.

In what is probably the most frequently cited comment from this period, Marianna Torgovnick characterizes Western conceptions of the primitive as "our ventriloquist's dummy": "the primitive can be—has been, will be (?)—whatever Euro-Americans want it to be. It tells us what we want it to tell us."[47] Accordingly, Torgovnick's object of study is the "image" of the primitive that formed in a wide range of intellectual disciplines and cultural practices at the beginning of the twentieth century. This image was consolidated when a range of "tropes" "slipped from their original metaphoric status" and were naturalized.[48] Whether a "rhetoric of control" or a "rhetoric of desire," primitivism constituted a self-deluding subsumption of the Other.[49] For Torgovnick the conceptual impasse between Western frames and the unrepresentable Other can only be solved by "making a space" for the authentic primitive. She sees hope in (then) recent approaches to the problem that use "dialogic models." These might afford the Other a "full voice."[50]

Torgovnick's stridency does not make hers a more notable scholarly achievement. Her broad and confident claims, however, allow us to see clearly the terrain onto which the subject of primitivism was drawn at the time. To be fair, her subject is not really primitivism but the "discourse" of the primitive. In conflating literary, theoretical, and other modes of discourse, though, primitivism was effectively eclipsed. The same moves can be perceived in more reserved studies such as Colin Rhodes's *Primitivism and Modern Art*, which concludes by considering the "dilemma of post-colonialism."[51] Rhodes cites what, in 1994, were recent examples of European artists who had used "extra-European material culture without attempting to conceal its particular identity."[52] The more the call to "make a space" for "the Other" was repeated, the more it started to resemble the idealizing logic it hoped to supplant. As Robert Young perceives with clarity: "The concept of the other, in short, simply comprises the modern form of the category of the primitive."[53] The obeisance to "the Other," not as a category for phenomenological reflection but as a designation for actual social groups, echoes the wishful *a priorism* of which primitivism stands accused. Rather than dismantling primitivism's idealism, deconstruction drove its logic deeper by further abstraction.

This process has been explained in detail by Victor Li. He shows that arguments like Torgovnick's were typical of a "neo-primitivist" trend at the time. This also includes the work of such figures as Hal Foster, Gayatri Spivak, Jean Baudrillard, and Jürgen Habermas. The postmodern critique of primitivism is, Li concludes, "primitivism without primitives."[54] It feels it can subtract the faulty concept of the "primitive" and retain the trace of the pure Other.[55] This "point-zero primitivism" thus believes it has avoided the constitutive problems of representation and authority: "if the referential absence of primitives absolves neo-primitivism of the 'Orientalist' sin of representing or speaking for concrete others, it also affords neo-primitivism the power to judge whether the speech or self-representation of others measures up to its non-referential, spectral ideal of the primitive. Neo-primitivism's safeguarding of the other from the power of representation is, at the same time, its power to police all representations of otherness by determining how far they fall short of the ideal Other."[56] Not only does neo-primitivism persist in making a fetish of absolute authenticity; it speaks as its witch doctor.[57]

Determinate negation and utopia are the cues for the current study, which aligns with the thinking of a different formation within postcolonial and world literary studies, one that begins with the assumption of a single, commonly experienced modern world-system.[58] The recasting in world-historical terms of notions of the "avant-garde" and "modernist utopianism," by Keya Ganguly and Nicholas Brown respectively, exemplify this trend. For Ganguly, provincializing the European avant-garde is not to confine it to an increasingly notional "Europe" or "West" but to situate it within the twentieth century as a "total conjuncture and geopolitical whole."[59] It includes not just the revolt of rebellious Europeans but the entire backdrop of global social ferment that also encompasses anticolonialism and nascent internationalism. Consequently, those artists and movements that might fruitfully be considered within the scope of the term *avant-garde* change, as well as which artistic techniques, or antiartistic ones, are considered as the manifestation of its praxis.

Likewise, in Brown's wide-ranging study works of modernism and decolonization are read alongside one another in such a way as to make them "comprehensible within a single framework within which neither will look the same. This framework . . . hinge[s] neither on 'literary history' nor abstract 'universal history' but on each text's relation to history itself."[60] Brown's study reminds us that the concept of totality does not block but rather enables a vision of the constitutive incompleteness of any given historical moment. Both Brown and Ganguly make it clear that direct historical connections between the artists that they discuss may well exist, but this is not their focus. They are concerned with the way diverse art practices align within a social totality as its historical shape evolves. We will observe direct connections between expressionism and D. H. Lawrence, Lawrence and Claude McKay, and McKay and negritude writers in the studies that make up the second part of this book, but the point is not to suggest a causal chain. Our purpose is to bring primitivism to shine forth by situating it in its proper totality and, thereby, to disclose its truth content.

If the postmodern fetish of the "Other" can be considered a kind of late incarnation of primitivism, the historical argument of this study might help to explain how such a metamorphosis came to pass. If there is continuity in the structure of primitivism beyond primitivism, it will also help to delineate the phenomenon if we can specify the moment at which the primitivist project gained urgency. We need to return to the period when there yet was belief in the primitive remnant.

Chapter 2

PRIMITIVISM AND PHILO-PRIMITIVISM

The postmodern assault on primitivism was caught up in the contradiction that besets all iconoclastic attacks: to will the destruction of the icon is to recognize the power that it holds. The Other was installed in the place of the decapitated primitive, but the body still kicked. In retrospect it is apparent that neo-primitivism formed part of the groundswell of a broader intellectual paradigm, one that Timothy Brennan has characterized as the "imperialism" of post-humanism: the elevation of a seemingly insuperable alienation under capitalism to a basic principle of thought.[1] If this has obscured our vision of literary primitivism, the question arises of what approach best will enable us to recover it—one that neither shies away from the labor of the concept nor breaks down literary works to the sum of propositions contained within them.

I have already discussed the necessity of adopting the "point of view of totality." This helps us to see that primitivism emerged at a particular conjuncture in the evolution of capitalist totality (on which I will expand further in the next chapter). I share with Brennan and Edward Said the conviction that the careers of concepts are best recovered through a humanist philology and with Theodor Adorno and Simon Jarvis a commitment to the articulation of the truth content of works of art. With regard to the former, Sheldon Pollock helpfully summarizes the basic aim of philology as the practice of expanding "the domain of truth by enlarging our capacity to see things the way other people, people earlier than or otherwise different from us, have seen them."[2] Rather than anachronistic moralism, a humanist philology helps us to recover the historical project of primitivism as it faced the undeclared future.[3] Expanding the domain of truth is not an exercise in historicism for its own sake but opens a path to the truth content of works of art, which we might paraphrase as that wish or desire inherent in the process of aesthetic making. A critical method centered on truth content will not examine particular passages or representations in isolation but seek to understand their immanent role in the work's formal organization. It is in the practice of trying to create meaningful forms, what Adorno at one point in *Aesthetic Theory* calls "blind making," that art presents us with "the unconscious writing of history."[4] We will attend to the ways in which primitivist literary works are put together rather than what they might *say* on any given page. Broadly, the procedure of the next two chapters is philological; the chapters following them will be concerned with articulating the truth content of exemplary primitivist works.

A suitable place from which to embark on the philological recovery of primitivism is Robert Goldwater's *Primitivism and Modern Art* (1938), the most accomplished attempt to define the phenomenon during the period of its flourishing. When concluding, Goldwater sets out to differentiate the primitivism that his work has identified from other aesthetic schools and modes. He wants to avoid the banal conclusion that primitivism is just "one more romantic exoticism."[5] The difficulty is that the concept's unity cannot be secured with reference to a single aesthetic movement or artistic group, or even broad formal or thematic commonalities. It is, he concludes, an "artistic attitude," which, above all, rejects stylistic decorum and seeks to absorb the viewer directly. There are explanations for the emergence of this attitude that are internal to the history of European art. He understands primitivism to be motivated by a desire to negate intricate late-Victorian styles. There are also external explanations. The primitivist artists drew inspiration from the so-called primitive arts that were arriving in Europe from far-flung societies. The sought-for qualities of immediacy and directness, Goldwater comments, were "read into the objects rather than objectively observed."[6] This is the classic coincidence of primitivism-as-modernism: the young radical who strays from the gallery halls to the ethnographic displays and suddenly discovers his stylistic solution in the objects deposited the week before from the anthropologist's ship.

Goldwater puzzles over why the primitivists in his study should have been stimulated by works from some regions but not others. Why were they drawn to objects from Africa and Oceania but not Central America? The possible explanation that there is greater formal complexity in "primitive" American arts does not satisfy him. "It may be explained chiefly," he concludes, "by the fact that the Inca and Aztec societies had long been destroyed and their lands occupied. They were thus no longer *living symbols of primitive simplicity* subject to aesthetic idealization and imperial conquest."[7] For the primitivist object to be a "living symbol," it seems it must come from a yet uncolonized, still "primitive" society. Goldwater does not ask why it is that the primitivist attitude should have taken hold so strongly at the start of the twentieth century. Why were earlier artists not similarly inspired to emulate Inca and Aztec artists when those societies were being subjected to imperial conquest? A partial answer is latent in his phrasing. It is no coincidence, we will see, that the societies that were still perceived to be capable of producing "living symbols of primitive simplicity" were at that very time being subjected to imperial conquest; one is the condition for the other. Delving into this paradox is essential for understanding emphatic primitivism, which erupted at the moment of the perceived liquidation of the primitive in the era of Imperialism. What is needed, then, is a historical vantage on this historical moment. To this end, I will now trace the trajectory of primitive idealizations leading up to it, especially with regard to the "noble savage."

The "Noble Savage" as Philo-primitivism

In their landmark study, Arthur Lovejoy and George Boas distinguish between two overarching types of primitivism: chronological and cultural. Whereas the former looks to a remote past in which one's ancestors once existed—a golden age, an Arcadia, an Eden—the latter looks to geographically remote societies—the Romans to the Germans, early modern Europeans to the New World, modernist artists to the Pacific Islands. "The one thing both variants have in common," Gaile McGregor usefully summarizes, "is the assumption that primitive cultures provide a viable or at least *instructive* alternative to civilized existence."[8] In both cases the primitive condition is both remote *and* internally self-sufficient—a primitive world unto itself.

Both also share the assumption that "primitives" exist in a "state of nature": an absolute against which to measure civilization's corrupting mediations. Where chronological primitivism tends to produce myths of a "fall," perhaps with selective appeals to the textual and archaeological record, cultural primitivism seeks out evidence of a form of life "actually lived by human beings."[9] Lovejoy and Boas further distinguish two modes in which either type of primitivism might be expressed. Whether chronological or cultural, the idealized primitive society might be one in which minimal time is devoted to procuring necessities, thereby maximizing the time available for the realization of desires and talents ("soft" primitivism), or it might be one in which continuous subjection to necessity produces a life of ceaseless struggle ("hard" primitivism). From their taxonomy we can abstract the following quadrant, into which I have inserted representative works:

	Hard Primitivism	Soft Primitivism
Chronological primitivism	Igor Stravinsky's *Rite of Spring*	Piero di Cosimo's *Vulcan and Aeolas*
Cultural primitivism	Pablo Picasso's *Ladies of Avignon*	Paul Gauguin's *Sacred Spring, Sweet Dreams*

Lovejoy and Boas believe that the axes of chronological/cultural and soft/hard can be used to analyze primitivism in any civilization from "cave-men" onward (7). The task they set themselves was exhaustively to categorize all the various primitivisms across the historical record (including in non-European societies).

This transhistorical primitivist spectrum can be differentiated from the emphatic primitivism that is the subject of this study by redescribing their subject as *philo-primitivism*: a broad interest in or felt affinity for the primitive. (Fittingly, Lovejoy and Boas's study opens with a discussion of the philosopher Philo's primitivism.)[10] This is not to suggest that the term *primitive* has ever existed as a stable historical category. Tony Brown recently reminded us of the concept's complex linguistic and cultural evolution. An eighteenth-century "philo-primitivism," when *primitive* generally signified "originary," would be very different from a nineteenth-century one, in which *primitive* and *savage* increasingly were used synonymously.[11] It is instructive to look at perhaps the most famous figure in the history of philo-primitivism: the so-called noble savage. Comparing the world-historical conditions that nurtured and sustained this figure helps to pinpoint those conditions in which emphatic primitivism burst forth.

The oxymoron is usually traced to the following passage in John Dryden's play *The Conquest of Granada* (1672):

Obeyed as sovereign by thy subjects be,
But know, that I alone am king of me.
I am as free as nature first made man,

> Ere the base laws of servitude began,
> When wild in woods the noble savage ran.[12]

Almanzor, the hero of the tragedy, inverts the conventional sense: the laws of sovereignty, which supposedly ennoble civilization, in fact produce servitude, so nobility is to be found in its opposite, free nature. In naming the ideal, though, Almanzor is making an *analogy* with his own free character. He is idealizing himself, not a condition toward which he aspires.

An ideal can have any number of purposes, and that of the noble savage tends to the analogous and instructive, not the transformative. In William Davenant's *The Cruelty of the Spaniards in Peru* (1663), written a decade earlier, primitivity extends into the work's texture only so far as loosening the syllables with the shifting stress meter of song:

> We danc'd and we sung,
> And look'd ever young,
> And from restraints were free,
> As waves and winds at sea.[13]

Perhaps the sight of song in a public theater during the Puritan Commonwealth may have caused the audience a certain frisson of spontaneity, but it is an exoticism within an overriding classicism.

The colonial theme and setting in Dryden's and Davenant's plays are not incidental. Anthony Pagden has observed that the inversion of "civilized" values offered in such works finds articulation by staging the process of colonial conquest.[14] In the course of scenes portraying their violent colonization, "primitive" characters have the occasion to voice the natural first principles by which they hitherto had lived. The brute facts of their conquest expose the religious hypocrisy of their colonizers. The didactic function of these noble savages, Pagden observes, is as *critics* rather than as ideals to be emulated.

In such works the image of the primitive is usually more familiar than it is strange, with form and aspect supplied by the stock of received mythic and classical ideals.[15] William H. Truettner's study of painterly representations of indigenous Americans in the eighteenth and nineteenth centuries shows how consistently indigenous people were portrayed in classical poses and tableaus.[16] We might say that "chronological" primitivism conditions the re-presentation of "cultural" primitivism. On the "cultural" side this philo-primitivist conjunction required eyewitness accounts or informants of one kind or another. In the early days of European conquest this was most often the explorer or travel writer,[17] but with settlement and the continuous advance of the frontier, the idealizing standpoint came within ever greater proximity to the idealized life-form. Not surprisingly, the idealizer soon crossed the frontier, and travel writing gave way to pseudoethnography.[18] The American artist George Catlin spent the greater part of the 1830s traveling through the yet uncolonized areas of northern America painting portraits of individuals from several communities. In a letter written in the early days of this undertaking, he makes the usual analogy with classical beauty: "the wilderness of our country afforded models equal to those from which the Grecian sculptors transferred to the marble such inimitable grace and beauty; and I am now more confirmed in this opinion since I have immersed myself in the midst of thousands and tens of thousands of these knights of the forest."[19] Not much, it seems, separates these knights from Dryden's savages in the woods. We might suppose that Catlin's purpose is principally artistic, and at first he indicates as much with the primitive serving as an instructive analogy.[20] Reading on, however, we find that there is also a historical urgency to his project:

> I have, for many years past, contemplated the noble races of red men, who are now spread over these trackless forests and boundless prairies, melting away at the approach of civilization. . . . and I have flown to their rescue—not of their lives or of their race (for they are "*doomed*" and must perish), but to the rescue of their looks and their modes, at which the acquisitive world may hurl their poison and every besom of destruction, and trample them down and crush them to death; yet, phoenix-like, they may rise from the "stain on a painter's palette," and live again upon canvass [*sic*], and stand forth for centuries yet to come, the living monuments of a noble race.[21]

His undertaking is thus also scientific and historic: to produce a representation that can survive as an enduring ethnographic record.[22] As the ideal yet exists, the imperative is to make a fair copy.

It is worth noting that these comments were written well before the publication of Darwin's *Origin of Species*. The systemic nature of the process of racial annihilation for which "social Darwinists" would later claim a scientific basis did not require a theory of evolution in order to be perceived. Indeed, if Darwin's work has so often been credited with catalyzing new conceptions of the primitive, we can see that it formed part of a much broader world-historical consciousness being produced by colonial expansion. Traveling in Australia at the same time that Catlin was roaming America, Darwin observed that "wherever the European has trod, death seems to pursue the aboriginal. We may look to the wide extent of the Americas, Polynesia, the Cape of Good Hope, and Australia, and we find the same result." Reflecting on this, he wondered whether there might be some "more mysterious agency generally at work": "The varieties of man seem to act on each other in the same way as different species of animals—the stronger always extirpating the weaker."[23] The priority often given to the theory of evolution in producing a new idea of the primitive needs to be turned on its head. The same global historical process that fomented the acute anxiety that later spurred primitivism enabled Darwin to formulate a unitary theory of humanity.

A century later, Claude Lévi-Strauss would comment on the paradoxical relationship between ethnographic empathy and colonial expansion: "I have only two possibilities: either I can be like some traveler of the olden days, who was faced with a stupendous spectacle, all, or almost all, of which eluded him, or worse still, filled him with scorn and disgust; or I can be a modern traveler, chasing after the vestiges of a vanished reality."[24] Catlin's paintings and Darwin's theory are at the historical hinge of these alternatives. As he "roamed," Catlin's artistic ambitions increasingly gave way to ethnographic necessity. He would paint several portraits a day in the attempt to produce a comprehensive survey. These works are consciously produced fossils, and Catlin presented them as such, showcasing them in a traveling exhibition accompanied by public lectures describing his time "amongst the wildest tribes."[25]

The historical trajectory leading to the moment of emphatic primitivism should now be apparent. I am not suggesting that this trajectory follows a straight line, and I do not doubt that a detailed diachronic study would throw up plenty of contradictory evidence. The overall picture, however, would not be greatly affected. The nature and cause of the historical process that led to human societies being integrated into a global totality might be matter of ceaseless debate but not the fact of its having occurred. It is especially interesting to revisit the work most closely associated with the discourse of the noble savage in view of this trajectory: Jean-Jacques Rousseau's *Discourse on the Origins of Inequality* (1755). Tor Ellingson points out, as have others before him,[26] that in this work Rousseau neither idealizes any existing "savage," nor does he recommend this condition.[27] His argument is conducted in the mode of genealogical conjecture, as is made clear at the outset: the "state of nature" is one that "no longer exists, which perhaps never existed, which probably never will exist, and about which it is nevertheless necessary to have precise notions in order to judge our present state correctly."[28] There is a clear distinction throughout the work between the projective fiction of the speculatively conceived "True Savage" and the reports Rousseau cites of "savage peoples known to us."[29] Reports of "Negroes," "Caribs," "American Savages," and "Hottentots" (see 108, 113, 152, 189–91) are used to speculate about the qualities of the True Savage. It is another philo-primitivistic synthesis of the empirical and ideal. In this case the ideal takes the form of a concept, "natural justice," rather than a classically framed representation.

Rousseau intimates that the gap between real and ideal might have something to do with the fact that they are "known to us," such as in the passing comment: "When one thinks of the good constitution of Savages, at least of those whom we have not ruined with our strong liquors,"[30] but this does not appear to him as an irrevocable process. Writing eighty years earlier than Catlin, he could yet convince himself that, like oil and water, primitive and civilized would remain separate.[31] By the time of Robert Louis Stevenson's "The Song of Rohero" (1890), penned in Tahiti, where he set up residence in 1888, the attempt to conjure an alternative primitive world by conjoining the classical past with the noncolonial present had acquired the tincture of anachronism:

> Ancient and unforgotten, songs of the earlier days,
> That the elders taught to the young, and at night, in the full of the moon,
> Garlanded boys and maidens sang together in tune.[32]

Stevenson's is a tale of "delighting maids" "garlanded green," of boys with "clean-lipped" smiles, of "scarcely nubile" elders, of naked men "plucking and bearing fruit" by moonlight, of "victuals rotting." The fusion of classical and anthropological ideals extends into the work's prosody, which, as Sean Pryor's careful analysis shows, produces an uneasy and uncertain tension between the "primitive" associations of the ballad and the sometimes "classical," sometimes "primitive" associations of the hexameter.[33] Not exactly swept away from their modernity, Stevenson's critics complained that he was either confused, an inept versifier, or both.[34] In his other Pacific writings Stevenson would vacillate between this romantic vision of life beyond imperialism's perimeter and a forthright engagement with contemporary colonial conditions that was "at once critical of and implicated by the colonial contract."[35]

We have arrived at the historical moment that political economists would soon call "Imperialism." It was established for consciousness that every human society could be known and that all would soon be synthesized in a single totality. Late-Victorian imperial fictions, from *King Solomon's Mines* to *Heart of Darkness*, showcase the final stages of this transition. At the level of psychology, the geographical space of the primitive, that which engenders "cultural primitivism," had all but been extinguished, and the existence of the primitive consequently was pushed permanently into a speculative chronological mode. Primitivism was the groan discharged when it was realized that the sense of alternative possibilities that had arisen in the encounters between radically different societies had been made possible by the expansion of a system that was suffocating them. Even if there remained communities in which humans lived according to entirely different social logics, the dramatic geographical extension of capitalism through late colonialism made them appear as tragic realities.

We start to see that any discussion of primitivism that is premised on a fixed separation of "West" and "non-West" will be flawed. The primitive ideal shifted within the purview of expansionist colonialism, and emphatic primitivism erupted at the moment when any remaining sense of an absolute separation of primitive and civilized was at the point of dissolution. Accordingly, we must be divested of the false dichotomy that has set the terms for nearly all discussions of primitivism: the binary of "civilized" and "primitive," and its recent corollary, "the West" and its "Others." Emphatic primitivism does not stand over and against any old "civilization," which could be the concentration of human population in any circumstance, but against a new kind of social domination, one that threatened to end the possibility of natural existence altogether. It is a peculiar form of spiritual rebellion immanent to the imperialist apotheosis of European colonialism.

Primitivism and Primitive Accumulation

The tendency to think of the historical formation of global capitalist modernity as a crescendo of Western cultural domination (i.e., "Westernization") rather than as the consequence of the progressive totalization of capitalist modes and relations of production has long been entrenched in scholarly and public discourse. As Neil Lazarus comments in his landmark 2002 essay "The Fetish of 'the West' in Postcolonial Theory," this tendency is shared by both its defenders and iconoclasts.[36] This is identity politics writ large, in which all features of the "modernity" disseminated through imperialism and globalization are notable above all for being "Western." In fetishizing the West, Lazarus argues, certain postcolonial iconoclasts have been sucked into a cultural politics that is invested primarily in trying to change concepts and representational frameworks (what certain conservatives call "political correctness"). It also leads to the a priori assignation of moral authority to dominated cultures, which is to say, that which is not "West." The casualty has been critical thought that works from a standpoint immanent to the globalization of capital.[37]

When a symphony orchestra appears to be a necessary accessory for any cosmopolitan, investment-friendly city, one cannot doubt that Eurocentrism has been a significant ideological manifestation. To critique this is different from an open-eyed assessment of the diverse ways in which the logic of capital has reorganized social relations and produced new ontological horizons across human societies. In the case of the scholarly discussion of primitivism, the "fetish of the West" has diverted attention away from both the specific historical conditions in which primitivism manifested itself and its systemic nature. Primitivism has been understood as a peculiar form of hypocritical self-abnegation that symptomizes the broader trend of "Westernization." Instead of approaching primitivism through a nebulous binary of the civilized (West) and the primitive (Other), we need to attend to the particular "civilizational" form in the course of whose development primitivism is thrown up as a project. Particularly, I want to stress that primitivism emerges at that moment when the capitalist world-system broadly was *perceived* to be at the point of subsuming all noncapitalist domains. (It would be inaccurate to claim that primitivism manifested itself at the point when every last human being had *in fact* been compelled into capitalist relations.) In the terms of Marx's *Capital* (in its English translation), I am referring to the climax of the process of "primitive accumulation," whether through direct conquest or indirect control.

There are two aspects of this moment in particular that ripened primitivist despair: (1) colonial expansion was reaching the point of geographical saturation, and (2) international financial competition had become, unambiguously, the engine of colonial activity. (These are the same conditions that incubated imperialist war.) I use the term *Imperialism* not as a retrospective theory of the diverse practices of European colonists from the fifteenth century onward but as the term was used by theorists and economists at the beginning of the twentieth century, most famously V. I. Lenin and fellow Marxists Rosa Luxemburg, Rudolf Hilferding, and Nikolai Bukharin. Thinkers participating in this discussion by no means comprised only Marxists, though—Norman Angell, Thorstein Veblen, and J. A. Hobson began the theoretical discussion, and Joseph Schumpeter would later join in—and journals of political economy and trade, as well as newspapers across Western Europe and North America, were littered with the term.[38] Across this discussion, "Imperialism" referred specifically to new finance-driven practices in international relations, in which private interests compelled state policies of monopolization, protectionism, and armament.[39] (I distinguish the historical nature of the term here by retaining the capitalization.)

The protagonists were not the more established European empires but the rising forces of Germany and the United States, states whose capitalists needed productive outlets for the immense stocks of capital built up during rapid and intensive industrialization but that did not have available large colonial domains for their deployment. They were thus compelled into colonial activity. Under Imperialism, theorists of the time argued, agency had been displaced from particular imperial powers to the financial system itself. It was no longer the exploitation of this or that community or land but a system that had become automatically expansionist. Hobson described this as "Imperialism without limit," Schumpeter as "the objectless disposition on the part of the state to unlimited forcible expansion."[40]

These theorizations of Imperialism came between a linear and teleological ("stagist") notion of primitive accumulation and later conceptions of the uneven nature of capitalism as a world-system. It was a moment when the spatial limits of accumulation seemed palpable but before spatiotemporal dislocations in patterns of accumulation, and attendant crises, could clearly be understood as systemic and ongoing.[41] In *Results and Prospects* (1905) Leon Trotsky may have begun the process of theorizing global capitalism as an integrated yet heterogeneous totality that fused past and present forms of production, but it was not until after the collapse of the European empires that such heterogeneity was widely perceived as systemic.[42] It is within the millenarian zeitgeist of this intermediate stage, when such dislocations were perceived to be signaling the system's imminent end, that the primitivist yearning for an organic social existence became most acute. It is not that "Western" artists were for the first time coming into contact with radically different "non-Western" art, as Goldwater surmised long ago, but that the radical difference of a social existence unmediated by exchange value—what Rosa Luxemburg was calling "natural economy"—suddenly appeared to be miraculous.

To put the particularity of this moment into relief, we can contrast the purpose and scope of Marx's discussion of primitive accumulation in the 1860s with Luxemburg's in 1913. For Marx primitive accumulation is that process by which peasants are forcibly separated from control over the means of their subsistence and are compelled to sell their labor as a commodity. This discussion completes the argument against classical political economists, whose ahistorical theories, he claims, naturalize the establishment of capitalist relations. Ostensibly, the discussion of primitive accumulation is genealogical—it was the "original" accumulation necessary to kick-start the process. Both the wealth that would become capital and the workers who would serve to increase its value were gained through the barefaced robbery of peasants. In practice, capitalism's expansion was global, so "original" accumulation was ongoing in Marx's time, most conspicuously through colonial conquest. It is in this section of *Capital* that he discusses "the entanglement of all peoples in the net of the world market" that sounds the knell for capitalist private property, but this was yet a vague endpoint.[43]

For Luxemburg primitive accumulation was not just the starting point for capitalist relations but "a kind of metabolism between capitalist economy and those pre-capitalist methods of production without which it cannot go on and which, in this light, it corrodes and assimilates."[44] The final crisis of capitalism would come when all remaining noncapitalist environments had been drawn into the procedures of accumulation. Imperialism was hastening the arrival of this point: "Imperialism is the political expression of the accumulation of capital in its competitive struggle for what remains still open of the non-capitalist environment."[45] It is of no concern whether this is a correct or even valuable revision of the concept of primitive accumulation. What is significant is that Luxemburg was convinced that Imperialism had revealed the fundamental contradiction of capital to be one obtaining between capitalist and noncapitalist spheres rather than something inherent in the commodity form or the relationship between capital and labor. From Luxemburg's perspective, capital simply could not coexist with "natural economy"; it must "always and everywhere fight a battle of annihilation against every historical form of natural economy that it encounters, whether this is slave economy, feudalism, primitive communism, or patriarchal peasant economy."[46] Thus, she confidently pronounced the system's imminent collapse, and Lenin would reiterate her conclusion shortly after. It is this sense of the impending extinction of all "natural economies" that was the precondition for the primitivist striving for "living symbols of primitive simplicity."[47] What to earlier generations had seemed an inexorable process, whose endpoint nevertheless was distant, suddenly appeared to have reached its denouement.

The Sublimation Thesis

Words and concepts are inherited from the past, and their use pertains not only to existing reality but also to one's sense of the way the present will unfold into the future. That which is primitive is not only a matter of what has been and currently is primitive but also that which will continue to be or become so. By the turn of the twentieth century it was clear that any "primitive" society could not maintain its autonomy in the face of Imperialism's "objectless disposition." This did not lead to the concept's obsolescence but a reorientation of the conception of the relationship between the civilized and the primitive. Increasingly, civilization came to be regarded as the result of a sublimation or repression of the primitive rather than as its Manichean opposite. We might call this the *sublimation thesis*, and its paradoxical logic was succinctly captured in Walter Benjamin's claim that "there is no document of civilization which is not at the same time a document of barbarism."[48] In their *Dialectic of Enlightenment* Theodor Adorno and Max Horkheimer formalized this insight into a critique of the epistemological paradigm of mature capitalism. For the purposes of the present study we might paraphrase their central theses regarding myth and enlightenment: (1) the primitive is already civilized, and (2) the civilized has an inherent tendency to revert to the primitive.[49] According to Adorno and Horkheimer's analysis, instrumental reason's inexorable drive to dominate nature has an unreflective mythic dimension, and the apparatuses of social discipline and control in societies organized using myth were always already civilized. Such materialist conceptions of the sublimation thesis stood alongside other, usually ahistorical, conceptions, whether these took the form of positing civilization's primitive unconscious, its primitive origins, its primitive Dionysian intuitions, its primitive flow of consciousness, or the notion that technology was in fact an eruption of primitive forces. The many forms of appearance of the sublimation thesis point to the breadth of the historical and epistemological shift taking place.

It is crucial to recognize, therefore, that the act of positing the sublimation thesis, in whichever form, is not of itself *primitivist*. If Freud speculates that taboos in modern Europe have "some essential relationship with these primitive taboos and that an explanation of taboo might throw a light upon the obscure origin of our own 'categorical imperative,'" it does not follow that artistic explorations of taboo have a primitivist telos.[50] The sublimation thesis just as often played into antiprimitivism, perhaps nowhere more forcibly than in Joseph

Conrad's work. Even more crucially, we should not assume that when an artist or group of artists invoke the sublimation thesis as the basis for an aesthetic program—for instance, futurist technologism, expressionist intuitionism, or surrealist explorations of the unconscious—the sublimation thesis is necessarily the source of a given work's primitivism. We must look to the structure of desire that leads an artist to call on the sublimation thesis and then look at how the sublimation thesis is concretely drawn into the internal constitution of the artwork.

As with the false dichotomy of the civilized "West" and its primitive "Other," we need to get beyond claims that assign causality to the author of any given version of sublimation thesis, such as when David Pan asserts that "the origins of twentieth-century primitivism lie in the work of Friedrich Nietzsche"[51] or when Raymond Geuss suggests that "the idea specifically derived from *The Birth of Tragedy* which has become perhaps most influential in the twentieth century is . . . the view that destructive, primitively anarchic forces are a part of us (not to be projected into some diabolical Other)."[52] As we have remarked, the urge to identify particular thinkers as the progenitors of primitivism leads to the view that identifying a work's primitivism is a matter of cracking its aesthetic shell to extract the primitivist idea that lies within.

In the case of Nietzsche the writings do not even conform to the vein of primitivism that he is supposed to have sponsored. Take, for instance, his notion of the "blond beast." As first formulated in the *Genealogy of Morals* (1887), the concept refers to the "noble" "barbarian" spirit that wants only to satisfy its own desires and repeatedly breaks free from any form of social control.[53] If this appears to affirm unencumbered instinct as against moralizing *ressentiment*, the historical argument of the book in fact takes us in the opposite direction. For Nietzsche the instincts of the "blond beast" have long been lost—he calls them "the old instincts." *Ressentiment* and asceticism now condition the habits and instincts of Europeans.[54] These do not sit above a residual or repressed layer of bestial instinct that need only be unleashed; the conscience of the moral subject *is* the animal instinct of the contemporary European. Nietzsche's whole argument therefore turns against the unmediated expression of instinct. His intellectualist project of recovering the "blond beast" is undertaken in order that it might serve as a shield *against* primitivism *qua* the unencumbered demand for equality, universal political agency, and constitutional justice.

As Timothy Brennan has shown, Nietzsche's antiprimitivism arose from a twin phobia of socialist and anticolonial agitation. Brennan quotes these lines from the *Genealogy*: "who can give any guarantee that modern democracy, the even more modern anarchism, and indeed that predilection for the 'commune,' the most primitive form of social structure which is common to all Europe's socialists, are not in essence a huge *throw-back*—and that the conquering *master race*, that of the Aryans, is not physiologically being defeated as well?"[55] (The anti-Nietzsche in this respect would be Diego Rivera, whose majestic scenes of the lost Aztec universe point to a utopian communist future.)[56] If primal instincts are directed toward the communal and democratic, then conceptual reflection is required to initiate a regimen that would restore to Europeans the instincts of nobility and domination.[57] Nietzsche looks to the colonial space as the terrain for this reeducation:

> The workers in Europe . . . should introduce an era of vast swarming out from the European beehive, the like of which has never been experienced, and with this act of emigration in the grand manner protest against the machine, against capital, and against the choice with which they are now threatened, of becoming of necessity either slaves of the state or slaves of a revolutionary party. . . . What at home began to degenerate into dangerous discontent and criminal tendencies will, once outside, gain a wild and beautiful naturalness and be called heroism.[58]

Citing this and numerous other comments, Brennan has reconstructed the relationship between Nietzsche's thinking and the intensification of colonialism and industrialization in Germany in the 1870s and 1880s. For Nietzsche the primitive ideal is not to be attained beyond the colonial perimeter but by reconceiving of the colonial territories as pastures for the *Übermensch* as he escapes the trappings of the barbarian industrial left.

Misperceptions are historical, though, and if Nietzsche was perceived by his contemporaries to have promulgated an ideal of primitive intuition, we must acknowledge the complex afterlife of his peculiar tropes and rhetorical postures. If some grafted the concept of the Dionysian onto that of the unconscious in order to affirm the artistry of primal drives, it did not necessarily carry the weight of Nietzsche's antiprimitivism. It is notable, however, that there was a strain of antiprimitivism that fell into line with his assumptions, as is evident in Lothrop Stoddard's association of Bolshevism with Rousseau and "the lure of the primitive."[59] In any case this short excursus on Nietzsche has served only to show the falsity of equating the sublimation thesis with primitivism. Primitivism will not reveal itself through intellectual genealogy or the history of ideas but by situating the primitivist project within its proper totality.

Chapter 3

PRIMITIVISM AND NEGRITUDE

Primitivism and Totality

Emphatic primitivism is more than an expressed affinity or preference for the primitive. It is the urgent desire to become primitive, a condition whose fulfillment would require no less than an exit from the capitalist world-system. To realize its project, primitivism seeks guidance from the remnants of noncapitalist societies conceived as self-sufficient totalities. On this point we encounter a potential contradiction. If the desire for alternative social worlds originates in an anguish caused by the new realities produced by the totalization of capital, then the primitivity perceived in any particular "remnant" might only be the projection of the discontented. That is, if an alternative is sought ahead of any specific notion of what the "primitive" form of life being pursued would actually entail, then its content must be supplied only by the primitivist's fancies. This study steadfastly refuses the temptation to treat the primitive remnant as only a "construction," as though alternative social totalities had never existed or should not be affirmed as preferable to capitalism. Nevertheless, it is certainly the case that the remnant is mediated through and through by primitivist longing.

Rather than persist with social constructivist or psychoanalytic lenses that emphasize only the objectification of subjective desires, it is better to conceptualize primitivism dialectically. For this we can return to Bloch's concepts of "subjective" and "objective" nonsynchronicity. We noted in the first chapter that subjective nonsynchronicity refers to the discontent of the individual who feels out of step with the times, while objective nonsynchronicity refers to the remnant objects and social practices that persist beyond their strict necessity within the present political economy. From the position of nonsynchronous discontent, which in this case might be described as the felt loss of natural being, primitivism desires access to that mode of reality perceived in the remnant. Reaching this state cannot be achieved simply by producing a representation of it. It is the process of opening up the possibility of an alternative social condition to that lived under capitalism.

If this is starting to sound implausibly abstract, the manifestoes and essays that I will discuss in this chapter reveal that such was the language of the time. Contemporaneous articulations of the primitivist project did not talk about "the Other"; they talked about capitalism and what it would take to reenliven destroyed social realities. We might start with a speculative fragment from Carl Einstein's "On Primitive Art" (1919): "Primitive art: that means the rejection of the capitalistic art tradition. European mediateness and tradition must be destroyed; there must be an end to formalist fictions. If we explode the ideology of capitalism, we will find beneath it the sole valuable remnant of this shattered continent, the precondition for everything new, the masses of simple people, today still burdened by suffering. It is they who are the artist."[1] There are a few things to highlight here. We can begin by clarifying that "European mediateness" refers to the way that European art is "tangled up in the processes of sophisticated capitalism" (124), a comment Einstein makes just before this passage; next, to end "formalist fictions" is not to leap out of the mediate into the immediately primitive but to break through the "ideology of capitalism"; third, primitive art, as a process rather than a category of objects, reaches its fulfillment in recuperating the "masses of simple people," which is easily decoded as a call to proletarian revolution. If Einstein was influenced by Nietzsche's work in some respects, comments such as these show that his political commitments led him in the opposite direction.

As the translator of this essay notes, for Einstein the "primitive" in "primitive art" is synonymous with "unmediated" and "immediate," and its temporality is to be distinguished from that of a vulgar Darwinist chronology.[2] In his essay "African Sculpture" (*Negerplastik*), published three years earlier, Einstein refers to African sculpture as "so-called primitive art," showing that he was conscious of the distinction.[3] In *Negerplastik*, Einstein had argued that the study of the formal principles in certain African sculpture could assist Europeans to reconcile the visual experience of objects with those objects' concrete materialization. This would mean conceiving of plastic expression as an act of projective knowing rather than the artful representation of objects in the world. It would ensure that the reification of experience was not misrecognized as sophistication and direct expressiveness as barbarity.

Einstein's fragment on primitive art appeared in Ludwig Rubiner's collection *Der Gemeinschaft* in early 1919. According to Charles W. Haxthausen the essays in this volume were full of "confident tidings of the passing of capitalism and recklessly utopian hopes for the revolution."[4] It is notable that this sense of possibility should have prompted Einstein to push the analogy of "primitive art" and the revolutionary masses to the point of direct identification. It reveals the outline of a political trajectory that comes with an aesthetic commitment to the primitive at this time. To affirm the primitive was to make oneself an antagonist of the social arrangements in which it had come to seem impossible.[5]

Haxthausen is right to call such sentiments recklessly utopian. The dangers of a politics driven by an aesthetics of immediacy would soon become apparent, especially with the ascendency of the twin of fascist populism and consumer satisfaction. It would be learned that ideology manifests itself all the more acutely at just the point that one believes oneself to have come into possession of the authentic: *this* is a German *volk*, or *this* tune is love. Hence Adorno's warning that "[thought] falls prey to the mediated as soon as it tries to grasp the unmediated directly." To be vigilant against mediation is not to give up on the immediate, though: "Thought remains faithful to the idea of immediacy only in and through what is mediated."[6] The aspiration to the immediate—to natural society, to unmediated necessity—encounters at every turn the dissolution of nature in culture. This is why primitivism takes the form of an "aesthetic modification of the human project" (a Sartrean formulation that I discuss in detail in Chapter 5). Stated in the broadest possible terms, primitivism is a movement through the mediate toward the immediate. Just as any claim to the spontaneous reappearance of the German *volk* is bogus, so negritude poets discovered that any claim to an immediate access to "Africa" is blocked by colonial mediations.

Staying for the moment in the central European context, it is helpful to recall some aspects of the famous debate on expressionism that took place in the darkness of the 1930s as the German left looked back on the spirit of its youthful utopianism.[7] When György Lukács denounced expressionism as "the literary mode corresponding to fully-developed imperialism,"[8] it was also an attack on a section of the left that he believed could not own up to the fallacy of equating aesthetic spontaneity and left politics. To this Bloch countered: "what if authentic reality is also discontinuity?"[9] For him expressionism's wrought subjective utopianism should not be regarded as a symptom of capitalist crisis but as an authentic rebellion whose motivations, if not its methods, were the same as a "lucid humanist materialism."[10] Lukács shot back that to celebrate the reflected surface of reified experience is to give up on comprehending it as a totality. These discussions would spin off in a number of directions. What is important for our purposes is that the standoff centers on the aesthetics of immediacy. Expressionism's pursuit of a primal immediacy *either* is the ideal that fascism wants to suppress *or* betrays an unconscious alignment with it. Accordingly, Bloch would have argued that the inclusion of Emil Nolde's work in the exhibition of degenerate art demonstrated an aesthetic inassimilable to fascism; Lukács would see Nolde's expressed fascist sympathies as confirmation of the internal logic of his aesthetic.

The present study does not aim to decide this matter—not because it cannot be decided but because such discussions need to be situated in their proper totality if their relevance to primitivism is to be made intelligible. The totality, that is, in which the elements in view can be understood in the fullness of their interrelations. Although the term *imperialism* regularly surfaced in the expressionist debates, the participants were only peripherally conscious of the global imperial context. Take the following passage from the section on nonsynchronicity in Bloch's *Heritage of Our Times*:

> The ignorance of the white-collar worker as he searches for past levels of consciousness, transcendence in the past, increases to an orgiastic hatred of reason, to a "chthonism," in which there are berserk people and images of the cross, in which indeed—with a nonsynchronism that verges on extraterritoriality— Negro drums rumble and central Africa rises up. The reason: the middle class (in distinction to the proletariat) does not directly take part in production at all, but enters it only in intermediary activities, at such a distance from social causality that with increasing ease an alogical space can form in which primal drives and romanticisms, wishes and mythicisms come to the fore.[11]

Chthon is the subterranean correlate of Olympia—a dark place of underworld deities. Where working-class nonsynchronism clings to the concrete remnants of surpassed political economy, the middle-class worker, in his desire to remain entirely aloof from the productive sphere, burrows all the deeper into irrationalism. Africa, for Bloch, evidently is to be regarded as entirely separate from the arena in which the German white-collar worker operates. The continent may have been divided up among the imperial powers at a conference in Berlin fifty years earlier, and Germany a late but determined mover into the colonial game—there was a small diasporic African community in Berlin from the late nineteenth century—but the capacity to connect local mentalities to this imperial totality had not yet developed.[12] The complex interpenetration of societies through the agency of the world market remained for Bloch and his peers an abstract consideration.

It is interesting to contrast this sense of chthonic with its sardonic use in the following passage from T. E. Lawrence's *Seven Pillars of Wisdom* (1922). Lawrence is pointing out the ironies of encouraging British colonial subjects to cultural pride: "God had not given it them [the colonized] to be English; a duty remained to be good of their type. Consequently we admired native custom; studied the language; wrote books about its architecture, folklore, and dying industries. Then one day, we woke up to find this chthonic spirit turned political, and shook our heads with sorrow over its ungrateful nationalism—truly the fine flower of our innocent efforts."[13] As in Bloch, *chthonic* signifies nonsynchronicity. In this case a cultural past that has been suppressed under colonial rule is elevated by colonized intellectuals to the status of a protonational culture. To speak of "chthonism" in this context is to bring into view a material historical process, one reflected in, say, Gandhi's transition from top hat to dhoti. A nonsynchronous appeal to "Africa" from a discontented English colonial administrator would be entirely intelligible in this context—such is the narrative logic of Conrad's most successful stories. A chthonism that exits home territory indicates its fundamental irrationality to Bloch, but for a Lawrence or Conrad, such are the daily contradictions of colonial practice.

Primitivism as Negritude

If literary primitivism is reconceived as a nonsynchronous negation of the imperial world-system, the scope of possible authors and works that might fruitfully be interpreted within its bounds must also be reconsidered. In the light of the above exposition we might expect that primitivism was *more* likely to have been pursued by those in the peripheral zones of the capitalist world-system, or by those who felt themselves more readily to belong to them, or, at least, by those who felt compelled to move toward them—the areas, that is, where the discontent of those dispossessed by colonialism was the most acutely felt and where the remnants and mental habits of destroyed political economies and structures of feeling seemed more present and alive. So we find that it was hardly only "Western" writers who were drawn to the charge of the noncapitalist remnant. In a now globe-encircling world-system characterized by combined and uneven development, it was those writers and artists who were most violently torn from previous forms of social organization that most keenly felt the remnant's revolutionary possibility. For them, these previous social worlds yet seemed real, or they more urgently needed to believe in the illusion of their reality. Accordingly, it is not D. H. Lawrence, Georges Bataille, or Gottfried Benn who occupy the center-ground of this study but writers among those of the New Negro, negritude, nativist, and indigenist movements of the global peripheries: the colonized, the "conscripts of modernity," for whom Imperialism was, irrevocably, their social horizon but for whom the primitivist project hummed with greater urgency.

This claim will probably attract skepticism. Habitual associations need to be loosened in order for us to perceive that the negation in the name of the "primitive" was system-wide. It was a negation entangled with racial ideas and illusions but that was nevertheless enacted across a number of different communities within the uneven global system. I am assisted in making this claim by a number of anti-Eurocentric correctives in recent humanities scholarship, above all that which has identified the "Black Atlantic" as integral to the constitution of the so-called West rather than as something to be considered off to the side in subject/object terms. Instead of reaching for the tool kit of subtextual reading that seeks always to find the "appropriation" and "subversion" of "Western discourse" wherever a "colonial subject" speaks, or notions of "resignification" based on anachronistic and *ad hominem* assumptions, we need to immerse ourselves in the historical sensibilities of this time and the full scope of its radical and often racialized idealism.

Listen to this group of francophone students addressing their fellow "conscripts of modernity" as they issued their manifesto *Légitime défense* in Paris in 1932:

> And if, by its content, this collection is primarily addressed to young French Caribbeans, it is because we think it opportune to aim our first effort at people whose capacity for revolt we certainly do not underestimate. If it is especially aimed at young blacks, it is because we consider that they in particular suffer from the effects of capitalism (apart from Africa, witness Scottsboro) and that

they seem to offer—in having a materially determined ethnic personality—a generally higher potential for revolt and joy. For want of a black proletariat, from which international capitalism has withheld the means of understanding us, we are addressing the children of the black bourgeoisie. We are speaking to those who are not already branded as killed established fucked-up academic successful decorated decayed provided for decorative prudish opportunists. We are speaking to those who can still accept life with some appearance of truthfulness.[14]

We can observe parallels with Einstein's fragment on primitive art. These are not thoroughgoing, but it is hardly a stretch to see that both issue from within the same zeitgeist and are motivated by a common desire to discover the social and aesthetic basis for a negation of "international capitalism." As with Einstein, the authors believe that the potential for revolt lies with those who have endured the worst of this system; nevertheless, they find themselves making their appeal through bourgeois channels. Also, they characterize this in the terms of a fight against time, seeking out those instincts for joy and revolt that are *yet* unmediated. The most obvious difference is that the voice of declaration occupies a standpoint that is much closer to the subject of insurrection. "They" are also "we," and, it can be expected, this has much to do with what the students refer to as a "materially determined ethnic personality."

This brings us to Aimé Césaire's coining of the word *négritude* two years later in the third issue of *L'étudiant noir*. Trying to envision a "revolution" that would be more than "a mere shaking of surfaces," he calls for his black readers to "apprehend in ourselves the immediate Negro, plant our negritude like a beautiful tree until it bears its most authentic fruits" (saisir en nous le nègre immédiat, planter notre négritude comme un bel arbre jusqu'à ce qu'il porte ses fruits les plus authentiques).[15] As a statement of the aims and means of the primitivist project, this seismic utterance, which only recently has been recovered, could not be more concise. Read in the broader context of the groundswell of utopian primitivism, it articulates not as a novel aspiration but a more forthright declaration of the task ahead. Above all, we can see that "immediate Negro" is an oxymoron that a successful negritude would render a tautology. Immediacy and authenticity come from the activities of "apprehension" and "planting," not from naming and identifying. What this passage does not do is enact these processes. In Chapter 5 we will give full attention to Césaire's activation of negritude's project.

If the received vision of primitivism has been almost entirely diachronic and dualist, this study will verge on overemphasizing the synchronic and global experience of imperialism's apotheosis. *Qua* primitivism, the works of D. H. Lawrence share more with those of Césaire than with the ideas of Rousseau or the romantic poets, however readily certain of Lawrence's enthusiasms might be situated within a history of a nature-idealism that habitually is associated with Europeans. Also, to identify the morphology of the primitivist project does not entail claiming a unity of intention or method. What constitutes the remnant and its perceived potentiality is different for writers in different locations within the imperialist totality. It is worth keeping in mind that this is not a roll call of primitivists but a study of literary primitivism—of primitivizing aesthetic acts, not the stated philosophy of any particular writer. The manifestoes and essays under discussion in this chapter help only to delineate the sphere of primitivist activity. They do not define its purpose or meaning.

A decade after *Légitime défense*, and within the flowering of the negritude movement that it presaged, Suzanne Césaire published an essay in *Tropiques*, "A Civilization's Discontent." Again we find the broadsides against bourgeois "civilization" ("The rat race. Diplomas. Naked ambition. Struggle reduced to the bourgeoisie's level. Buffoon's race"), in this instance accompanied by a short narrative that traces the progressive alienation of the Martinican. In the "depth of his consciousness" he is a "plant-man" [l'homme plante], someone whose instinct is to "abandon himself to the rhythm of universal life" and who "makes no effort to dominate nature."[16] This form of selfhood, she asserts, is the continuation of an "*Ethiopian sentiment of life.*"[17] Slavery and then assimilationist colonial society estranged the Martinican, who no longer recognizes his "true nature." Césaire claims that there had been an "explosion of the primitive self" with the abolition of slavery in 1848 when freed Martinicans briefly spurned commodified labor, but the imperative to suppress the plant-man self only intensified over time, especially with the formation of a comprador middle class. The first imperative of negritude, she counsels, is to "recognize ourselves": "It is not at all a matter of a return to the past, of the resurrection of an African past that we have learned to understand and to respect. It is a matter, on the contrary, of the mobilization of all the combined vital forces on this land where race is the result of continual mingling. It is a matter of becoming conscious of the formidable mass of different energies that until now have been trapped within us."[18] The remnant cannot be restored to the reality in which it once thrived, but consciousness of it can form the basis for mobilizing pent-up forces. Surrealism has provided certain techniques for initiating this project. Césaire's call, now, is for the Martinican people to find their own aesthetic solutions.

It has often been observed in cultural theory that the colonial situation produced a belief that the "Negro" or the "Aborigine" or the "colonial subject" writ large is constitutively nonsynchronous—"belated" in Homi Bhabha's lexicon. If some would characterize negritude's surrealism as belated, we must keep in mind the quite different modalities of primitivism and the variety of contexts in which its project took hold. It is not a question of who first but of the peculiar resources and trajectories that the primitivist project acquired in different zones of evolving capitalist totality. Unlike the protagonists of European expressionism and surrealism, whose quests for noncapitalist remnants were often scattergun and uncritical, for these artists and thinkers, primitivization necessarily involved an exacting encounter with social identity.

To demonstrate what I mean by this, we can compare Alain Locke's essay "A Note on African Art" with Einstein's "African Sculpture." Both take the surge of interest in African sculpture among European artists as their point of departure. Both believe that ethnographic and aesthetic lenses can help to make sense of this surge, and both choose to focus their efforts on the latter. Both maintain a distinction between fraudulent notions of the "primitiveness" of African art and perceive a dialectic of primitivity and refinement that is internal to African art. But where Einstein's argument ultimately goes in the direction of the fragment in *Gemeinschaft*, according to which "primitive art" can provide an external foothold from which to attack Europe's "formalist fictions," Locke's essay, which addresses fellow educated blacks, concludes with an inward turn:

> Because of our Europeanized conventions, the key to the proper understanding and appreciation of it [African art] will in all probability first come from an appreciation of its influence upon contemporary French art, but we must believe that there still slumbers in the blood something which once stirred will react with peculiar emotional intensity toward it. If by nothing more mystical than the sense of being ethnically related, some of us will feel its influence at least as keenly as those who have already made it recognized and famous. Nothing is more galvanizing than the sense of a cultural past.[19]

"European mediateness" is no less relevant for Locke than for Einstein or Bloch. He does not pretend that his reflections on African art can be removed from the intellectual and cultural climate in which he lives and thinks. Yet his interest is not derivative of French art. It arises from a need for "vitalizing influence" that is, in some ways, shared.[20] He finishes by intimating that this vitalization will lead to new techniques of expression and revelations of a "mysterious substrata of feeling." Consciousness of mediation does not mean that the artistic results will be the same, though. For Locke the promise of immediacy in African art appears, well, more immediate, even if it is only on the basis of a "sense" of ethnic affinity. Significant, in this respect, is the imperative in the first sentence of the passage: we, "American Negroes," "*must believe*" in the connection. That which slumbers in the blood may only be an illusion, but it is one that is necessary to stimulate the yearned-for vitality.

It is obvious but of the greatest significance that in the primitivism of New Negro and negritude writers, objective and subjective nonsynchronicity are always on the verge of collapsing into each other. The charged remnant holds the promise of the charged self. The project of recovering and reigniting that self presents the most fraught and therefore most pungent possibilities for primitivist writing, a tension well-captured by René Ménil: "Negritude is an aesthetic *that mistakes itself for its identity* and so takes itself for an anthropology—for the truth of an actually existing mentality."[21] And so we find Aimé Césaire frequently making ironic gestures of ontological identification: "I am a pyramid planted by a dynasty vanished from all memory."[22] The great work of literary primitivism turns out to be Césaire's *Cahier d'un retour au pays natal*, in which ironic reflection and earnest vitalism, civilized mediateness and primitive immediacy contend in an explosive dialectical struggle.

Perhaps the suspicion arises that in order to make the case for a utopian anticapitalist primitivism, a politically correct mask is found for it. There is no politically correct primitivism. Indeed, it is only after the failure to dissolve racialized consciousness in decolonization that political correctness could be deemed any kind of a solution to the inertias of racial oppression. Concretely, this means that we cannot overlook Léopold Senghor's affirmation of Nazi blood and soil ideology in the early 1930s any more than we can Lawrence's statements about strong leaders and blood consciousness. Senghor would later recant, claiming that such gestures were a rhetoric unleashed, but this study is not interested in excuses.[23] Worldviews at the time were soaked in racial illusions. Even as I maintain the distinction between language as shaped into works of art and as a blunt instrument for ideology, I recognize that the former absorbs rhetorical force from its potential misrecognition as the latter. This produces putrid ironies: "I accept . . . I accept . . . completely, with no reservation . . . / my race which no ablution of hyssop mixed with lilies / could purify."[24] The question is why this illusion, so evidently tied up with the language of oppression, seemed necessary, even to such a careful thinker as Alain Locke. The significance of this will become clearer when we elaborate on the claim that primitivism was a *project* and undertake the long meditation in Chapter 5 on Fanon reading Césaire against Sartre.

Just as there can be no access to emphatic primitivism by first profiling the variety of ideas that it supposedly idealizes, so separating out ideas of the "Negro" or "Africa" in order to unlock negritude's emphatic primitivism would be misguided. The deconstruction of negritude's supposed essentialism only draws attention away from that movement of primitivist striving that tends inherently to surpass any fixed representation or form. It also needs to be clarified that negritude is not a subcategory of primitivism, nor does primitivism encompass the range of aesthetic and ideological practices that have been called negritude. For this study, particular works of negritude *are* primitivism; we cannot make intelligible the broader phenomenon except from the vantage of these works.

This also allows us better to demarcate the "window of opportunity" of which I spoke in the preface. If emphatic primitivism erupts at the moment of Imperialism, we see now that its terminus is decolonization. The "chthonic" spirit of primitivism turns against globalizing capital in its guise as unlimited expansion through colonizing agents. After decolonization, there is no such specific agent of capital, and the ensuing subsumption of postcolonial national economies in a deterritorialized global market extinguished the smoldering light that had given the primitivist project its impetus.[25]

It remains in this first part of the book to advance a little further what is meant by an "aesthetic project" and to put to rest any lingering doubts around the question of representation.

Chapter 4

THE QUESTION OF REPRESENTATION

The Representation-to-Abstraction Fallacy

Questions of representation cannot be ignored in discussions of literary primitivism. If they were ignored, we would be in the realm of absolute alterity: the neo-primitivists' "primitivism without primitives." When the consideration of primitivism is restricted to questions of representation, though, we miss that movement in the work that surpasses any particular representation or fixed notion of the primitive. In the light of the historical argument of the previous two chapters, the basis for this claim should now be clearer. The perceived subsumption of all "natural economies" into the world-system at the time of Imperialism and, with it, the encroaching sense that primitive experience was at the point of its final liquidation meant that this condition could no longer merely be portrayed by artworks but would need to be renewed through their agency.

We need, therefore, to inquire into the ways in which the primitive *qua* remnant gets absorbed into and transformed by the work. What is the remnant, and in what respect is it primitive? To what social reality is it perceived to belong? How can that reality be known? What would it take to rekindle the social condition perceived within the remnant? What problems are encountered when trying to do so? The answers in any given instance cannot be generalized, because primitivism is not a single tendency but a process pursued in different ways and in accordance with quite diverse intuitions about the desired primitive destination. Primitivism is an emphatic concept in the dialectical sense that Adorno uses the term: at once categorical and qualitative. There are no criteria one could use to ascertain whether a given work is or is not primitivist. Judgments concern *intensity*, and this can only arise in the experience of primitivist works and be articulated through interpretive reflection.

This means that we need to attend to the kinetic movement of representations of primitive remnants within the overall dynamic of literary works and, at the same time, to appreciate the protean nature of techniques of representation themselves, which, as any account of modernism will alert us, were especially volatile at this time. In this chapter I will consider the work of four artists working respectively in the media of painting, narrative fiction (long and then short), and poetry to investigate how the question of representation arises in different ways across these different media and genres.

In his 1938 study Robert Goldwater observes a tendency in a certain class of primitivist paintings toward the fusion of representation and form: "a continual extension and expansion of the type of object represented, its vaguer and vaguer iconographic definition, until all its qualities as object and even as type of object are lost, its formal and representational aspects are merged into one, and it is impossible to tell (but not because of any unclarity of technique) what is geometry and what the subject matter."[1] The suggestion that the tendency in primitivist works is always toward abstraction has led to what I will call the representation-to-abstraction fallacy, something particularly prevalent in the discussion of primitivism in visual art. It is assumed that primitivism has an inherent drive toward abstraction and, therefore, that full abstraction equates to a fully realized primitivism. The inherent tendency of primitivism is thus identical to that of modernism, conventionally conceived.

When we start to inquire into how works pursue the primitive as a *project*, and not as a subject, and set out to make judgments about the intensity of their primitivism rather than the fact of it, we start to see quite different patterns. The work and career of the German painter Emil Nolde is an interesting case. In her excellent discussion of Nolde in *German Expressionism: Primitivism and Modernity*, Jill Lloyd shows that the artist's persistent attraction to non-European subjects and styles prompted different artistic approaches at different stages of his life. Early drawings of Assyrian and Egyptian sculptures exhibit "painstaking attempts to copy his models as accurately as possible according to inherited traditions of nineteenth-century vision and technique."[2] Nolde commented later in his career that these efforts were conducted not for the sake of making an accurate copy but came from the same questing impulse that would eventually lead him to "seek guidance from vigorous primitive peoples."[3] Like many European painters, he became interested in ethnographic museums in the first decade of the twentieth century. In 1911–12 he conducted studies of objects at the Berlin Ethnographic Museum that he then used as material for a series of still lifes.

These fascinating works occupy, with volatility, a "complex zone" between representation and abstraction, mimesis and the free play of color.[4] Lloyd notices that in his *Mask Still Life I*, the bright blue background shines equally through the eye holes of five overlapping masks, reducing the sense of spatial depth and rendering them as flat superimpositions.[5] This loosening of objects from spatial context was intensified when Nolde started bringing together objects from a variety of places and times into "theatrical encounters," such as in *Man, Woman and Cat*.[6] The figures in this work were taken from sketches of a Cameroonian throne and a carved Nigerian door that were displayed in different sections of the museum.[7] The figures are a flat mat, set against a textural background, drawing attention not so much to the individual characteristics of the objects as their mystical relations and oppositions as types. There is an even more radical juxtaposition of objects in *Figure and Chickens* and *Still Life, Exotic Figure, Mask and Rider*, in which there is no sense of a narrative that might connect the figures. They produce an "autonomous rhetoric of gesture."[8]

At this point we might expect that this will follow the familiar story told of Nolde's contemporaries, most frequently Picasso, according to which the "primitive" object is just one means European artists used to free themselves from conventions of perspective and representation. The teleology of these autonomous gestures will be full abstraction. (And the cultural critic will not fail to add that Nolde's mix-and-match approach reveals a flippant and appropriative attitude to the cultures from which the objects were drawn.)

Nolde's work would take quite a different path vis-à-vis the primitive. In 1913 he accompanied an expedition of the German Imperial Colonial Office to New Guinea. A generation after Gauguin, and in the longer tradition of Europeans questing for the primitive in the Pacific, another artist travels to the region with the project of revitalizing the language of color and form.[9] What Nolde discovered was a fallen colonial reality: a "crude and extreme colonialism" that is a "brutal business."[10] With the arrival of missionaries and then soldiers, he commented in his diary, "The first, great door is opened . . . for adventurers, for dubious European rubbish carrying venereal diseases, and for greedy salesmen. The colony is secured." The life forms of Nolde's would-be "nature-humans"

(*Naturvölker*), like Rousseau's "savages known to us," had long been disrupted by colonial conditions.[11]

Nolde occupied an ambivalent position in the colonial expedition. Although he was disgusted and ashamed by the visible effects of colonialism, his task was to carry out a demographic study of "the racial characteristics of the population."[12] This brief supplies the frame for his watercolor sketches of New Guinean laborers. As Andrew Zimmerman observes, these were the subjects of primitive accumulation—indigenous laborers who had been expropriated and drawn into the colonial labor economy. The watercolors display neither an attempt to resolve general problems of painterly practice nor attempts to gain an exact ethnographic image. Lloyd describes them as striking a "delicate balance between observation and expression."[13] Thick outlines and a range of colors are used selectively to convey nuances of light and mood in the faces of his subjects.[14] Unlike his primitivist works, these seem to be more aware of the potentially contradictory relation between colonialism and representational mode.

The paintings and woodcuts that Nolde worked up from his sketches and memories of his New Guinea trip once he returned to Germany, however, are much closer to the expressionistic aesthetic of the still lifes of 1911–12. At a remove from the all-too-mediated presence of his "primitive" subjects, Nolde was once again ambitious in his approach to color, texture, and form, for which a "primitive" content seems once again only the prompt. Lloyd comments that the fluctuation between realist sensitivity and expressionist hyperbole, and Nolde's ambivalence toward the "primitive" as seen over the span of his career, typifies the primitivism of the German expressionists more generally: a response to modernity that is simultaneously reactionary and revolutionary.[15] Her verdict is that the production of a forward-looking aesthetic to express a backward-looking *völkische* ideal "uncovers a deep-rooted paradox."[16]

This paradox, I am contending, extends well beyond German expressionism and European modernism as they are conventionally delineated. It is characteristic of the primitivist project, which fluctuates between the desire to be true to specific instantiations of the primitive but realizes, in so doing, that it must renew the condition of possibility for that existence. Nolde found he was not able to go to New Guinea and declare "like that." His works become primitivist precisely in the attraction toward and then movement away from conventions of representation. A descriptive realism would only fossilize the primitive, a fully realized abstraction would suggest that one could, in one leap, gain the wished-for immediacy.

This is not the same thing as claiming that *Nolde*, the biographical subject, was a primitivist. We have traced a trajectory in his career toward works that are alive in the complex zone between representation and abstraction, in which, it turns out, the remnant is something more like a wish.[17] Just because the appropriation by early twentieth-century artists of African and Oceanic resources have been placed within an art-historical narrative that designates the "primitive" as a stepping stone toward abstraction, this should not prescribe those works' incipient intentions. We may well decide that some of Picasso's works are emphatically primitivist but not others.[18] These can only be understood by engaging with each work in its dynamic relation to its material. The purpose of this excursus on Nolde has been only to demonstrate the ways in which questions of representation must look to the fluctuations of style and form, not simply the presence, or transcendence, of a galvanizing "primitive" remnant.

D. H. Lawrence's *The Rainbow*

The primitivist project must pursue its ends or, we might say, conduct its primitivizations, using different means where the medium is linguistic. As Erhard Schüttpelz has commented, the fame and notoriety of primitivism in the visual arts has meant that the inner workings of literary primitivism have largely been understood by invoking the borrowed representation-to-abstraction narrative.[19] In turning now to a primitivist novel, D. H. Lawrence's *The Rainbow* (1915), we must keep in mind that novels are temporal objects, read over large spans of time. It is not enough simply to focus on evidently primitivist images in the narrative. We need to trace the movement of the narrative as it manifests the work's primitivism. I will work my way through the generic and stylistic shifts in *The Rainbow* in order to identify the buildup of primitivist energy that bursts forth at its end—that is, those sections that typically get cited when discussing Lawrence's primitivism.

The Rainbow opens with a parable-like account of the rhythm of the generations of the Brangwen family. They are "fresh, blond, slow-speaking people . . . living on rich land, on their own land."[20] They have a look in their eyes "as if they were expecting something unknown, about which they were eager" (*R*, 9). The generations of the family exist in vibrant interchange with their land and have a stable relationship with the nearby town of Cossethay. Prose repetitions suggest organic cycles, made even more conspicuous in the following lines with the use of anapests: "they took the udder of the cows, the cows yielded milk and pulse against the hands of the men, the pulse of the blood of the teats of the cows beat into the pulse of the hands of the men" (*R*, 10). The men are bound to the earth and realize their life-force working the farm. The women, however, face two ways: behind, to the "blood-intimacy" (*R*, 10) of cattle, but also outward, to "the spoken world beyond" (*R*, 10)—that is, to civic life. Here the parable starts to lose its timelessness with the introduction of a particular, if unnamed, female Brangwen. In line with her type, she is reflective and speaks often with the local vicar, recognizing in him a power that she does not find in her husband. She tries to work out how this can be when her husband has more wealth and a sturdier frame. She concludes that it is the vicar's education; he has "the power of thought and comprehension" (*R*, 13).

The next section begins: "About 1840, a canal was constructed across the meadows of the Marsh Farm, connecting the newly opened collieries of the Erewash Valley" (*R*, 13). The clock is set and started: the farm is now presented as a part of evolving material conditions, and we learn that it had only been through luck that it had not previously been encroached on by the mines. In a few lines we are taken through the lives of the Brangwens of 1840. Alfred marries Heanor, the daughter of a local publican, and they have four sons and two daughters. The oldest son runs away to sea. After a "savage rebellion" the second son trains as a draughtsman and moves to Nottingham to work in a lace factory, where he marries the daughter of a chemist. Frank becomes a butcher, Alice marries a collier, and Effie remains at home. Each of these stories might be a novel, but the narrative comes to focus on the youngest, Tom, who rides out the process of education and the lure of broader aspirations to stay on and work the land. This does not mean that his life plays out in neat conformity to archetype. After a distressing encounter with a prostitute, he represses his "sex-desire" throughout his twenties (*R*, 28). It is a stranger in a black bonnet, Lydia Lensky, the exiled widow of a Polish revolutionary, who reawakens him. She enters Cossethay from world-history—political contest, revolution, exile— bringing with her a four-year-old daughter, Anna.

Their union is not the collision of History and Archetype that might be expected. They marry, have two sons, and live a steady existence on the farm. Much later in the novel, we learn that Lydia believes that Tom had "made himself immortal in his knowledge with her. So she had her place here, in life, and in immortality" (*R*, 240). She has been reabsorbed from History into the immortal rhythms of Archetype. Lydia, we learn, was the figure at the start of the novel who reflects on the power of education and who we might have thought would take us beyond the perimeter of the parable. It transpires that she has no interest in pursuing "the power of thought and comprehension."

The novel shifts to Anna, who takes her stepfather's name. We are guided through her childhood and marriage to her step-cousin Will Brangwen. With this couple desire comes into contradiction with the necessities of their union, and there is an intensification of what I will call Lawrence's "techniques of immediacy": the stretching and repetition of conceits, images, and metaphors over many passages that nonetheless describe only brief moments in time. When Will and Anna first make love, Lawrence uses the conceit of the "rind": "He surveyed the rind of the world: houses, factories, trams, the discarded rind; people scurrying about, work going on, all on the discarded surface. An earthquake had burst it all from inside. It was as if the surface of the world had been broken away entire: Ilkeston, streets, church, people, work, or rule-of-the-day, all intact; and yet peeled away into unreality, leaving here exposed the inside, the reality, one's own being" (*R*, 139). The "rind" conceit is then used to characterize Will's struggles with Anna, who frustrates him by remaining turned outward to the "rind of the world." Pages of contest follow, as the pair wrestle both to possess one another and yet remain independent, especially Anna from Will's attempts to dominate her.

The conflict comes to a climax with Anna's first pregnancy, and her bid for total independence. In one scene she dances in exaltation of herself. Will enters, and she pauses but then continues: "With slow, heavy movements, she swayed backwards and forwards, like a full ear of corn, pale in the dusky afternoon, threading before the firelight, dancing his non-existence, dancing herself to the Lord, to exhortation. He watched, and his soul burned in him" (*R*, 170–71). Although expressed in Christian terms, the scene is pagan in character, as if a birth-rite surges up through Anna.

She is victorious; Will accedes to her elemental motherhood and no longer tries to command her affections. Around this time he visits London and experiences a moment of nonsynchronous dislocation (one not dissimilar to that which Marlowe seeks to elicit from his companions toward the start of Conrad's *Heart of Darkness*). Will marvels that this civilization had been built up by people who were once "helpless savages, running with their spears on the riverside" (*R*, 179). This insight gives him inner confidence: "sweep away the whole monstrous superstructure of the world today, cities and industries and civilisation, leave only the bare earth with plants growing and waters running, and he would not mind, so long as he were whole, had Anna and the child and the

new, strange certainty in his soul. Then, if he were naked, he would find cloth-
ing somewhere, he would make a shelter and bring food to his wife" (R, 179).

The couple reach equilibrium but only after they have rebuffed a more
forceful incursion from the world beyond their immediate sphere than that
endured by the previous generation. In union they keep themselves closed off
from the world, something that is confirmed when they visit Lincoln Cathedral. The building previously had made Will's spirits soar, but he now finds that
its peculiar power lies in the fact of its being a *relic*. Pursuing a career as choir-
master and then as artisan, Will moves into the nostalgic mode of the "arts and
crafts" movement.

The narrative next turns to their firstborn, Ursula. Unlike the previous generations, her story is open-ended and breaks decisively with the circuit of the
Brangwen archetype. With Ursula, the philo-primitivist idealization of organic
social relations and fertility becomes a questing, individuated, outward-driven
primitiv*ism*. The novel's genre also shifts. What had been a cyclical novel of
generational succession is pushed into a linear, open-ended *Bildungsroman*.

With each of the novel's first two generations, the narrative moves relatively
quickly to scenes of courtship, marriage, and procreation, and the fates of the
characters are cast within a more localized temporality and ontological horizon
than the *Bildungsroman*'s "national-historical time."[21] When it comes to Ursula,
many more episodes from her girlhood are related and more attention given to
the travails of an emergent self: "how to act, that was the question? Whither
to go, how to become oneself? One was not oneself, one was merely a half-
stated question" (R, 264). When her first flame, Anton Skrebensky, eventually
enters, there is the same intensity as there had been with the previous couples.
Yet, from the start, her stance toward these encounters is related in the terms of
self-realization: "it was begun, now, this passion, and must go on, the passion
of Ursula to know her own maximum self, limited and so defined against him"
(R, 281). At the same time, the affairs of nation and empire encroach on their
love. Ursula is repulsed by Anton's desire to fight in war, but it only deepens
their desire. After their first sexual encounter at her uncle's wedding, Anton is
absorbed by History, leaving to fight in the Second South African War: "one
had to fill one's place in the whole, the great scheme of man's elaborate civilisation, that was all" (R, 304).

Over the next six years Ursula has an affair with her schoolmistress, a suf-
fragette; becomes a school mistress herself, a vocation she finds cruel and hard-
ening; and goes to university. For the first time in the novel, lovers are realizing

themselves outside of marriage, and it is in the novel's penultimate chapter that we are plunged finally into a declared primitivism. Or, better, the primitivist energy building up beneath the surface of the narrative makes itself apparent.

Just before Anton reenters the narrative, Ursula meditates on the disjuncture she feels between her essence and the wider world into which it wants to emerge:

> This world in which she lived was like a circle lighted by a lamp. This lighted area, lit up by man's completest consciousness, she thought was all the world: that here all was disclosed for ever. Yet all the time, within the darkness she had been aware of points of light, like the eyes of wild beasts, gleaming, penetrating, vanishing. And her soul had acknowledged in a great heave of terror, only the outer darkness. This inner circle of light in which she lived and moved, wherein the trains rushed and the factories ground out their machine-produce and the plants and the animals worked by the light of science and knowledge, suddenly it seemed like the area under an arc-lamp. (*R*, 405)

It takes a moment of profound dislocation for her to perceive that the totality that constitutes her world has a perimeter. This realization might be detached from any concrete situation, but psychoanalytic critics long ago cracked the binary code of knowledge-as-conscious-light and desire-as-unconscious-dark, and soon after, postcolonial theorists demonstrated that this correlates to a binary of colonizing Europe and its colonized Others. Right on cue, Skrebensky returns from Africa, and these meditations are projected onto the geography of Empire:

> He was to her a voice out of the darkness. He talked to her all the while, in low tones, about Africa, conveying something strange and sensual to her: the negro, with his loose, soft passion that could envelop one like a bath. Gradually he transferred to her the hot, fecund darkness that possessed his own blood. He was strangely secret. The whole world must be abolished. (*R*, 413)

This is what Skrebensky relates by utterance:

> "I am not afraid of the darkness in England," he said. "It is soft, and natural to me, it is my medium, especially when you are here. But in Africa it seems massive and fluid with terror—not fear of anything—just fear. One breathes it, like a smell of blood. The blacks know it. They worship it, really, the darkness. One almost likes it—the fear—something sensual." (*R*, 413)

This, it would seem, is as straightforward a manifestation of primitivism as colonial discourse as there could be. The African "Other" is valorized within a structure of representations that correspond to the terms used to justify and sustain colonial conquest. The racist language essentializes "the negro" as inherently sensual, subsumed by primal forces, even as it intimates that such characteristics are the qualities of anticivilizational distinction. The valorization only serves to entrench the terms of this framework. As it is built on such assumptions, rather than bringing them into question, this primitivism is to be critiqued as racist ideology.

An argument that runs in this direction is certainly formidable. To seek to redeem primitivism from these overtly racist passages would be foolhardy, and I do not mean to do any such thing. What I would like to bring into question is the manner in which these racist mediations are situated in the movement of the novel's primitivism. What has come to be theorized as colonial discourse here draws the perimeter beyond which primitivism strains. The "terror" that breathes through Skrebensky is not, for Ursula, the end point—some achieved primitive state—but the sense of a possible condition beyond, which is only fractionally more concrete than her circle-of-light epiphany. In Lawrence's historical moment and place such limits can still just about be perceived as geographical and only just adhere to some putative "primitive" human in that dark space. On the cusp of the integration of all human communities into a single world-system, Ursula, through Skrebensky, strains to intuit an ideal life-form beyond what are only just still spatial limits.

In the scenes that follow, Ursula despairs that she cannot go there. Skrebensky is to join the colonial elite in India, and she asks him: "'What do you govern for, but to make things there as dead and mean as they are here?'" (R, 427-28). In the same scene she is exasperated by trains running through the meadows in Sussex: "So little, yet its courage carried it from end to end of the earth, till there was no place where it did not go. . . . The blind, pathetic, energetic courage of the train as it is steamed tinily away through the patterned levels to the sea's dimness. . . . The train had tunnelled all the earth, blindly, and uglily" (R, 429–30). These broodings on the limitless scope of Empire, on where light meets darkness, on whether there is any darkness left, are driven inward into the dynamics of Ursula's and Skrebensky's passion. What in previous generations was a struggle for reconciliation within marriage is now a struggle between two states of desire: Anton's desire for containment within orderly marriage and Ursula's desire to go beyond the limits of the known. Sex is unleashed from its social function. They fuck everywhere, and everywhere it is a contest because they do not share a common end. The affair ends with this following exchange: "'Is it my fault?' he said, looking up at length, challenging the last stroke. 'You couldn't—' she began. But she broke down" (*R*, 446). Within days Skrebensky is engaged to another woman and moves with her to India.

Ursula breaks definitively from the organic cycle of the rural archetype. This does not mean, however, that she has shed her Brangwen qualities. There have been wayward Brangwens before, and the British Empire is hardly new. Ursula's primitivism, the narrative encourages us to conclude, is not that of a discrepant subjectivity but the moment that History breaks the Archetype. Will and Anna were driven from immediacy into nostalgia. When this new generation seeks refuge, they find that everywhere has been made gray by "civilization." With Ursula the Brangwens vault over the national-historical time within whose bounds protagonists typically developed in the nineteenth-century *Bildungsroman*. Her trajectory conforms to what Joshua Esty has identified as the arrested development of the genre's protagonists in the age of Imperialism. This "unseasonable youth," Esty comments, "condenses into the language of character and plot this new, open-ended phase in imperial/finance capitalism."[22] Marriage no longer presents closure, and there is no readily available alternative form of equilibrium toward which to develop.

Unexpectedly, the novel ends with an image of hope, a rainbow, which could easily come across as trite. Every now and then, though, a cliché can be invested with new energy:

> And the rainbow stood on the earth. She knew that the sordid people who crept hard-scaled and separate on the face of the world's corruption were living still, that the rainbow was arched in their blood and would quiver to life in their spirit, that they would cast off their horny covering of disintegration, that new, clean, naked bodies would issue to a new germination, to a new growth, rising to the light and the wind and the clean rain of heaven. She saw in the rainbow the earth's new architecture, the old, brittle corruption of houses and factories swept away, the world built up in a living fabric of Truth, fitting to the overarching heaven. (*R*, 459)

I would like to suggest that this passage brings to a climax the novel's primitivism. The remnant has been progressively emptied of specific content and has given way entirely to abstraction. The image (the rainbow's pure spectrum of color), the world to emerge ("Truth"), and the attributes of the beings that will emerge with it ("new," "clean," "naked") push beyond our capacity to think a concrete situation. The primitive condition is now entirely a speculative one. The risk is that the level of abstraction needed to express this leads only to banalities—a hopeless hope forced by total immanence. The potency of the novel's primitivism comes in the realization that such a trite image might be the only available exit.

Is there a correlation between the seemingly inexorable movement toward abstraction in *The Rainbow* and the "complex zone" in which representation and abstraction vacillate in Nolde? To answer in the affirmative would be to conflate questions of form and technique in Nolde's work with those of genre and theme in Lawrence's. The remnant's potentiality and its capacity for aesthetic activation operate within the single visual field in works like *Man, Woman and Cat*. In *The Rainbow* the remnant, whether it be the organic social relations of Tom Brangwen's farm, Will Brangwen's Lincoln cathedral, or Anton Skrebensky's racialized "negro," and the moment of primitive renewal, the rainbow, have a relation through the temporal movement of the narrative. If one wanted to push the correlation harder, it could be argued that the prose in Lawrence's novel becomes increasingly abstracted, pointing perhaps to the stylistic shifts accompanying the heightened psychologism in the Ursula section. But even this would assume that "representation" and "abstraction" are fixed categories that apply equally to different materials. "Abstraction" is a metaphor for artistic method, so what we actually would be identifying is a rather tenuous analogy between processes. It seems wiser, then, to conclude that the primitivist project can be undertaken in multiple ways and will produce quite different manifestations in different artistic media and materials.[23]

As this discussion develops, we will find that the terms *mediation* and *immediacy*, rather than *representation* and *abstraction*, will better help us to specify primitivism's morphology. When we come to *The Rainbow*'s sequel in Chapter 6, I will consider in greater detail how Lawrence's narratives attempt to move through mediated existence into immediate life.

Negrophilia, Negrophobia, Negritude

The Negro is life; the Negro is the jungle; the Negro's blood throbs to the rhythm of the tom-tom. The Negro *is* primitive. This is the tense, and these are the clichés, of *negrophilie* or, on the other side of the Atlantic, the "Negro vogue" of the 1920s, and there is nothing nonsynchronous about the simple present. If this is the primitive, here in its immediacy, then representing it will be a straightforward exercise.[24] A bit of cubism, some stream of consciousness, the odd shock of chromaticism might help to give the image an appropriate sense of animation, but it cannot be doubted that it is that flash of dark skin that embodies the principle of animation.

Perhaps the most thoroughgoing deconstruction of negrophilic representation was undertaken by Langston Hughes in his collection *The Ways of White Folks* (1934), most pointedly in the second story, "Slave on the Block": "They were people who went in for Negroes—Michael and Anne—the Carraways," it sarcastically begins, and does not let up.[25] Unlike most white liberals, this bohemian couple have no pretense to a social concern for "Negroes"; their interest is purely aesthetic. They are particularly excited when they encounter the nephew of their recently deceased cook:

> "He *is* the jungle," said Anne when she saw him.
> "He's 'I Couldn't Hear Nobody Pray,'" said Michael.
> For Anne thought in terms of pictures: she was a painter. And Michael thought in terms of music: he was a composer for the piano. (*WW*, 21)

They hire him on the spot, ostensibly for odd jobs but really to be an in-house model for Anne and an ethnomusicological specimen for Michael. Before long Luther is at his ease, singing work songs half-naked around the house during the day, crawling around Harlem and sleeping with their maid at night.

The title of the story is also the crux of the satire. Anne has the idea of painting Luther as a slave for sale—"She wanted to paint him now representing to the full the soul and sorrow of his people" (*WW*, 24)—and asks him to pose on a box. Michael comes in, goes into raptures and immediately resolves to "put him into music": "a modern slave plaint, 1850 in the terms of 1933" (which sounds like "Deep River in the jaws of a dog" [*WW*, 25]). Things fall apart when Michael's negrophobic mother arrives from Kansas City and insists that Luther be dismissed. Michael carries out her wishes in spite of Anne's protestations that she hasn't yet finished her work.

The story allegorizes the essentializing folly of negrophilic representation (something that pertains as much to music here as it does painting). When the Carraways get carried away by the image of Luther as a slave, they reveal that their perception of his supposedly uninhibited sensuality is not nature but history. They are seduced by the image of their own racial domination, which is sublimated into their philo-primitivism.

"Rejuvenation Through Joy" is a different kind of satire. Eugene Lesche, whose racial identity is kept deliberately ambiguous throughout the story, is a handsome man who uses his charms to swindle money from middle-class white women through various schemes. When he discovers the profitability of what would now get called mindfulness retreats, he hits on an idea to capture market share: " 'Looks like to me,' said Lesche, 'a sure way to make money would be, combine a jazz band and a soul colony, and let it roll from there—black rhythm and happy souls' " (WW, 77). He hires a "young Yale man" to write pseudoscientific articles like "Contentment and Aboriginal Rhythms" (WW, 78), gives a series of lectures in New York expounding the "curative values of the Negro jazz" (WW, 73), and establishes a client base among New York's high society.

Lesche's "Cult of Joy" is unabashedly philo-primitivist: "Move to music, he said, to the gaily primitive rhythms of the first man" (WW, 70); "*See how the Negroes live, dark as the earth, the primitive earth, swaying like trees, rooted in the deepest source of life*" (WW, 84), and so forth. Unlike the Carraways, these purveyors of racial ideology know what they're doing. Lesche's business partner briefs the colony's band, "the Primitives," that they are to provide "real primitive jazz out of Africa (you know, Harlem) to help 'em learn to move, to walk, to live in harmony with their times and themselves" (WW, 81). At first everything goes according to plan, but when clients start falling in love with Lesche and members of the band, jealousy turns the celebration of spontaneity against itself. One woman fires on the drummer. Seizing the gun, another turns on Lesche: " 'How right to shoot the one you love!' she cried, 'How primitive, how just!' " (WW, 94).

"Rejuvenation Through Joy" satirizes the commodification of black culture, which stands alongside "German eurhythmics, psychoanalysis, Yogi philosophy, all of Krishnamurti, half of Havelock Ellis, and most of Freud" (WW, 80) as just one more cure for instrumental reason and associated ills of modernity. In a perceptive essay on this story, David Chinitz recognizes that although Lesche's theories are a mockery, they are nevertheless "a mockery of something important."[26] To critique the falsity of commodification does not mean that the thing being converted into exchange value is itself false.

This rings especially true when the satires of negrophilia in *The Ways of White Folks* are read alongside the satires of negrophobia. In "The Blues I'm Playing" Hughes turns to the racial politics of patronage. Mrs. Dora Ellsworth is a wealthy widow who has turned her energies and financial means toward the arts. She is particularly keen on nurturing and grooming up-and-coming artists. When she is tipped off by a music critic about a talented pianist, Miss Oceola Jones, her interest is piqued. She has not supported a black artist before, and the appeal of uncovering talent from what seems to her to be an unlikely source is an appealing project. She pays for all of Oceola's living expenses, as well as lessons with the world's best classical pianists, including two years with a master in Paris. She is worried, though, that her investment will come to nothing if Oceola marries her Harlem sweetheart or is drawn toward her musical roots in the playhouses and jazz parties. Despite success in the concert halls, Oceola goes against her patron's wishes. She marries and moves back to Harlem, and Mrs. Ellsworth gives up on her.

In the final scene she goes to Mrs. Ellsworth's place to give a last recital. She plays exquisitely, and Mrs. Ellsworth starts to harangue her for getting married. As she rants, Oceola slips into the blues: "blues that deepened and grew into rollicking jazz, then into an earth-throbbing rhythm that shook the lilies in the Persian vases of Mrs. Ellsworth's music room" (WW, 119). Mrs. Ellsworth freezes in her chair as Oceola makes "the bass notes throb like tomtoms deep in the earth" (WW, 120). The vocabulary used to characterize her playing in the final scene is consistent with that used earlier when she plays at nightclubs in Paris.[27] They also match those used with sarcasm in the satires on negrophilia. In those tales Hughes employs free indirect discourse to ensure that the bad faith informing the language of negrophilia is readily identifiable. There is no such sarcasm in these more detached descriptions of Oceola's playing. No narratorial cues suggest that we ought to read the description of bass notes throbbing like tom-toms deep in the earth as anything but a genuine evocation. These are descriptors of music, not racial type, but Hughes knows the risks involved in playing with that line.

We are not dealing, then, with tropes and stereotypes only but also with generic expectations and the inflections of narrative voice. If the commodification and fetishization of black culture in the "jazz age" present two hazards for Hughes's descriptive language, the phobias of Eurocentric taste and race hierarchy likewise need to be confronted without euphemism. Hughes is negotiating a negritude between the twin perils of negrophilia and negrophobia, essentialism and assimilation. His solution is not to purge his work of all compromised signifiers, ceding the language of authenticity to the salesmen of black culture; rather, he makes use of the apparatus of narration to create an opening in which the truth in contemporary black culture might find expression.

In his article, Chinitz presses the case that the scathing satires of *The Ways of White Folks* follow from a clear break in Hughes's oeuvre after he realized the errors of his earlier negrophilia. While there can be no doubt that the stories in *The Ways of White Folks* show a keen awareness of the ways in which the tropes of racial idealization reflect a damaged social reality, this awareness was nevertheless already present in his earlier poetry, even where it appears outwardly "negrophilic":

POEM
For the portrait of an African boy after the manner of Gauguin

All the tom-toms of the jungles beat in my blood,
And all the wild hot moons of the jungles shine in my soul.
I am afraid of this civilization—
    So hard,
      So strong,
        So cold.[28]

It is difficult to determine the function and significance of the line beneath the title and, thus, the way the reference to Gauguin frames the poem. Is it a subtitle? Is it a dedication? Is it a directive? Is it the poem that is "after the manner of Gauguin" or the hypothetical portrait it portrays? It might be that the poem emulates Gauguin, or that it emulates a hypothetical pictorial emulation of Gauguin, or that it is imagining the way in which a Gauguin-like portrait might speak. It could be ventriloquizing the European primitivist's "dummy," to borrow Maria Torgovnick's metaphor, or invoking Gauguin's lurid aesthetic to endow the voice with vivid presence. The "tom-toms" and "wild hot moons of the jungles" could be the conscious invocation of the sham voice of negrophilia or that of an earnest negritude, for which Gauguin is a positive resource.

Of course, these are not just words or cultural discourse; they are formed poetic utterance. The poem opens with the boy making two forthright declarations about his blood and soul. The line break comes at the caesura, so these utterances have a prose rhythm. Breaks continue to follow the punctuation, but when it comes to characterizing the civilization that confronts the boy, there are three short clauses with an advancing margin, each consisting of a monosyllabic adjective with anaphoric intensifier. The poem produces a distinct, if short-lived, rhythm that echoes the two-beat "tom-toms" of the first line. The poem does not give the image just interiority but also rhythmic force.

The interpretation that most tempts me is that the poem gives expression to the otherwise mute "primitive" subject of Gauguin's work. It occupies the perspective of the image as it gazes back at the artist and gallery viewers. The mimesis of the tom-tom animates his fear in the rhythm that he declares to be innate, giving force to the confrontation. The poem's strength, though, is to hold a number of possibilities in tension at the same time. We have no access to the boy's interiority, let alone his "nature," except through the surface of the evoked Gauguin-like image, one that might either be impeding or intensifying our connection to this nature. To use the language of the fragment of Carl Einstein discussed in the last chapter, European "mediateness" must be pushed through; it cannot be summarily dismissed.

In "Danse Africaine," another poem from *The Weary Blues*, Hughes's rhythmic mimesis is even more emphatic: repetition, assonance, ellipsis, and apostrophe are all deployed to create the effect of the "low beating of the tom-toms" that "Stirs your blood."[29] The question here concerns the addressee: *whose* blood is being stirred? If the French title is taken as a self-conscious affectation, we might imagine that the poem's "night-veiled girl" is performing for the cultured white audience of the ballet, whose blood is stirred by the *frisson* of her difference. If not, it might address a middle-class Harlemite who is stirred by a neo-African sense of self. Again, the ambiguity is constitutive of the poem's primitivism.

In Hughes's early poetry the song of negritude never quite sings freely. The awareness of mediation restrains the voice from abandoning itself to the intimation of the immediate, sending it in the direction of the lament or the blues, and a wistful subjunctive. "Afro-American Fragment" reflects on the loss of culture, beginning with the short lines "So long, / So far away, Is Africa." The lines swell in length to the stanza's central utterance, which promises hope of recovery through song—"Save those that songs beat back into the blood—," before then receding with the knowledge that these are sung in mediated language: "Beat out of blood with words sad sung / in strange un-Negro tongue—."[30] This is fragment as generic description but also as residue of a lost African world. Perhaps it is even a triple pun, acting as verb to convey the fragmentation of African selfhood. The poem's end holds the promise that the song will sound through "some vast mist of race," yet even this is one "Of bitter yearnings lost, without a place—."[31] Not only is Africa lost but perhaps also the bitter yearning for it. It is a song that has lost contact with the remnant.

Reflecting on the period when these poems were written forty years later, Hughes commented that "had the word *negritude* been in use in Harlem in the twenties, Cullen, as well as McKay, Johnson, Toomer, and I, might have been called poets of *negritude*."[32] To bring his work within the frame of negritude is an anachronism that, it seems, he welcomed. Nevertheless, there is a tonal and, perhaps, deeper aesthetic shift when it comes to the work of emphatically primitivist negritude, which will be discussed in the second part of this book.

To intimate what this might be, and to bring this discussion of representation to a close, we can look at a poem by Hughes's Haitian friend Jacques Roumain, whose verse adopts a register that is both more forthrightly primitivist and political. Roumain does not baulk at contrasting "the murmuring water where / your fathers bent their dark faces" with "the white man . . . this bit of / sea spume cast out, like spit, upon the shore" ("When the Tom-Tom Beats").[33] In the frankly hostile anticolonial poem "Sales Nègres" ("Filthy Negroes"), from his final collection, *Bois-d'Ébène* (*Ebony Wood*, 1944), Roumain cultivates a Manichaean poetics in which the distinction between negrophilia and negritude is unambiguous, delineated according to a critique of commodification. It is better to quote from the original to perceive the pan-African, transatlantic arena in which its confrontation is staged:

> un nègre
> n'est qu'un instrument
> à chanter, n'est-ce pas,
> à danser, of course
> à forniquer, naturlich
> rien qu'une denrée
> à acheter à vendre
> sur le marché du plaisir
>
> (nothing but a commodity
> to buy or sell
> on the pleasure market)[34]

These "filthy negroes" are starting to play "another rhythm":

> deep into the heart of infernal jungles
> will throb the terrible telegraphic beating
> of the tom-toms beating tirelessly beating
> beating[35]

The beating does not emerge from the jungle but beats into it—a movement toward the source, not a memory of it. The poem closes with a call for all the "wretched of the earth" (Fanon knew this poem) to overthrow "this world / of negroes / niggers / filthy negroes," for "even the tom-toms will have learned the language / of the *Internationale*."[36] The remnant has become the medium of a primal class confrontation, whose racial lineaments have been constituted in global imperialism.

PART II

Studies

Chapter 5

CÉSAIRE, FANON, AND IMMEDIACY AS A PROJECT

I argued in Part I for a conception of literary primitivism as a historically contingent phenomenon specific to the period between the apotheosis of imperialism and the dissolution of the European empires. Given that primitivism has long been understood as a transhistorical tendency according to which those discontented by "civilization" idealize whatever notions of the "primitive" are prevalent at the time, I focused on the theoretical and historical considerations required to reconceive of primitivism in this way. It was necessary, in particular, to dismantle the assumptions that have led in recent scholarship to a nearly exclusive focus on questions of representation and ideology. In the works discussed in the last chapter of Part I, we began to establish that emphatic primitivism is characterized not by a drive to represent the primitive but the attempt, through art, to renew the possibility of primitive experience. The works vacillate between appeals to the nonsynchronous remnants of lost "primitive" worlds (whether by representative or other means) and intimations of a primitive world to come, for which a new aesthetic language is sought. To identify this vacillation is not to suggest that we should revert to the primitivism-as-modernism thesis that is still embedded in some histories of visual art whereby primitivism was one means by which Western artists broke with long-standing perspectival conventions and embraced abstraction. Adopting "the point of view of totality," I have argued that primitivism was an aesthetic mode promulgated across the world-system at the height of European imperialism, a time when it was widely believed that the precondition for primitive experience, what Rosa Luxemburg termed "natural economy," had been decisively overwhelmed by a geographically totalized capitalism.

This argument is materialist in two senses: one associated with an orthodox Marxist viewpoint, the other as practiced by critical theorists, especially Theodor Adorno. The violent disruption of relations of production as the productive means across diverse social realities either were co-opted into or eliminated by the political economy of the commodity prompted widespread nonsynchronous longing for those previous social realities, especially given the new kinds of domination and violence experienced by those forcibly conscripted into this world-system. The totalization of capitalist political economy may have been global—it *combined* all previously existing non- and semi-capitalist societies—but it was not experienced in a uniform way—its social consequences were *uneven*. New and old fused and *developed* in highly localized and contingent ways, producing a world-historical situation marked by profound social contradictions, constitutive inequality, and psychotemporal dislocations. To understand this situation as primitivism's material *precondition* is not to say that these conditions *determined* or directly were registered in primitivism's aesthetic forms. Literary primitivism is not the immediate manifestation of social contradictions; it wants to understand and negate those contradictions, using the peculiar materials of literature to do so.

As outlined in *Aesthetic Theory*, Adorno's notion of "the material" of artworks helps us to perceive the specific expressive possibilities available at any given time in a particular medium. The material refers not to the raw matter artists use to make objects but "the sum of all that is available to them, including words, colors, sounds, associations of every sort and every technique ever developed. . . . It is everything that artists encounter about which they must make a decision."[1] Artistic material, in short, combines physical stuff with the received conventions of expression. Thinking about art in terms of its material allows us to see that artistic decisions do not manipulate matter but the existing techniques for manipulating matter. If this at first appears to suggest materials are gathered from one enormous quarry of possible expressive means, the progressive, which is not to imply improving, character of art means that only particular materials can be meaningfully employed at any given moment. Superficially, we might think of the waxing and waning of artistic fashions and the way these affect technique: the use of the long take in neorealist cinema, flashbacks in science fiction, or found objects in Dada, for example. The notion of the material is historical, but its theoretical purpose is not to furnish historical explanations. For Adorno it provides the basis for perceiving the unique meaning-making capacity of artworks. He suggests that by attending to the specific demands made by artistic materials, and the way in which works respond to these demands, we can interpret their *truth content*. Truth content is not the propositional or image-making dimension of artworks, that which they explicitly say or represent, but that which they implicitly *wish*, something that can only be known by understanding the aesthetic logic that informs their making.[2]

If Part I was concerned largely with identifying the historical and material precondition for literary primitivism, the three studies in Part II undertake to elucidate primitivism's truth content. These two procedures, or, perhaps, materialisms, can hardly be separated. Already we have looked at the ways in which particular works harness the capacities of form in an attempt to re-awaken primitive experience, and we will continue to give studied attention to the world-historical circumstances of the works discussed. Nevertheless, a clear shift in the critical approach will be evident moving into the detailed studies in Part II. Having established new historical parameters, the task now is to make present the aesthetic *event* of primitivism, something that calls for what might be called slow reading. In the first study, at the center of which stands the most significant literary primitivist work, Aimé Césaire's *Cahier d'un retour au pays natal*, I slow read Frantz Fanon's remarkable critical narrative "The Lived Experience of the Black." If this approach to the *Cahier* appears at first circuitous, it is a route worth taking: Fanon's self-conscious primitivization affords a unique opportunity to seize upon the historical forces that the *Cahier* both channels and wields.

The "Process of Regression"

If we wanted to pinpoint the moment that literary primitivism, as an aesthetic mode and historical phenomenon, gained full self-consciousness, we could do worse than supply the date on which the following passage was written:

> I had rationalized the world and the world had rejected me <u>in the name of</u> color prejudice. Since no agreement was possible on the level of reason, I threw my-self back toward unreason. *I had, out of the necessities of my quest, adopted the process of regression*, but it remained an unfamiliar weapon; here I am at home; I am made of the irrational; I wade in the irrational. <u>Irrational up to the neck</u>. And now how my voice vibrates![3]

The past tense, the clear sense of purpose, the cool, even sarcastic tone with which the program of unreason is undertaken, all indicate that primitivism's Owl of Minerva is stretching its wings. I have emphasized the phrase that I would like specially to bring to attention. For reasons that I will consider over the course of this chapter, the speaker has come to understand that primitivism ("the process of regression") is a project ("quest") that a particular set of circumstances has made necessary—most evidently that which has made him unassimilable to the world. This forms the background to the unsettling disjunction between the rhetoric of intellectual inquiry and the brief of regression.

Immediately following this comment, the speaker cites several lines from Aimé Césaire's *Cahier d'un retour au pays natal* (*Notebook of a Return to My Native Land*; herein *Cahier*)—the utterances, that is, which make the speaker's voice "vibrate":

> Those who have invented neither gunpowder nor the compass
> those who have never known how to subdue either steam or electricity
> those who have explored neither the seas nor the sky but those who
> know all the nooks and crannies of the country of suffering
> those whose only voyages have been uprootings
> those who have become flexible to kneeling
> those who were domesticated and christianised
> those who were inoculated with bastardisation . . . (*BS*, 123)[4]

These lines demarcate what we can now identify as the domain of the primitive at the historical moment of emphatic primitivism with all its attendant paradoxes: a condition defined in the negative as something beyond the perimeter of capitalist civilization but that, in being known and identified, reveals itself as subject to colonization. The speaker goes on to quote two further passages from the *Cahier*, which I will consider later, interspersed with his own increasingly hysterical commentary:

> Eia! The tom-tom babbles the cosmic message. Only the Negro has the capacity to convey it, to decipher its meaning, its import. Astride the world, my strong heels spurring into the flanks of the world, I stare into the shoulders of the world as the celebrant stares at the midpoint between the eyes of the sacrificial victim. . . . Blood! Blood! . . . Birth! Ecstasy of becoming! Three-quarters engulfed in the confusions of the day, I feel myself redden with blood. The arteries of the world, convulsed, torn away, uprooted, have turned toward me and fed me. . . .

Black Magic, primitive mentality, animism, animal eroticism, it all floods over me. (*BS*, 124–26)

The speaker self-consciously embraces the delirium of the *Cahier*'s primitivism, alchemically transforming into ontology the terms by which the "Negro" has been socially negated: the quintessence of the non- or even antimodern, the jungle, the "life" that capital has wrung out of its European avatars. It is an irrationalism, we must keep in mind, that the speaker has decided to enter into by rational means, as the conscript to this modernity that racially excludes him.

The year is 1951, the speaker is Frantz Fanon, and these passages are from the essay "The Lived Experience of the Black," which first appeared in the leftist Catholic magazine *Esprit* before being included as the fifth chapter of *Black Skin, White Masks* the following year.[5] Researched and written alongside the other chapters of *Black Skin* over a seven-year period, it is noteworthy that this essay first appeared as a standalone piece. It is the most essayistic and tightly narrated of the chapters in the larger study. It is an epochal piece of writing, in the dual sense of embodying and producing the spirit of its time. It becomes ever harder to imagine how we would think about colonialism, racial alienation, or decolonization and its aftermath without this essay, but also how history would have unfolded without the effects his insights had on his and following generations. With respect to those historical conditions in which literary primitivism emerged, the essay both marks their late apotheosis and anticipates their surpassing with the movements of decolonization, which, for better or worse, brought to a close primitivism's epoch of possibility.

The rhetorical stridency, the vivid dramatization, the unpredictable fluctuations in temperament make it a gripping narrative, and its mix of existential philosophy, psychiatry, psychoanalysis, anthropology, sociology, and cultural and literary criticism produces a dense intellectual fabric. The essay can be read as an intervention in any of these fields, and a focus on only one aspect would diminish its circumference. In other words, it can hardly be read as an essay *about* literary primitivism. What I will argue over the course of this chapter is that it stages an encounter with the psychosocial reality that had made negritude's primitivism, its "process of regression," necessary. Fanon calls on all of these fields of thought both to embody and critically appraise the process of *primitivization*; and here I use the term both in the weak philo-primitivist sense of being assailed by the racial norms and ideals of the colonial metropolis and the emphatic primitivist one of undertaking primitivism as a project of transformation toward the primitive. In addition to Césaire the essay cites or, more precisely, vocalizes poetry by Léopold Senghor, Jacques Roumain, David Diop, and, tellingly, A. M. Vergiat, from his anthropological study *Les rites secrets des primitifs de l'Oubangui*. As will be made clear, among these voices Césaire's is pivotal. Not only is the *Cahier* cited several times, but Fanon splices particular phrases and rhetorical shapes from it into his own essayistic voice. "The Lived Experience of the Black" activates the poetics of negritude in the sarcastic-surrealist mode of Césaire's primitivism. It is a peculiar kind of inter-pretation of the *Cahier*, channeling the force of its poetic knowledge to wield its fusion of satire and neo-African commitment.

The latter aspect, its commitment, is easy to overlook, especially when it has become habitual to condemn or explain away racial tropes and race-based claims, regardless of register or intent. When Fanon cries, "Blood! Blood! . . . Birth! Ecstasy of becoming!" it is easy to assume that his sarcasm is our post-modern irony—how else to hear the hyperbolic exclamations? Those familiar with the *Cahier* will be aware that these words have in fact also been appro-priated from Césaire's text. When he returns to his "own" voice, Fanon is still channeling Césaire's poem.[6] If "Blood! Blood!" is mocking the citation from *Cahier*, then it is a mockery that may well already be present in the poem.

The plot thickens as we read on. It turns out that the motions of self-realiza-tion in negritude, however consciously undertaken, really *did* need to be pur-sued with an absolute resolve, for when a critic comes along to pronounce that his "process of regression" ultimately has a rational, universalist end, Fanon jumps on him:

> Jean-Paul Sartre, in this work, has destroyed black enthusiasm. Against histori-cal becoming he should have opposed the unforeseeable. I needed to lose myself absolutely in negritude. One day, perhaps, in the depths of that unhappy roman-ticism . . .
>
> In any case, I *needed* not to know. This struggle, this redescent had to take on an aspect of completeness. Nothing is more unwelcome than this notion: "you'll change, my boy; when I was young, I too . . . you'll see, all will pass."
>
> The dialectic that introduces necessity at the fulcrum of my freedom drives me out of myself. It shatters my unreflected position. Still in terms of conscious-ness, black consciousness is immanent to itself. . . . My Negro consciousness does not hold itself out as a lack. It *is*. (*BS*, 135)

The work in question is Sartre's essay "Black Orpheus," which served as an introduction to an anthology of negritude poetry edited by Senghor and published in 1948. Fanon is objecting to a passage from Sartre's essay that he cites before the passage I have just cited, in which Sartre speculates that negritude's inversion of white colonial supremacy is not in the name of the black racialism that it appears emphatically to declare but is really a call for all immiserated peoples to rise up against the bourgeois order. Fanon's retort that he "needed not to know this" seems odd, though. The paradoxes of bad faith are casting a long shadow, and it will require close attention to figure out what is going on. As with the rest of the essay, there are abrupt tonal and rhetorical shifts that unsettle the decisive tone. By the time that he says "My Negro consciousness does not hold itself out as a lack. It *is*" we might wonder if the italics in fact signal a surly defensiveness. The aim of this chapter is to put us in a position to comprehend fully the conceptual, rhetorical, and literary aspects of this passage. To do so will require a philological reconstruction of the philosophical and literary environment in which Fanon was writing and, especially, an understanding of why he would channel Césaire's primitivism to rebuff Sartre's theory of negritude.

We might begin by trying to get a handle on the obviously crucial contention that "the dialectic that introduces necessity at the fulcrum of my freedom drives me out of myself"—something that needs to take place without breaking the immanence of "black consciousness." Like many similarly stark philosophical pronouncements in *Black Skin*, it presumes a readership that is familiar with the Hegelian and phenomenological underpinnings of French existentialism. Fanon's notes are suffused with the postwar French intellectual milieu: there are several titles by Sartre, learned engagements with Lacan, and passing references to figures like Michel Leiris, Maurice Merleau-Ponty, Karl Jaspers, Anna Freud, and Francis Jeanson, as well, of course, as Césaire and a number of writers within the *Présence Africaine* group. A thoroughgoing reconstruction of Fanon's intellectual debts and positioning within this milieu, which, it is a surprise to find, has not been undertaken within the voluminous body of scholarship on his work, would take up more space than is available here. I will focus on his various engagements with Sartre, for in them there is an opportunity to get the measure of his productive yet tense relation to the existential moment in Paris, and the way in which he turns the methods and language of French phenomenology against itself as he reflects on the wider colonial reality. Fanon was drawn above all to Sartre's long essay

What Is Literature?, which he explicitly acknowledges as a guiding influence for the entire project of *Black Skin*: "Ever since Sartre's decisive essay, *What Is Literature? (Situations II)*, literature has been committed more and more to its only real task, which is to make the collective pass to reflection and mediation (faire passer la collectivité à la réflexion et à la médiation): this work [i.e., *Black Skin*] wants to be a mirror with a progressive infrastructure, in which it will be possible to discover the Negro on the road to disalienation" (*BS*, 183–84).[7]

Fanon's criticism of "Black Orpheus" on the basis that only a freedom immanent to experience can break the spell of immediacy takes the terms of *What Is Literature?* as its impetus. It resonates particularly strongly with the following passage from Sartre's work: "I shall say that the writer is committed when he tries to achieve the most lucid and the most complete consciousness of being embarked, that is, when he brings himself and others to pass from the commitment of immediate spontaneity to the reflective [fait passer pour lui et pour les autres l'engagement de la spontanéité immédiate au réfléchi]. The writer is a mediator *par excellence* and his commitment is the mediation."[8]

The theoretical disposition of this passage can be found throughout *Black Skin*. In the conclusion, for instance, Fanon comments that an effective understanding of racial objectification cannot proceed by summarily dismissing racial categories but must come through an understanding of a life already "embarked" in a "situation" that has internalized racial categories (*BS*, 230). Fanon's conception of his writing as a "mirror with a progressive infrastructure" likewise echoes several passages in which Sartre refers to literature as a mirror that mediates and transforms what it reflects.[9] Evidently, he had absorbed the notion that the expression of raw immediacy cannot bring on its own transformation, and, following Sartre, he turns to literary experience as a privileged medium in which to think about how such transformations might be possible. Read in the light of this, "The Lived Experience" appears in a way that has not always been apparent in the many exegeses of it: as a *dramatized literary critical essay* in which Fanon enacts the developments of consciousness of negritude poetry in order to challenge Sartre's reading of it.[10]

My discussion will be conducted in four parts. First, I read Sartre's *What Is Literature?* to understand the notion that literature can facilitate a passage from immediacy to reflection, particularly Sartre's claim that narrative fiction had become the medium best able to carry out an "aesthetic modification of the human project." Moving to "Black Orpheus," I show the ways in which he then was forced to modify his argument in order to claim negritude poetry as a significant literature of "commitment." I next come to the mode of Fanon's critique, which, I show, cannot be understood without attention to the effects of style and rhetoric and the influence of Césaire's primitivism. Finally, I look to the complex intertextual fabric of Fanon's polemic against Sartre in "The Lived Experience of the Black." Fanon seeks to embody the movement of experience that he believes is so integral to negritude's project of immediacy. This is a study, thus, of Césaire's primitivism as it was activated by Fanon in the course of pursuing primitivism's decolonial horizon.

"The Aesthetic Modification of the Human Project"

The notion that literature has a unique capacity to bring immediacy into a state of reflection forms part of a general effort by Sartre to describe a "committed literature" (*littérature engagée*) for his times. He wants to show that "at the bottom of the aesthetic imperative, we discern the moral imperative" (*WL*, 47; translation modified). The argument is advanced on two overlapping fronts: with regard to the medium and form that artists employ and in relation to the historical circumstances in which they write.

Sartre begins by distinguishing literature from other arts, particularly music and painting. "Notes, colours and forms are not signs," he writes, and the significance of each is "but the dim little meaning which dwells within it, a light joy, a timid sadness, remains immanent or trembles about it" (*WL*, 2). Music, in particular, has a unique ontological status: "A cry of grief is a sign of the grief which provokes it, but a song of grief is both grief itself and something other than grief. Or, if one wishes to adopt the existentialist vocabulary, it is a grief which does not *exist* any more, which *is*" (*WL*, 3; Sartre's emphasis). (Note the way Fanon will echo this with "My Negro consciousness does not hold itself out as a lack. It *is*.") A lament will not tell you anything about the circumstances that have caused grief, but it gives you a sense of its weight and force. This is not conducive to commitment, however. The committed artist requires the semiotic dimension of language.[11] For Sartre, when narrative fiction engages language as a system of signs, names spring into networks of signification, and one is "embarked" in the world that it fabricates. Once embarked, "there is nothing you can do to get out of it" (*WL*, 15).

He is well aware that there is no guarantee that names will fix on their objects. Whether written or spoken, they are just as much physical entities as strokes of paint or sounds. This gives rise to the distinction between prose and poetry and to the central phenomenological distinction of *What Is Literature?* Whereas the former, in naming and connecting things and events, uses language transparently, the latter treats them as physical substances. Poetry does not undergo the "radical conversion" that enables fiction to negate immediate reality.[12] This distinction is not at first a historical or even formal one but the question of one's stance toward language.

The theoretical basis for Sartre's coupling of "literature" and "commitment" comes in the final section of the second chapter, where he discusses aesthetic experience as an experience of human freedom that enables us to intuit how we might act to improve the world. Sartre calls this the "aesthetic modification of the human project" (*WL*, 44), a phrase to which I will return frequently. He first claims that the complex sensation of "aesthetic joy" is essentially the intuition of a transcendent purpose. The capacity to fabricate and enter into fictional realities reveals the underlying "appeal . . . of a value" in structuring our perceptions of and actions in the world. By leading consciousness to an awareness of its preconscious disposition, aesthetic joy makes us aware of our capacity to intervene in and change our deep structures of desire. The reader's consciousness is the medium through which fictional worlds come into existence and so is constitutive of its freedom. As the reader draws on her experiences of daily reality when imagining this other world, literary experience allows that reality "to be seen as it is, but as if it had its source in human freedom" (*WL*, 43). The decisive moment of mediation does not come in the act of writing the fictitious world but through the thoughts and reflections of the reader who can activate its commitment. There are conditions, however, regarding what sort of literature can awaken aesthetic joy and so rightfully attain literary status. Only literature that reveals the world as it calls for the reader to exceed that world is capable of producing aesthetic joy. Sartre regards mimetic realism as misguided because it feigns to provide a complete and final image of the world. Through the aesthetic modification of the human project one necessarily experiences injustice as a human and not natural fact and is embarked in an unfreedom of which one is a part creator.[13]

At this point the argument moves from the phenomenology of reading to literature's historical situation. Sartre believes that commitment must be proposed by a writer to specific readerships at a specific time. This "pact between human freedoms" (44) ultimately is premised on transcending circumstances they both share. It is helpful briefly to sketch Sartre's historical narrative of

French literature as it will enable us to situate his later claims regarding negritude poetry. He begins in the eighteenth century and the moment when writers found themselves in a new position, between the monarchy and the rising bourgeoisie. "Unclassed," they began to articulate their solitude as a universal condition of individual autonomy. They did not intend to speak on behalf of the bourgeoisie, but it so happened that by insisting on their autonomy at this time, they aligned themselves with the bourgeoisie as it also asserted its independence. This cultivated a literature that named its commitments: "it was *this* institution that had to be denounced and at once, *that superstition* that had to be destroyed immediately" (*WL*, 84). On assuming power, the bourgeoisie then went about creating institutions that produced new forms of control. In reaction, literature's intrinsic demand for autonomy led it to dramatically change its aspect. If bourgeois positivism proposed the complete integration of all life into a unified progressive system, literature discovered its "unassimilable matter" (*WL*, 88). In the longer run this led to the absolute subjectivism of surrealism: "[the surrealists] squandered literary traditions, hashed together words, threw them against each other to make them shatter" (*WL*, 102). Surrealism removes literature from history and makes literature's "commitment" a "poetic fiction" (*WL*, 146).

In the final essay Sartre calls attention to two converging developments that he believed were leading (French) literature from such poetic fictions to the committed fiction that he advocates: the fallout from the Second World War and the negation of pure formalism that arises from literature's own internal dialectic. In turning to the concrete and utilitarian, literature again coincides with what Sartre regarded as the paradigmatic political struggle of the day: proletarian revolution. The difficulty for Sartre, then, becomes distinguishing a prose that serves utilitarian ends from one that engenders freedom. Here he has recourse to "being." Literary beauty will not be defined by "the form nor even by the matter, but by the density of being" (*WL*, 176). Prose is a "toboggan" that hurls the reader into the midst of this density.

Throughout *What Is Literature?* the American novelist Richard Wright is Sartre's exemplar of this new literature of commitment (see *WL*, 58–61, 83, 119–20, 185). Sartre's comments on Wright give us the most concrete sense of what he means when he talks about the movement of immediacy into reflection: "He mediates, names, and shows them [black Americans] the life they lead from day to day in its immediacy, the life they suffer without finding words to formulate their sufferings. He is their conscience, and the movement by which he raises himself from the immediate to the reflective recapturing of his condition is that of his whole race" (*WL*, 60). Mediating immediacy is a matter of finding a name; naming is showing, and showing activates the freedom frozen in the immediacy of life lived under oppression. Wright's particular importance, Sartre continues, comes in addressing a dual readership of educated blacks and sympathetic whites. It is through these black and white middle-class readerships that Wright reaches out to his "virtual" readerships, the illiterate black peasants and southern white racialists who are caught up directly in the institutions and structures of feeling of segregation. To adapt the term Sartre uses for the autonomy of the eighteenth-century French writer, we could say that Wright performs an "unracing."[14] His novels enable his readers to experience racial segregation through the strength of a consciousness emancipated from its position within it.

"Black Orpheus"

When Sartre accepted an invitation to contribute an introduction to an anthology of francophone poetry in French, a volume that would appear in the same year as *What Is Literature?*, we might anticipate that he would use the opportunity to extend and deepen his argument about commitment. The poetry of negritude, however, would not slot easily into his critique of formalism. Not only is the work poetic, but several of the major figures evidently were influenced by the surrealists that *What Is Literature?* had just declared redundant. We might therefore anticipate that Sartre will seek to steer these poets toward the example of Wright. Instead, he tries to capture the polemical spirit of this poetry by tacitly revising the historical argument of *What Is Literature?*: "Black poetry in the French language," he asserts, "is the only great revolutionary poetry of our time" (*BO*, 117).[15] This is quite an about-face; one that could easily expose his notion of commitment as the literary expression of whatever political position has been decided on in advance.

Sartre sees, though, that negritude poetry confounds his phenomenology of narrative fiction. It is not for want of maturity that language is the scene of revolt for negritude:

> The herald of the black soul [*l'âme noir*] has gone through white schools, in accordance with a brazen law which forbids the oppressed man to possess any arms except those he himself has stolen from the oppressor; it is through the

shock of white culture that his negritude has passed from <u>immediate existence</u> to the reflective state. But at the same time, he has more or less ceased to live his negritude. In choosing to see what he is, he has become split [*dédoublé*], he no longer coincides with himself. (*BO*, 119–20)

For a number of reasons, becoming conscious of racial objectification by claiming an African ancestry cannot be a matter simply of naming things. Sartre understands well that slavery and colonialism forced Africans from various regions and language groups into the single identity category "nègre." The galvanizing paradox of negritude is that the urge to articulate the value of African origins must pass through the concepts born of the destruction of African social particularities. Sartre's consciousness of this predicament evidently extends only so far. In his commentary on Wright, Sartre did not intimate that there could be a problematic relation between the linguistic materials of the novelist's world-disclosure and the racial situation it mediates. Now he goes to the opposite extreme: the pane of each referent is obscured by the history of racial oppression—"the colonist has arranged to be the eternal mediator between the colonized" (*BO*, 121)—so Sartre must retrace all the steps of his critique of poetic formalism.

To characterize the forlornness of a quest undertaken in the medium of the colonizer's language, he invokes the Orpheus myth.[16] When the writer turns through language to look at his negritude, it vanishes and he sees only the disturbed matter of that language:

White words drink his thoughts like sand drinks blood. If he suddenly gorges himself, if he pulls himself together and takes a step backward, there are the sounds lying prostrate *in front of him*, strange, half signs and half things. He will not speak his negritude with precise, efficacious words which hit the target every time. He will not speak his negritude *in prose*. As everyone knows, <u>this feeling of frustration that one has when confronted with a language that is</u> <u>supposed to be a means of direct communication is at the origin of all poetic</u> <u>experience</u>. (*BO*, 122)

How, then, can negritude achieve the movement to reflection that unlocks free consciousness without possessing the means to fabricate fictional worlds? The unavoidable connection here between the substantiality of language and the corporeal objectifications of race brings into question his earlier account of what can be known in the experience of literature and how it can be thought. In the opening discussion of poetry in *What Is Literature?* Sartre discusses poetic writing as a kind of corporeal extension: "He [the poet] feels them [words] as if they were his body; he is surrounded by a verbal body which he is hardly aware of and which extends his action upon the world" (*WL*, 6). There is no mention here of the possibility that the capacity for words to act in accordance with the poet's desires might be frustrated.

Language thus fails negritude twice: as prose it will not say what the writer means to say, and as poetry it will not extend corporeality. (Fanon will comment that for "Negros" "consciousness of the body is solely a negating activity" [*BS*, 110].) Negritude "passes" from "immediate existence" into the "reflective state" not because of any cognitive capture of its immediacy via the agency of "aesthetic joy" but through the shock of a split consciousness caused by the attempt to harness the colonizer's language. The question, then, concerns the medium of negritude's "reflective state" and the way in which this can unlock freedom. Is it vested specifically in poetic expression, or is this simply a general problem of language and colonialism? In trying to answer this, Sartre draws on the stock of ethnographic stereotypes: "And since French lacks terms and concepts to define negritude, since negritude is silence, these poets will use 'allusive words, never direct, reducing themselves to the same silence' in order to evoke it. Short-circuits of language: behind the flaming wall of words, we glimpse a great black mute idol" (*BO*, 123). Faced with mounting contradictions, Sartre can only conjure this vague image of tribal menace. Perhaps, though, this empty gesture testifies to a real predicament. Negritude's linguistic crisis reflects an imaginative state restricted to vague intimations of lost fetishes—the lost remnant.

The "great black mute idol" is not negritude's destination, though, but a stage in its further unfolding. What we are witnessing are the projections of a gathering ontology: "Negritude—like liberty—is a point of departure and an ultimate goal: it is a matter of making it pass from the immediate to mediate [*faire passer de l'immédiat au médiat*], of *thematizing* it. . . . It is not for him a matter of *knowing*, nor of his ecstatically tearing himself away from himself, but rather of both discovering and becoming what he is" (*BO*, 125). On cue Sartre calls on Heidegger: the passage to the mediate is a revelation of the "negro's" being-in-the-world. All the organic metaphors, libidinal themes, and rhythmicity of negritude poetry in fact are directed toward sharpening the poet's consciousness of exploitation. Where the negritude poet tries hardest to bring immediate physicality into his poem, Sartre argues, he most clearly understands the suffering incurred in the loss of authentic embodied experience. Coming to this realization enables the negritude poet's commitment: "because he has suffered from capitalistic exploitation more than all the others, he has acquired a sense of revolt and a love of liberty more than all the others" (*BO*, 136). The attempt to realize Being by tearing apart the language of racial objectification allows access to a preconscious awareness of the historical situation that produced it, and, with it, the free desire to change the world. The failure to realize a "Negro" ontology has been necessary and serves as exemplary transcendence. We come, then, to the passage that will enrage Fanon:

> The subjective, existential, ethnic notion of *negritude* "passes," as Hegel says, into the objective, positive and precise, notion of the *proletariat*. . . . In fact, Negritude appears as the minor moment [*temps faible*] of a dialectical progression: the theoretical and practical affirmation of white supremacy is the thesis; the position of Negritude as an antithetical value is the moment of negativity. But this negative moment is not sufficient in itself, and these blacks who use it know this perfectly well; they know that it aims at preparing the synthesis or realization of the human in a society without race. Thus Negritude is for destroying itself, it is a passage and not an outcome, a means and not an end. At the moment that the black Orpheuses most tightly embrace this Eurydice, they feel her vanish from between their arms. (*BO*, 137)

The significance and weight of this passage will be explored in a number of ways over the rest of this chapter. To begin, I want to highlight the comment that negritude poets know "perfectly well" that the racial content of their work is self-transcending. As we have seen, Fanon will rebut: "I *needed* not to know." Both writers, however, seem caught up in contrary modes of bad faith. On the one hand, how could negritude be poetically successful if it conducts itself as though it were a procedure? On the other, if negritude pursues its ends through a genuinely oblivious racialism, why would Fanon credit Sartre with destroying "black enthusiasm"? For his part, Sartre seems aware that his dialectic of negritude is at least paradoxical if not self-negating.[17] One aspect of the verdict that Fanon reaches is that Sartre is being condescending, elevating himself to the position of master theorist who sees what the poets blindly must not. This effectively renders negritude a conceptual, rather than aesthetic, modification of the human project.[18]

Where does this leave poetic knowledge? Sartre sets out to argue that poetry can, after all, produce the kind of knowledge necessary for commitment, only then to pull the rug from under it. Toward the end of the essay Sartre discusses the following lines from Jacques Roumain's "Bois-d'Ébène":

> Africa I have held your memory Africa
> you are in me
> Like a splinter in a wound
> like a guardian fetish in the centre of the village
> make of me the stone of your sling
> of my mouth the lips of your sore
> of my knees the broken columns [les colonnes brisées] of your abasement . . .
>
> AND YET
> I want to be only of your race
> Peasant workers of all countries.[19]

Before looking at Sartre's commentary, it is helpful to observe some basic tensions operating in these lines. Most conspicuously, the majuscule on the conjugation suggests an internal wrenching, as though universalism were the compulsion of a superego conflicting with an intuitive desire to act in the name of Africa alone. The switch in the original French to the formal *vous* confirms the distinction. This is also latent in the pun on *colonnes*, which presents the broken foundations of the colonized self and society ("colonnes") and, menacingly, broken colonizers ("colons"). It might be difficult to channel the desire for revenge into the more general call for proletarian revolt when there are particular scores to settle that have to do with an unavoidable cultural memory and specific historical wrongs.

This tension finds a resolution of sorts in the poem's final image (lines not cited by Sartre but that Fanon will cite in "The Lived Experience of the Black"):

> Just as the contradiction of the traits
> create the harmony of the face
> we proclaim the unity of the suffering
> and the revolt
> of all the people on all the surface of the earth
>
> and we mix the mortar of brotherly times
> out of the dust of the idols. (*BS*, 118; my translation)

If negritude desires above all to reclaim its own idols, then any transition to universality will need to use the yearning for this remnant as its base substance (i.e., "the dust of idols"). The nonsynchronous desire is materially constitutive of the utopian act; it is not left behind.

Here are Sartre's remarks: "With what sadness he still retains for a moment what he has decided to abandon! With what pride as a *man* he will strip his pride as a negro for other men! He who says at once that Africa is in him like 'a thorn in a wound' and that he *wants* to be only of the universal race of the oppressed, has not left the empire of unhappy consciousness" (*BO*, 137). He completely misses Roumain's attempt to fashion an image that precisely does not abandon the urgency of its negritude. The impulse to theorize negritude gives him a tin ear for its poetics.

Misadventures of the Critical Discourse on the "Black Orpheus" Debate

There is now a broad consensus that Fanon's riposte to Sartre's "Black Orpheus" is decisive. Critics have applauded him for calling Sartre on his sham "dialectic" of negritude and for reminding Sartre that the *experience* of race cannot be properly understood if placed in a predetermined teleological scheme. The two positions are cast as a theory/experience binary in which Sartre proposes a false theoretical understanding of negritude, and Fanon issues the necessary corrective on the plane of experience. Underlying this view, no doubt, is the certainty that Fanon's experiences as a black man allowed him to perceive the experiential truth of negritude. Nevertheless, those who have contributed to this critical consensus have tended not to focus on those aspects of Fanon's writing that would make the primacy of experience manifest but to treat his argument as though it too were conducted on the theoretical level that he is supposed to be shunning. "Experience" is inserted into the space vacated by "dialectic" and proclaimed the superior theory of race. A quick look at some of these critical engagements will help to make clear why it will be necessary to work through the cognitive content of Fanon's rhetoric and style.

James Penney suggests that, in opposition to Sartre's dialectic of negritude, Fanon stipulates the "properly *experiential* dimension of black subjectivity in the Antilles" (56).[20] For Fanon, "racially or ethnically predicated assertions" (58) are a condition for solidarity in the anticolonial struggle. Penney regards these assertions in psychoanalytic terms as a "transferential relationship with French colonial culture" (58). In the final analysis, though, Fanon will see, with Sartre, that negritude is a transitional phenomenon. Fanon's stance toward negritude is "ambivalent" and its racial premise a "*symptom*" of colonial alienation" (58; Penney's emphasis). Fanon expresses "the black colonized subject's *right* to the expression of his symptomatic alienation" (58; my emphasis). Observe the use of a series of concepts—"ambivalence," "symptom," "rights"—that distance Fanon from negritude's confronting racialism. As Penney's argument is predicated strictly on the conceptual content of the essay—though he allows that it is "emotional" (56)—he believes the fallout from the history of conquest and physical violence Fanon confronts is, at heart, a theoretical problem: "Sartre's theoretical dialectic of colonialism inscribes itself onto the very materiality of the colonized subject's body" (57).

In two essays on the "Black Orpheus" debate, Robert Bernasconi adheres to much the same logic.[21] For him the debate really concerns the epistemology of race, and he, too, presents a Fanon that outmaneuvers Sartre's dialectic on the terrain of experience: "Sartre knew about the needs and the suffering of blacks in an intellectual way, but by saying what he said he showed that he did not really know it" ("On Needing," 234). Fanon's achievement, then, is a salutary reminder that black people experience racism in a way that white people do not. "[Fanon] told white men what we need to know, while at the same time reminding us that we will never really know it. Racism is inscribed on Fanon's body" ("The European," 109–10). Why do white men need to be told about the limits of their capacity to know about racial experience if only "experience" gives us any knowledge of it? Bernasconi breaks the strictures on cognition he himself puts in place.[22] As with Penney, we are informed that racial objectification is not the internalization of a political economy premised on brute oppression but a problem of "inscription."[23]

At first it seems Azzedine Haddour is cognizant of the literary dynamics of the debate, commenting that Sartre's interpretation of negritude finds its basis in the "medium of poetic expression."[24] He also sees that "Fanon accuses Sartre, by abstracting the experience of being black, of damning up its poetic source" (291). Yet Haddour believes that Fanon's objection is not finally an important one and that Fanon sees the dangers of negritude's "totalizing and essentialist rhetoric" (292–93). The "medium of poetic experience" suddenly becomes "essentialist rhetoric." The consequences of this shift can be seen clearly when he misreads a passage from Fanon's later essay "Racism and Culture." In the passage Fanon discusses negritude's yearning for a precolonial past, declaring that the "plunge into the chasm of the past is a condition and source of freedom" (la plongée dans le gouffre du passé est condition et source de liberté).[25] When he cites this, Haddour changes the tense and adds a pronoun ("their plunge into the chasm of the past [was] the condition and the source of freedom" [294]).

This is because, he claims, Fanon is speaking only of the past actions of Algerians in the specific context of Algerian anticolonialism. (There is in fact no mention in the essay of Algeria or the Algerian situation.) Haddour hopes to show that when Fanon speaks of the plunge into the past in this particular case, it is *"historical"* (Haddour's emphasis), whereas the negritude writers pursue a dangerous rhetoric of essences. When one reads the passage in full, however, it is clear that Fanon is making a claim for a direct connection between negritude's nonsynchronicity and the leap of liberation:

> The culture put into capsules, <u>vegetative</u> since foreign domination, is revalorized. It is not reconceived, <u>recovered</u>, dynamized from within. It is shouted. And this headlong, unstructured, verbal revalorization conceals paradoxical attitudes. . . . This rediscovery, this absolute valorization almost in defiance of reality, objectively indefensible, assumes an incomparable and subjective importance. On emerging from these passionate espousals, the native [*l'autochtone*] will have decided, "with <u>full knowledge of the facts</u>" [*en "connaissance de cause"*] to fight against all forms of exploitation and of alienation of man. . . . No neologism can mask the new certainty: the plunge into the chasm of the past is the condition and the source of freedom.[26]

The act of shouting what has been deadened cannot recover its previous life, but, as a value-creating act, it gives itself presence and can make concerted demands. The verb Fanon uses to describe the action of negritude—*plonger*—is the same used by Césaire in the *Cahier*'s most famous passage, one that Fanon cites several times in *Black Skin*. What we have here is a thoroughgoing political justification for negritude's emphatic literary primitivism. To respond absolutely to the call of the nonsynchronous remnant is the basis for pushing through alienated mediations and activating alternative futures.

To specify in what respect this plunge is a literary act, it is helpful to make a small digression on Wole Soyinka's oft-quoted put-down of negritude: "a tiger does not proclaim his tigritude, he pounces." Soyinka appears to be belittling negritude on the same grounds that Fanon would supposedly abandon it: politics requires practical action not literary indulgence. Janheinz Jahn has recorded Soyinka making a very interesting clarification of this comment: "I said: 'a tiger does not proclaim his tigritude, he pounces.' In other words: a tiger does not stand in the forest and say: 'I am a tiger.' When you pass where the tiger has walked before, you see the skeleton of the duiker, you know that some tigritude has been emanated there. In other words: the distinction which

I was making . . . was a purely literary one: I was trying to distinguish between propaganda and true poetic creativity."[27] The choice between a static and active negritude is not one between theory and experience, nor between literature and real political action, but different ways of using and responding to language. It is not a distinction that could be determined by only attending to the referential content of the language of negritude. It requires us to take seriously the effects of style, rhetoric, and form. It is on this plane that we should approach "The Lived Experience of the Black": not as the correct theorization of "black experience" but as an attempt to *do* negritude.

How to Do Negritude

In the preface to *Peau noire, masques blancs* (which unfortunately has not been included in either English translation) Francis Jeanson recounts comments made to him by Fanon regarding his attitude to writing: "When I write things like that, I am trying to catch my reader affectively, or in other words irrationally, almost sensually. For me, words have a charge. I find myself incapable of escaping the bite of a word, the vertigo of a question mark. . . . [I want to] sink beneath the stupefying lava of words that have the colour of quivering flesh."[28] The precocity is unmistakable, right down to the Césairean clash of "lava" and "quivering flesh,"[29] and some of his contemporaries and early critics took these pretensions to be a diversion from the urgency of the political situation that his work confronts. After meeting Fanon at a dinner with Michel Leiris, the anthropologist Alfred Métraux wrote in his diary that Fanon has "an unfortunate passion for literature."[30] An early Anglophone critic of *Black Skin* complained that "Fanon becomes so entranced with the sound of words that he sometimes obscures all content."[31] Such comments assume that Fanon's style is the surplus to an otherwise efficacious theoretical content. I will show that in *Black Skin, White Masks* style *is* method.[32]

If the received image of Fanon is one of a clear-minded, sharp, and relentlessly oppositional intellectual, it can be surprising to find that, on a second look, the rhetorical bearings of his polemic are not always easy to determine. Among his many antagonists it can be hard to work out which are the real targets. There is a particularly illustrative moment in "The Negro and Psychopathology," the chapter in *Black Skin* that follows "The Lived Experience of the Black." In it, Fanon targets Alioune Diop's introduction to Placide Tempel's *La philosophie bantoue*. He quotes a passage in which Diop claims that notions of political revolution are premised on European assumptions about civilizational progress and are thus contrary to the genius of "the Negro." Fanon pulls him up, crying, "<u>Watch out</u>!" (Attention!), before pointing to the unhistorical and unmediated basis of Diop's argument:

> It is quite true that Bantu philosophy is not going to open itself to understanding through a revolutionary will: but it is precisely <u>that degree to which Bantu society is closed that we do not find that substitution of the exploiter for the ontological relation of Forces</u>. Now we know that Bantu society no longer exists. And there is nothing ontological about segregation. <u>Enough of this outrage</u> (Assez de ce scandale).
>
> For some time there has been much talk about the Negro. A little too much. The Negro would like us <u>to forget</u>, so that he may regroup his forces, his authentic forces.
>
> One day he said: "My negritude is neither a tower . . ."
>
> And someone comes to Hellenize him, to <u>Orpheize</u> (orphéiser) him . . . this Negro who is looking for the universal. He is looking for the universal! (*BS*, 185–86)

Fanon is moving quickly through intellectual contexts and voices. The first point of reference here is a passage in Césaire's *Discourse on Colonialism*, which polemicizes against the work by Tempel that Diop is introducing.[33] Here is Césaire excoriating Tempel: "But <u>watch out</u>! [Mais, attention!] You are going to the Congo? Respect—I do not say native property (the great Belgian companies might take that as a dig at them), I do not say the freedom of the natives (the Belgian colonists might think that was subversive talk), I do not say the Congolese nation (the Belgian government might take it much amiss)—I say: You are going to the Congo? Respect the Bantu philosophy!"[34]

As well as appropriating particular words, Fanon absorbs Césaire's sarcastic asides, leading questions, and clipped rhythm, if not his parallelism. Both are performing an incredulity that "Bantu philosophy" could be spoken of without reference to the colonial situation into which it now articulates. Diop, in other words, is ontologizing colonial segregation. The words Fanon chooses to bring this engagement peremptorily to a close, "assez de ce scandale," also carry something of the weight of the outrage to which this other speaker refers:

> Torte
>
> o torte of the frightful autumn

where brand-new steel and perennial concrete thrive
torte o torte
where the air is rusting in great patches
of wicked glee
where sanious water scars the great solar cheeks
I hate you

one still sees madras rags around women's loins rings in their ears smiles on their
    faces babies at their breasts and I will spare you the rest:
ENOUGH OF THIS OUTRAGE!
[ASSEZ DE CE SCANDALE!][35]

This passage comes about a third of the way into Césaire's *Cahier*. What is the scandal, exactly, to which the speaker is objecting? The majuscule and exclamation seem disproportionate, if not self-ironical. One possibility is that the speaker is alluding to the kind of poetry that had constituted so much of the Martinican repertoire. What Suzanne Césaire dubbed "dou dou" (sweet sweet) poetry: "Literature of sugar and vanilla. Tourism literature."[36] Enough of the outrage of exoticism, of papering over reality. Carrie Nolan's comment that "[in the *Cahier*] we are never sure when a written unit (a word or phrase) will turn toward the 'reality of its content' or when that unit will spin away toward other verbal units found either within the poem or beyond" is apt: it is not certain whether the women are the scandal, the poetic mode in which they appear, or it is a spasm without direct cause.[37] If we were to read the stanza before this as an attempt more adequately to present the actual misery of Martinique, we would find only a surrealist ode to some tropical cake/island/sound object where physical properties do not match their objects. Césaire will not sanction the exotic image of the island, but this is not a cue for descriptive realism. What we have is more a psycholinguistic realism, in which the speaker is embittered by the incapacity to settle into a single mode of representation.

Fanon's adoption of "Assez de ce scandale" would probably not strike a reader unfamiliar with the reference as particularly noteworthy.[38] As we read on, however, the invocation shades the argument with its ambiguity and self-negating exasperation. In the next sentence Fanon tempers his hostility. It seems now that Diop's comments could be the legitimate expression of a metaphysical need: "The Negro would like us to forget, so that he may regroup his forces, his authentic forces." We might now hear the "scandale" as an affected outrage; the outrageousness of the quest to find any residual authenticity in the

"Negro"—the outrageousness, perhaps, of "black enthusiasm." Fanon returns to *Cahier*, quoting from that pivotal moment in the poem when negritude is openly declaimed:

> my negritude is not a stone, its deafness hurled against the clamour of the day
> my negritude is not an opaque spot of dead water over the dead eye of the earth
> my negritude is neither a tower nor a cathedral
>
> it plunges deep into the red flesh of the soil
> it plunges deep into the blazing flesh of the sky
> it pierces opaque protestation with its straight patience. (*BS*, 115)[39]

The line Fanon quotes, "ma négritude n'est ni une tour," comes at the end of a sequence of negative anaphora, each of which asserts that negritude is neither a specific object nor a tradition, and just before a mirroring positive sequence that describes negritude's vigorous actions. He is interpolating Césaire's negritude at the moment just before it pounces. Fanon has already cited this passage twice (once in its full poetic context) in the previous chapter and so prepared his reader to experience this citation as a thwarted climax. Now it is the voice of the critic who stymies Fanon by "Orpheizing" him, robbing "the Negro" of the particularity of his quest in order to render it in universal terms. This reference, of course, is to "Black Orpheus."

No sooner has Fanon critiqued Diop's naive affirmation than he is fending off the critical negation of Sartre. The triple deployment of Césaire reveals to us negritude's paradoxes and risks. This is why "assez de ce scandale" ends up being ambivalent: the outrage first is directed at false attempts, like Diop's, to ignore the colonial context when reaching for authenticity but then also at that context for producing such false immediacy in the first place. The rhetorical texture manifests the constitutive contradictions of the ontological impulse. Césaire and Diop both aspire to something essential, the yearning is not in question, but Fanon allows the differences in the manner in which they pursue it to rub against each other. We can turn again to René Ménil's comment that: "Negritude is an aesthetic *that mistakes itself for its identity* and which takes itself for an anthropology."[40] The thin, yet deep, fault line between Diop and Césaire is that between a bogus anthropology and the "aesthetic modification of the human project." Without attention to negritude's aesthetics we will lose sight of this distinction and will inevitably be guilty of that great crime: essentialization.

This is the gamble of "le grand trou noir" (the great black hole) of which Césaire speaks in the final passages of *Cahier*, a phrase that Fanon repeats to himself throughout his early work and that he cites immediately after this passage. When he says, "I need to lose myself in my negritude," he means precisely *lose*: he does not set the conditions; his negritude conditions him. Fanon's recklessness, and this is what politically correct critics have tried to suppress, is to then insist that this aesthetic plunge will be politically enabling. As he comments toward the end of "The Negro and Psychopathology": "The *eye* is not merely a mirror, but a correcting mirror. The *eye* should <u>permit</u> us to correct cultural errors. I do not say the *eyes*, I say the *eye*, <u>and we know to what this eye refers</u>; not to the crevice in the skull but to that very uniform light that wells out of the reds of Van Gogh, that glides through a concerto of Tchaikovsky, that <u>clings</u> desperately to Schiller's *Ode to Joy*, that allows itself to be conveyed by the worm-ridden bawling of Césaire" (*BS*, 202).

The distinction between the biological eye and the "eye" that sees from the perspective of the artwork aims to specify a mode of perception enabled by aesthetic objects. It calls for the kind of submission to the cognitivity of aesthetic objects affirmed by another Hegelian thinker: "The identification carried out by the subject was ideally not that of making the artwork like himself but rather that of making himself like the artwork."[41] It is the transfigurations of the aesthetic object that allow Fanon to see a way out of the web of psychic projections inhibiting black subjectivity in the colonial context. If negritude simply gave him an echo of himself as he immediately felt himself to be, he might only resublimate, à la Diop, an objectified form.

Fanon's Nausea

Returning, now, to "The Lived Experience of the Black," we have gained insight both into the Sartrean rationale for Fanon's polemic ("the aesthetic modification of the human project") and the Césairean stylistic and rhetorical mode in which it is enacted. At the level of plot the critical narrative of "The Lived Experience" moves dialectically through the stages of estrangement and existential struggle experienced by an assimilated francophone black man as he encounters the social field of white metropolitan France. It begins with the primal realization of his racialized identity, something that he perceives when a white child exclaims: "Look a Negro!" This shocks him out of his immediate unreflective experience of the world. At first, he tries to find rational arguments to rebut the irrational associations that this identity pins to him, but these prove ineffective. He comes to understand that this irrationalism is the symptom of social relations that cannot be argued out of existence. He therefore resolves to embrace the irrational notions about "the Negro," turning on its head the value structure that demeans him. This new confidence in his negritude is brought to a halt when an ostensibly sympathetic white critic announces that these experiences of racial confidence are only transitory. Trapped in his skin but diverted from his negritude, the speaker intimates at an uncontrolled and violent denouement.

Fanon only addresses Sartre directly toward the end of the essay, but there are signals throughout that anticipate the climactic confrontation. Following the excruciating moment with the white girl, and her mother's ham-fisted attempt to save the situation ("Look how handsome that Negro is!"), Fanon comments: "I took myself far off from my own presence, far indeed, and made myself an object. What else could it be for me but an amputation, an excision, a haemorrhage that spattered my whole body with black blood? But I did not want this revision, this thematization. All I wanted was to be a man among other men" (*BS*, 112–13). This may well allude to that moment in "Black Orpheus" when Sartre speaks of negritude "*thematizing*" the Negro's immediate experience (*BO*, 125). We have already noted that Fanon adopts the notion that literary knowledge makes manifest to consciousness the mediated nature of what had previously seemed immediate. At this early point in the essay, though, it seems that a distinction is emerging between a "thematization" brought on externally and a truly empowering cognitive capture of mediation.

On discovering his peculiar fate, he makes further allusions to Sartre, although now to different sources: "In the train it was no longer a question of being aware of my body in the third person but in a triple person. In the train I was given not one but two, three places. I had already stopped being amused. It was not that I was finding febrile coordinates in the world. I existed triply: I occupied space. I moved toward the other . . . and the evanescent other, hostile but not opaque, transparent, <u>absent</u>, disappeared. Nausea" (*BS*, 112). A theoretically minded gloss of this passage might go as follows: Fanon's nausea is not an individual psychic aberration but a symptom of the overall normative conditions of late-colonial French society. That something like this point is being made cannot be denied, but if we seek only to extract this theoretical kernel we will miss the purpose latent in the decision to adopt a first-person perspective rendered in a jagged, elliptical prose style replete with literary and philosophical allusions. Most conspicuously, whether for the purposes of harmonization or dissonance, Fanon is inviting us to think his nausea in relation to that of Roquentin in Sartre's 1938 novel *La nausée*.

Before delving into that intertext, we might quickly note an allusion to another of Sartre's works. In *Being and Nothingness* (1943) Sartre devotes attention, almost tediously, to the ontological implications of those moments when one is discovered gazing at another, of being caught spying through a keyhole, for instance. The shock causes an acute awareness of oneself in the third person, a state Sartre calls "being-for-others."[42] Fanon is making a socioexistential pun: he does not just see himself as though in the third person but literally has three places on the train to himself as no one will sit near him. His experience of "being-for-others" is a fact of the social field.

In one of *Nausea*'s longer episodes Roquentin has the experience of being subjected to the judgment of another whom he is powerless to affect with his own judgment. He is in a municipal gallery, looking at portraits of the town's distinguished men. Standing before the portrait of a particularly shrewd looking merchant, Roquentin thinks: "I realized what separated us: what I might think about him could not touch him; it was just psychology, the sort you find [in] novels. But his judgement pierced me like a sword and called in question my very right to exist. And it was true, I had always realized that; I hadn't any right to exist. I had appeared by chance, I existed like a stone, a plant, a microbe. . . . He had never gone any further in examining himself: he was a leader."[43]

The encounter might only be with a representation, but Roquentin nevertheless finds that it is he, not the portrait, who lacks ontological resistance. Above all, the *chef*'s judgment is buttressed by his self-certainty and the capacity to take for granted his place in the order of things. Roquentin has no such certainty. The next portrait is of another local *éminence grise*. He sits with his grandson on his lap and smiles at the viewer. Roquentin does not feel judged by this man but potentially included in his emotional horizon: "In the evening of his life, he spread his indulgent kindness over all and sundry. I myself, if he saw me—but I was transparent to his gaze—I myself would find grace in his eyes" (125). Roquentin is included in the fold of this man's benevolence but only because it is indiscriminate. It is not true recognition.

As far as Roquentin is concerned, these are not encounters with visual representations but ways of inhabiting the world. Yet, as with Fanon, only the isolated man truly sees the "Other." Roquentin's transparency before the town fathers, however, is of a different order. He is no longer able to distinguish himself from other objects in his world because he does not trust any inherited belief in the innate meaningfulness and purposefulness of the existence into which he is "embarked." Fanon finds his world interrupted midstream, and his personhood stripped down and fixed. David Trotter comments with acuity: "Nausea, which could happen any time in any place, at random, *had* to happen when and where it did, to Fanon, because it is colonialism's necessity."[44]

Fanon's experience on the train also resonates with an episode in Césaire's *Cahier* that takes place on public transport. In it, the poem's speaker encounters a disheveled man on a tram. He spends several lines describing the man's wretchedness and, as he does, feels the judgments of the people around him, as well as an internalized set of associations, shaping his vision:

> It was the perfect composition of a hideous nigger, a grumpy nigger, a gloomy nigger, a slumped nigger, his hands together prayer-like upon a knotty stick. A nigger shrouded in an old threadbare jacket. A nigger who was comical and ugly, and behind me women were looking at him and giggling.
>
> He was COMICAL AND UGLY.
>
> COMICAL AND UGLY, for sure.
>
> I exhibited a wide smile of connivance . . .
>
> My cowardice recovered! (*NR*, 109; translation modified)

The majuscule suggests that a voice other than the speaker's is forcing its way into his or that it is the spasm of an unconscious reflex. Either way, the judgment that sketches the portrait possesses the voice. The speaker knows full well that his mania is "cowardice," but that does not prevent his vision from being mediated by the judgments of others.[45]

Fanon's encounter with his own racial uniform on a train reveals the ways in which this judgment-complex turns in on itself. With this encounter with facticity, Trotter observes, "ontology has finally begun, for Fanon," but it is an ontology that "enfolds an inaugural taste of racism." Hence the ontological moment in the train scene is a "surpassing of as well as a surpassing towards ontology."[46] The question becomes what this ontology will be and from what source it derives.

Césaire's Primitivism

Coming, finally, to Fanon's primitivism, we might revisit the passage from which we set off:

> Jean-Paul Sartre, in this work, has destroyed black <u>enthusiasm. Against histori-</u> <u>cal becoming he should have opposed the unforeseeable.</u> I needed to lose my-

self absolutely in negritude. One day, perhaps, in the depths of that unhappy romanticism . . .

In any case, I *needed* not to know. This struggle, this redescent had to take on an aspect of completeness. Nothing is more unwelcome than this notion: "you'll change, my boy; when I was young, I too . . . you'll see, all will pass."

The dialectic that introduces necessity at the fulcrum of my freedom drives me out of myself. It shatters my unreflected position. Still in terms of consciousness, black consciousness is immanent to itself. I am not a potentiality of something, I am wholly what I am. I do not have to look for the universal. Probability has no place inside my breast. My Negro consciousness does not hold itself out as a lack. It *is*. (*BS*, 135)

On some matters we have gained clarity. Negritude's objective is unforeseeable because it can only be attained through "the aesthetic modification of the human project." Fanon embarks on the experiment of negritude's inverse racialism without the safety-belt of a preordained universalism. This is its "night of the absolute," which the "born Hegelian [Sartre] had forgotten" (*BS*, 133–34). We recall, at the same time, that the transformation made possible in aesthetic experience is only confirmed when one becomes aware and takes hold of one's preconscious disposition—to be able to make a choice about that disposition rather than be subjected to it. This is different from the estrangement caused by the nausea of racial alienation or the thematization of a "symptomatic" rebellion against it.

Yet, and we now see that this is the pivotal phrase, he means to stress that "black consciousness is immanent to itself." Fanon gives a series of clarifications for this curious claim in the terms of ontology (he is not awaiting ontology but already possesses it; he does not need the universal to have ontology; and so on). As he does so, it is surely significant that he shifts from "black" to "Negro" consciousness. This suggests that although it might be impossible to circumvent the mediation of the Negro when reaching authentic blackness, this does not in the first place preclude ontology.

Immediately following this passage Fanon cites large chunks from three poems in quick succession (Roumain's "Bois-d'Ébène" and two by David Diop)—a series of proofs, it would seem, for these ontological claims. Nevertheless, after the second Diop passage, he admits that in attaching such claims to poems, "one runs the risk of finding only the nonexistent." In spite of his aggression and forthrightness, we see that Fanon is trying to keep a grip on something that requires a certain delicacy. This something is and is not accessible through language. Of one thing he is certain, though: "at the very moment when I was trying to grasp my own being, Sartre, who remained The Other, <u>in naming me removed from me all illusion</u>" (*BS*, 137). He was undertaking something by means other than the act of naming: an utterance that is, by turns, an "unhappy romanticism," an immanence of consciousness, and an illusion.

He understands that much of what formerly had felt like immediate and true experiences were behavioral patterns established in the social relations of plantation and stock exchange. To bestow on it a timeless ontological status would only install the sham of a "Bantu ontology." At this point Césaire and Sartre, polarities throughout the essay, are brought directly into collision:

> While I was saying to him [Sartre]:
>
>> My negritude is neither a tower nor a cathedral
>>
>> it plunges deep into the red flesh of the soil
>> it plunges deep into the blazing flesh of the sky
>> it pierces opaque protestation with its straight patience.
>
> while I was shouting that, in the paroxysm of my being and my fury, he was reminding me that my blackness was only a minor term. (*BS*, 137–38)[47]

If Fanon really is caught up in paroxysms of his negritude, why should it matter whether Sartre "names" it as one thing or another? Addressing this, one might think to comment on the implicit power relation between the then unknown black commentator and the preeminent white public intellectual of the day. It will be hard for Fanon to intervene effectively in a public sphere so dominated by Sartre. One might also take into account the institutional dynamics that led to the decision to invite Sartre to write the preface to Senghor's anthology in the first place. In robustly speaking *for* negritude, Sartre had eclipsed the poetry's own potentiality. Without wanting to dismiss these factors, I am nevertheless drawn to explanations that stay within the theater of contest that the essay itself establishes, for which Fanon's chosen weapons are poetry and speculative interpretation.

It strikes me as crucial that on this occasion Fanon quotes from the *Cahier* as it moves into positive anaphora, with negritude shifting from being defined as *not this or that noun* to *verb acting upon*. This realizes and surpasses the main thread of the poetic argument in *Cahier d'un retour ay pays natal*. I could cite dozens of relevant passages from any edition of the *Cahier* that prepare us for the power of the "plonger" sequence. Indeed, it would be hard to select passages in which the dialectical struggle of referential impulse and ontological wish were not present. The following two excerpts are selected only because they succinctly capture this struggle:

> I would rediscover the secret of great communications and of great combustions. I would say storm. I would say river. I would say tornado. I would say leaf. I would say tree. I would be soaked by all the rains, moistened by all the dews. Like frantic blood over the slow stream of the eye, I would roll words as crazy horses as fresh children as bloodclots as curfew as vestiges of temples as gems deep enough to discourage miners. Whoever would not understand me would not understand the roaring of the tiger either. (*NR*, 87)

> I have looked and looked at trees and so I have become a tree and this long tree's feet have dug great venom sacs and tall cities of bones in the ground
> with the force of thinking of the Congo
> I have become a Congo rustling with forests and rivers
> where the whip cracks like a great banner
> the banner of the prophet
> where the water goes
> likwala likwala
> where the lightning of anger hurls its greenish axe and forces the wild boars of putrefaction into the beautiful violent edges of the nostrils. (*NR*, 95; translation modified)

Both passages employ Césaire's most characteristic technique: relentless parallelism that seems at once to intensify the encounter with an object and to undermine its presence. The repetition in the passages of, respectively, saying and looking suggests an attempt to seize an originary ontology as though by the determination of will alone—magic by means of syntax. In the first the grammatical medium is the conditional: *if* circumstances were right, the speaker would have direct communion with, successively, natural phenomena, wildness, naiveté, the remnant of past mythology, and, finally, beauty beyond the reach of exchange value. In the second passage it is the present-perfect: the force of gazing effort has elicited natural being, which blooms present-continuous into a landscape.

With uncanny prescience Césaire defines cognitive success in the first passage not by referential accuracy but by animal force: negritude always already was tigritude. In the second the "Congo" conjured through the force of gazing is one in which nature produces the domain of reference—Likwala (or Kwala) being one of the large family of Niger-Congo languages—because in this utopian place there is no nature/human distinction. In these passages reanimating the remnant is not about finding the right signifier but bringing attention to the aesthetic modes of world-constitution. We are in a cognitive dimension of an entirely different order from that privileged by Sartre in *What Is Literature?* and passed over in "Black Orpheus." It is a dimension for which Césaire would attempt a prosaic explanation in his well-known essay "Poetry and Knowledge" (delivered as a lecture at a philosophy congress in Haiti in 1944 and published in *Tropiques* a year later).[48] I would like quickly to bring to attention three aspects of its argument: (1) the critique of analytical judgment; (2) the characterization of poetic achievement as the recuperation of primitive experience; and (3) the privileging of humor as a method for breaking the spell of the former and opening up access to the latter.

Césaire conducts the critique of analytical judgment, of knowledge as the formula $A = A$, in terms of the image, which is to be extended beyond correspondence through surrealist techniques of aleatoric association and as driven by a revolutionary desire: "*motor* for *sun, dynamo* for *mountain, carburettor* [*sic*] for *Caribbean* and so on" (143).[49] This is carried out not so much with the aim of affirming the negative (that A is not A) as of bracketing it in order to discover language in a "pure state." This state is an unabashed primitivism: "by pure state, I mean not submitted to habit or thought, but to the flow of the cosmos alone. The poet's word, the primitive word: a rupestral outline in sonic matter" (140). He talks of the emergence of "ancestral essence" (143) and stipulates that "the poetic attitude is an attitude of naturalization brought about by imagination's demented impulse" (145). This forthright primitivist utopianism, however, cannot be conducted as though the primitive word were the low-hanging fruit of a naive affirmation of nature. It must be seized by "poetic violence, poetic aggressivity and poetic instability" (141), and in the mode of a vicious humor whose role is "to cleanse the fields of the mind" and "dissolve with a blow torch the connections that . . . threaten to become encrusted in the mental pulp" (141).

If such formulations promise more than the poetry reasonably can deliver, we should remember it has its own rhetoric and poetics. These are hyperbolic conceptual strokes designed to clear away the temptation to the subtlety, irony, and exaltation of ambiguity that formally ambitious literature so often consigns itself: "beware of crossing your arms in the sterile attitude of the spectator" (*NR*, 89), says the speaker of the *Cahier*, words that Fanon repeats to himself in *Black Skin*. They are also claims that lack the historical content that supplies humor with its impetus. The violent merging of multiple images is not inherently funny; it is humorous in a situation where analytic judgment has replaced the true, yet social reality is so obviously untrue.

Much of the humor in the *Cahier* plays on the relation between truth and perception, with neither holding fixed positions:

> No, we have never been amazons of the King of Dahomey, nor princes of Ghana with eight hundred camels, nor doctors in Timbuctoo under King Askia the Great, nor architects in Djenne, nor Madhis, nor warriors. We do not feel that itch of those who used to hold the spear in our armpits. And since I have sworn to suppress nothing in our history (I who admire nothing so much as sheep grazing on the afternoon shadow), I will admit that for as long as I can remember we have always been quite pathetic dishwashers, shoeshiners with no ambition, looking on the bright side, rather conscientious witch-doctors, and the only undeniable record we ever broke was at endurance under the whip. (*NR*, 105)

The objective denial of African histories compels the assent to the subject position of the slave, whether by bondage or wage. There is nothing subtle about this passage, but neither is it entirely predictable. The lines evidently drip with sarcasm, but the parenthetical comment about sheep grazing and "conscientious witch-doctors" has an uncertain effect. The poem's politics will not take the form of knocking over cultural tropes like dominoes.

Just as Fanon is embittered when his rational appeals to the historical record go unnoticed, so Césaire is compelled to sarcasm:

> Or else they simply love us so much!
> Gaily obscene, doudou about jazz in their access of boredom.
> I can do the tracking, the Lindy Hop and the tap dance.
> And as a last delicacy our muted complaints muffled in wah-wah. Wait . . .
> Everything is in order. My good angel grazes on neon lights. (*NR*, 103; translation
>   modified)

The discrepant image of the angel could be symbolic or absurd; the poetic mode allows for both. Not only is the speaker unconcerned by the imperative to accuracy but uses the misperceptions of negrophilia to disrupt the basis of identity thinking altogether. In this sense its sarcasm pushes on from that which we encountered in Langston Hughes's *The Ways of White Folks* in Chapter 4. With a nod to Gramsci, we might call this Césaire's *passionate sarcasm*.[50] To paraphrase

Gramsci on Marx, Césaire is not mocking the intimate feelings of those under the sway of negrophobia and negrophilia (as though hurting someone's feelings could be enough) but the "contingent forms" of these social modes. This is in the service of demonstrating that the illusions they produce are formed within a certain "perishable world." Passionate sarcasm is, for Gramsci, also a "positive sarcasm" whose purpose is to give "new form to certain aspirations."[51]

The power of this fine-tuned yet seemingly spontaneous poetic register is apparent when we see it go to work on a phrase that Césaire recycles from the essay in which he first coined *négritude* (see Chapter 3; this repetition has also been noticed and discussed by Christopher L. Miller and Natalie Melas).[52] In the essay, Césaire speaks of the necessity of banishing false perceptions and placing "racial values, like so many liberating bombs, under the prisons that white capitalism has built for us." He then tells "those" who call for black revolt without also telling "the Negro" that "it is fine and good and legitimate to be a Negro (nègre)" that they have omitted that which is most vital for stimulating black revolutionary will. The passage is somewhat ambivalent. On the one side, it places racial categories at the center of a Marxian politics; on the other, this legitimation is still to be bestowed externally, which hardly sounds like a recipe for revolutionary success. In the *Cahier* the phrase reappears in a series of invocations leading to the poem's final utopian exclamations:

Come to me my dances
my bad nigger dances
come to me my dances
the breaking-the-yoke dance

the jump-jail dance
the it-is-beautiful-and-good-and-legitimate-to-be-a-nigger (nègre) dance (*NR*, 133)

Melas notes that the recycling of the phrase in the *Cahier* highlights "the manner and circumstance of its delivery," which she characterizes as the "ironic or knowing repetition of something oft repeated."[53] She sees the way in which the poem attacks the contingent forms of the language of authenticity but then diminishes its rhetorical force by portraying its effect as ironic. What is radical about these lines, and the poem's mode, is that they are both sarcastic and earnest.[54] We come, then, to the most crucial claim of this study, one that is also the kernel of the world-historical phenomenon of primitivism: Césaire's passionate sarcasm does not seek to demolish negrophilia/-phobia for the purpose of destroying illusions but to attack their contingent forms in order to regenerate the aspiration to a black ontology. This is Césaire's primitivism, and it is this which Fanon channels when asserting that black consciousness is immanent to itself. Césaire has found a way to the kind of direct affirmation that had eluded Hughes with his subtle frames and gravitation to the lament—a rapturous affirmation without naivety, an immediacy plunged into with full awareness of the mediations that condition its desires.

This brings us back to Fanon's preamble to the *Cahier*'s plunge sequence, which I cited at the start of this chapter. A "strange pride suddenly illuminates" the speaker. The being he thought he had lost becomes an opportunity yielded by his denied humanity:

> Those who have invented neither gunpowder nor the compass
> those who have never known how to subdue either steam or electricity
> those who have explored neither the seas nor the sky
> but those without whom the earth would not be the earth
> gibbosity all the more beneficial as the earth more and more abandons the earth
>
> silo where is stored and ripens what is earthiest about the earth
> my negritude is not a stone, its deafness hurled against the clamour of the day
> my negritude is not an opaque spot of dead water over the dead eye of the earth
> my negritude is neither power nor a cathedral
>
> it plunges into the red flesh of the soil. (*BS*, 124)[55]

Césaire's earlier sarcasm has established (in the negative) the continuities between the histories of past African civilizations and the imperialist world-history of guns, exploration, and conquest, so the parallel phrases about "those who" can hardly be taken literally. But nor is it possible to read these lines as an ironic comment on the philo-primitivist notion of Africans as being excluded from world history. It is a passage in which the eclipsed remnant is reincarnated as ontological act, which we could just as easily call the aesthetic modification of the human project.

In the pages leading up to the confrontation with Sartre, Fanon speaks of his "ecstasy of becoming," of no longer looking at sources but "The Source," of the Negro "raining his poetic power on the world," of discovering "the primeval One"; but he also discusses white ethnography, bogus black essentialist philosophy, and the perverse drives that lead white society to bestow a redemptive role on the Negro. When we see how deeply Fanon has absorbed the aesthetic and political logic of Césaire's *Cahier*, we can see that he is *not* taking an ironic view of "black enthusiasm." Fanon's primitivism is Césaire's passionate sarcasm. It seeks to dissolve the contingent forms of "the Negro" in the course of salvaging and enacting the remnants of an authentic blackness. For even as Fanon knows his primitivism is mediated by colonial habits of mind, it is a primitivism that nevertheless holds true to the immediacy that it must satirize.

This still does not entirely explain why he considers Sartre's act of naming to be such a decisive blow. The answer, I believe, lies not in looking at the conceptual plane but in looking at its place in the essay's unfolding narrative. We must remember that Sartre's verdict on negritude is the last straw, so it is not as if Sartre single-handedly punctures black enthusiasm. Fanon is saying that there truly is no hope if this ostensible ally cannot *get it*. As so many critics have pointed out, this means not getting that "the Negro suffers in his body quite differently from the white man" (*BS*, 138). Yet Fanon stipulates that he does not hold his negritude out as a lack. Not getting it also means not hearing negritude's humor and its aggressive satire. Sartre can speak of the "great black mute idol" and keep a straight face. In the most profound sense Fanon is accusing Sartre of reading the poetry without humor.

Primitivism and Realism

In the final passages of "The Lived Experience" Fanon turns his attention from negritude poetry to narrative fiction and drama and briefly touches on Sartre's play *La Putain respectueuse* and Richard Wright's *Native Son*. In *Black Skin*'s earlier chapters, novels are treated in a way that could be described as discourse analysis *avant la lettre*. He reads René Maran's *Un homme pareil aux autres* and Mayotte Capécia's *Je suis Martiniquais* as manifestations of French racial discourse and not aesthetic works in their own right. By contrast the works by Wright and Sartre are introduced for their value specifically as literary mediations. It is a measure of the breadth and complexity of Fanon's relationship to Sartre that having just claimed to have been betrayed by "Black Orpheus," he takes a passage from a Sartre play to illustrate the condition of black consciousness following that betrayal. Fanon quotes a scene in *La Putain respectueuse* in which a falsely accused black man is given a gun by the play's protagonist, the prostitute Lizzie, and told to kill the white men who are about to come through her door:

> THE NEGRO. I can't shoot white folks.
> LIZZIE. Really! They have no qualms about it.
> THE NEGRO. They're white folks ma'am. (*BS*, 139; my translation)

Fanon then directly identifies this "Negro" with the protagonist of Wright's novel: "It is Bigger Thomas,—who is afraid, terribly afraid. He is afraid, but of what is he afraid? Of himself. No one knows yet who he is, but he knows that fear will inhabit the world when the world finds out. And when the world knows, the world always expects something of the Negro. He is afraid lest the world know, he is afraid of the fear that would be in the world if the world knew" (BS, 139).

This turn from poetry to narrative at the end of the essay signals a shift from a focus on psychic states to the political situation of that consciousness. The examples of Native Son and, to a lesser degree, Chester Himes's If He Hollers Let Him Go are apt: the plots of both center on a sudden transition from an internal will-to-violence and its external actualization. In the following passage from Wright's novel, for instance, we find Bigger trying to work out whether or not his murder of Mary Dalton really had been accidental: "And in a certain sense he knew that the girl's death had not been accidental. He had killed many times before, only on those other times there had been no handy victim of circumstance to make visible or dramatic his will to kill. His crime seemed natural; he felt that all of his life had been leading to something like this."[56] Bigger realizes that he feels no guiltier having smothered the white woman than he did before the act. He had long before internalized that guilt. If anything, her death has equalized the relation between internal and external reality. It could well be that Mary Dalton's bones at the bottom of the furnace are to him what the bones of the Duiker are to Soyinka's tiger: evidence of his negritude.

Simply knowing that he has acted is not enough. Bigger burns with desire to have his act known and acknowledged. He is caught between the need to conceal his crime in order to frame the Daltons and the desire to reveal to anyone, even anonymous strangers on a Chicago streetcar, that he has indeed acted: "He looked out of the car window and then round at the white faces near him. He wanted suddenly to stand up and shout, telling them that he had killed a rich white girl, a girl whose family was known to all of them. . . . He wished that he could be an idea in their minds; that his black face and the image of his smothering Mary and cutting off her head and burning her could hover before their eyes as a terrible picture of reality which they could see and feel and yet not destroy."[57] This is a further development on the tram scenes in Césaire and Fanon. If Césaire's experience is external to the "tram nigger" and Fanon's is the shock of his own alienation, Bigger wants to impress on the white commuters around him the new reality he has brought into being. This is a composite picture, the simultaneous effect of his face and the stages of Mary's execution, with each conjunction raising the pitch of Bigger's enthusiasm.

"In the end," Fanon writes, "Bigger Thomas acts. To put an end to his tension, he acts, he responds to the world's anticipation" (*BS*, 139). Having seen the fundamental difference between Fanon's and Sartre's understanding of negritude's poetics, we now see that they also diverge in their reading of Wright. Sartre sees Wright as an exemplar for committed narrative fiction. Wright is important because he gives African Americans a name that allows them to mediate and reflect on their suffering. For Fanon the moment of mediation is the narration of Bigger's accidental-on-purpose murder. The importance of the novel, for Fanon, is not that we understand, in sociological detail, the social climate that led to Bigger's crime but that we confront the life that Mary's death gives him: "He was more alive than he could ever remember having been; his mind and attention were pointed, focused toward a goal. For the first time in his life he moved consciously between two sharply defined poles: he was moving away from the threatening penalty of death, from the death-like times that brought him that tightness and hotness in his chest; and he was moving toward that sense of fullness he had so often but inadequately felt in magazines and movies."[58]

Wright is often labeled a social realist and would probably find the label of primitivism unsuited to his work. It is Fanon's achievement in "The Lived Experience" to show that Césaire's surrealist primitivism and Wright's prose realism are not mutually exclusive literary projects. It is in their capacity as aesthetic modifications of the human project that the work of each writer discloses contradictions in consciousness in the late colonial moment. A paradox of the above passage is that Bigger experiences a fullness he could not obtain through magazines and movies, yet we, reading Wright's novel, are asked to believe in his new fullness. It is only in the mode of literary experience that Fanon can make this true for his readers.

Postlude

The conclusions I have reached over the course of this first study pertain in their entirety only to "The Lived Experience of the Black."[59] There are times in other essays when Fanon seems to agree with the thrust of the argument in Sartre's "Black Orpheus," particularly with regard to black American forms of music. In the essay "West Indians and Africans," for example, Fanon characterizes the embrace of the blues as part of negritude's plunge into its primitive self: "For after all, if the color black is virtuous, I shall be all the more virtuous the blacker I am! Then there emerged from the shadows the very black, the 'blues,' the pure. And Césaire, the faithful bard, would repeat that 'paint the tree trunk white as you will, the roots remain black.' Then it became real that not only the color black was invested with value, but fiction black, ideal black, black in the absolute, primitive black, the Negro."[60]

There is no reason, at least in the terms of "The Lived Experience," that the blues could not be a viable medium for negritude's aesthetic modification of the "Negro" as part of a liberating reflective capture of immediacy. Yet comments made by Fanon in "Racism and Culture," an essay written a few years later, suggest the blues are reducible to their historical conditions: "Thus the blues—'the black slave lament'—was offered up for the admiration of the oppressors. This modicum of stylized oppression is the exploiter's and the racist's rightful due. Without oppression and without racism you have no blues. The end of racism would sound the knell of great Negro music. . . . Literature, the plastic arts, songs for shopgirls, proverbs, habits, patterns, whether they set out to attack it or to vulgarize it, restore racism."[61]

The voice that here defers to the consensus that the blues is the visage of a racist society is certainly not the same as that which wants to enter into blackness as an absolute. Now the claim is made that to take the "plunge" would simply redouble the objectification of the "Negro." If the blues is "stylized oppression," can any "aesthetic modification of the human project" work from within oppressed conditions? Unless the blues happens to be a form of expression that is not up to this task (Fanon makes no such indication), negritude would have to be realized in a nonracist society before it could express anything that did not restore racism. Aesthetic experience is given a second-order and passive role, and Fanon appears to lose his grip on the insight that propels "The Lived Experience of the Black."

What a close engagement with Fanon reading Césaire with and against Sartre has shown is that earlier primitivisms, to which we will turn in the next two studies, were rhetorically and stylistically much less dexterous. As we will see in the works of Lawrence and McKay, there is a tendency to get backed into a bad choice between despair and false transcendence. Césaire's *Cahier* remains a startling work because it discovered a mode in which poetic abandonment was not premised on naiveté and in which the immediate could be seized without succumbing to the mediate. The *Cahier*, and Fanon's activation of it, also serves as a riposte to those later critics who would, in proclaiming that everything is mediated and constructed, jettison any faith in or evidence of alternate social worlds. When Fanon comments that "what was necessary was to shatter the current situation and to try to apprehend reality with the soul of the child" (*BS*, 193), he shows us that he has understood this aspect of Césaire's work. Fanon's primitivism is self-infantilizing, in the strong sense of wanting to recover the possibility of naive experience.

Chapter 6

D. H. LAWRENCE'S NARRATIVE PRIMITIVISM

What does the blood know? Long after the end of National Socialism and institutional colonial racism, this question sounds odd and certainly anachronistic. It is jolting to think that at the beginning of the twentieth century, questions of blood and knowledge still felt new and were at the center of various intellectual and social enterprises whose outcomes were yet uncertain. The combination of the rise of the biological sciences, the surge of human populations around the globe, and racial stratifications within and between metropolitan and colonial societies created an intellectual atmosphere in which hypotheses about the cognitivity of "blood" were both common and earnestly debated. Social Darwinism and eugenics are now notorious, but they were part of a much broader convergence of discourses around blood. The concept of "genes" was coined at this time, and with it came the notion that blood carries specific inherited traits.[1] If strains of human blood have character-defining contents, then political ideologies, social policies, and aesthetic movements can legitimately be founded on the differences between them.

There is a difference, though, and this needs to be stressed, between seeking to know the determining properties of blood and countenancing the idea that the blood itself *knows* something—that it has agency and the power of will. Thinking along this line provokes the double-take that comes when nature is assigned intentional consciousness—when activities like rabbits burrowing, birds singing, or trees pushing their leaves toward the sun are characterized as cognitive. In the case of the human person, though, we are dealing with two kinds of knowledge in the same entity: blood knowledge coexists with that mode of cognition usually assigned to the "mind." By investigating the peculiar historical consciousness that asks "what does the blood know?" I do not intend to revisit discourses of eugenics and scientific racism, even as we must acknowledge that the historical milieu is the same. As far as the eugenicists were concerned, "knowledge" is scientific knowledge: the ordering of things under concepts according to observable, repeatable patterns. The notion that blood holds certain active elements that bear on cognitive functions does not mean that its activity is believed to enact "knowledge" as such.[2] The cognitive agency implicit in the question "what does the blood know?" appealed more to artists and speculative thinkers.

D. H. Lawrence, in particular, was taken with the idea that the blood has its own specific way of knowing the world: "the blood has a unity and a consciousness of its own. It has a deeper, elemental consciousness of the mechanical or material world. In the blood we have the body of our most elemental consciousness, our almost material consciousness."[3] The distance of these comments from our now commonsense understanding that blood stores our DNA is evident in the use of the definite article: this is not blood as carrier but as distinct force. The syntax is the same as that usually reserved for "the unconscious." If human blood has a special kind of knowledge of the world, distinct from and more profound than those acts commonly regarded as cognitive, why does Lawrence persist with the same term? Why, indeed, not just call it "the unconscious" or "instinct"? There seems to be an irony in Lawrence's writing a work like *Fantasia of the Unconscious* (1922), in which he has recourse to making arguments *about* blood knowledge in the hope that it will bring his reader closer to it. There is the risk that secondary, "mind" knowledge will overwrite the immediate blood kind.

It seems, though, that there is little to lose: "We have almost poisoned the mass of humanity to death with *understanding*. The period of actual death and race-extermination is not far off."[4] There can be little doubt that this is connected to his belief that blood knowledge and mind knowledge are locked in opposition: "Blood-consciousness overwhelms, obliterates, and annuls mind-consciousness. Mind-consciousness extinguishes blood-consciousness, and consumes the blood. We are all of us conscious in both ways. And the two ways are antagonistic in us."[5] Lawrence does not consider what the world would be like if blood were to overwhelm mind, but the dominance of mind-consciousness clearly is a bad thing.

In the preface to *Fantasia of the Unconscious* Lawrence announces that his "pseudo-philosophy" has been "deduced" from intuitions explored when writing novels and poems. Where literary writing is the emanation of "pure passionate experience," the analyses of *Fantasia* are the "inferences made afterwards."[6] Contrary to his comments about the poverty of "understanding," he acknowledges that there is value in trying to "abstract some definite conclusions from one's experience."[7] Unlike "the blood" and "the mind," art and criticism, it seems, can work together toward mutual ends. Criticism can even assist art, sniffing out those moments when the artist betrays her own work by trying to make its truths explicit. In *Studies in Classic American Literature*, for instance, he dismisses as "Blarney!" Crèvecoeur's "idealist" speculations in his novels on the "noble savage and the innocence of toil" but insists that "Crèvecoeur the artist gives us glimpses of actual nature, not writ large."[8]

The central thread of this chapter concerns the capacity of literature to act as a medium for the revelation of blood knowledge and the problems that Lawrence encountered when trying to wield it for this purpose. I want to work out why an artist so invested in the presentness of experience writes such long novels. Lawrence the idealist wants us to believe in the unity of word and flesh; Lawrence the artist, working in the medium of narrative fiction, is forced to travel a different path. Here the historical background to Lawrence's argument is relevant. When he indicts Crèvecoeur for the falsity of his idealizations (that "blarney" about the "the noble savage"), we already have a hint that his own quest for blood knowledge will encounter pitfalls. We earlier observed in *The Rainbow* a drive toward the primitive that pushes the novel's symbolism to the limit of concrete representation. The purpose of this chapter is to explore the ways in which Lawrence nevertheless persisted in trying to give a language and artistic form to the process of becoming-primitive. These fictional manifestations, I will show, were shaped within an atmosphere of emergent anticolonialism, whose decolonial horizon Lawrence, in his strange way, attempted to channel. His literary primitivism becomes distinct when read in counterpoint to negritude as a kind of hyperbolic anticipatory mirror. From the vantage of the primitivism of Césaire and Fanon, which will serve as counterpoint throughout this chapter, he reads as a brash yet haphazard precursor, struggling to fashion a literary style that might embody blood knowledge without succumbing to philo-primitivist naivety.

I will begin with Wyndham Lewis's critique of Lawrence's primitivism, which targets the same tendency to idealize "the Other" that the neo-primitivist critics later in the century would condemn. Lewis's critique, though, is in the service of an ironic defense of "palefaces," a kind of rear-guard *blancitude* rather than the neo-primitivists' submission to an absolutized alterity. Asking whether Lawrence's primitivism, in fact, culminates in such passages of idealization, I look first to the presentist prose style that he fashions in order to make immediate consciousness manifest in *Women in Love* before examining the programmatic place of representations of primitive remnants in the unfolding of the novel's narrative. The remnant, it transpires, is not a benchmark but something used by Lawrence to tell his own story of blancitude. In his late novel *The Plumed Serpent*, to which I turn in the final section, Lawrence makes a flawed attempt to narrate primitivist redemption in the form of a fascist anticolonial revolution.

Wyndham Lewis's *Paleface* as Blancitude

The cultural politics of Lawrence's primitivism came under sustained attack as early as 1929, in Wyndham Lewis's *Paleface*. This work has never been republished and is read only by specialists. If not entirely forgotten, it certainly has been overlooked by cultural historians, which is a pity because it discusses the relationship between race and culture with an unusual degree of self-consciousness for its time. Encountering Lewis's polemic, one is struck by the fact that colonial racism had a rhetoric and a style. This forces us to contend with racism in the mode of self-conscious performative assertion, making it harder to chalk up anachronistic moral victories. His essay is evidence of the ways in which whiteness as a sensibility and way of being was compelled to justify itself by the nascent anticolonial challenge. He mounts his ironic defense of the "palefaces" in full knowledge that his opponent's position is the only morally defensible one. His tactic is Nietzschean, using irony and blithe self-contradiction to say the unsayable and yet prevent his opponents from holding him to his word. At its core the work is a recapitulation of Nietzsche's critique of Christian *ressentiment* and affirmation of the principle of strength. Written as European imperialism's greatest crisis loomed, Lewis's polemic in a sense proves that Nietzschean irony and dissimulation were the natural rhetorical strategies for justifying white rule.

Vincent Sherry describes *Paleface* as an early experiment in cultural studies.[9] The range of the work will surprise those used to pigeonholing white and nonwhite modernisms. Lewis reads Lawrence and Sherwood Anderson alongside W. E. B. Du Bois and Parisian *négrophilie* (which he calls "white phobia"). In setting out the antiprimitivist position, this work connects the dots at the moment of emphatic primitivism's maximum flourishing. In its diversity of reference and racial theme it anticipates *Black Skin, White Masks*, only as if in parodic photographic negative—"White Skin, Black Souls" perhaps.

A constant tendency in Fanon's thinking is the attempt to hold on to humanist absolutes, or at least their possibility, in a colonial situation in which relativism appears to be inevitable. It could be imagined, then, that he would welcome Lewis's assertion that "the 'principle of an absolute value in the human person as such,' of whatever race or order, I am eager to advance."[10] He would also concur with the following comment about the failures of European colonialism:

> For the most part the White peoples who overran the world, and, with the help of their rapidly developing Science, enslaved the greater part of it, wiping out entire races and cultures, were possessed of a meagre cultural outfit, and only a borrowed religion. It is a commonplace that Cortez or Pissarro were less "civilised," on the whole, than the Aztecs, Mayans or Incas they subdued. The Anglo-Saxons, who were responsible for the major part of this european expansion and colonization (although not the first in the field) possessed less cultural equipment, and a more naive and crude variety of religion (their well-thumbed genevan bible in their breast-pocket), than the other White partners of this World-conquest. (*P*, 125)

Lewis goes on to argue that there was a basic disproportion between the technical superiority that enabled colonial subjugation and the moral and spiritual accomplishment of those who undertook it. The tools of science and industry came to dominate the dominators, displacing the absolute from the human person to the "towering babylonian monument to Science" (*P*, 126). The "crystallisation" of a white "inferiority complex" caused by this alienation is the theme of Lewis's polemic.

In spite of this decline, Lewis takes it on himself to affirm the basic value of whiteness. Negritude's utopia of Africa is here the utopia of the enduring gentleman: "But ultimately whiteness is, in a pigmentary sense, aristocratic, perhaps—the proper colour for a 'gentleman': and blackness irretrievably proletarian. May not this be an absolute, established in our senses?" (*P*, vi). The shock provoked by this is calculated. Lewis wants us to register the effect when the widespread presumption of white superiority is openly declared at a time when it was beginning to be papered over by late colonial liberalism. In this he again mirrors Fanon. For Fanon the act that initiates negritude—the unilateral affirmation of blackness—is necessarily artificial.[11] What we might call Lewis's blancitude is likewise set in motion by the necessities of negation:

> I am really driven into the position of the Devil's Advocate to some extent (the devil or villain-of-the-piece being now of course the overbearing, stupid, wicked *Paleface* as seen by the conventional revolutionary tract) by the excesses of the anti-Whites—not, I am afraid, from what I have called *esprit de peau*. But flung violently into that diabolical position, I did I must say at first find myself developing what was a sort of *esprit de peau*, of a quite respectable dimension. I detected myself looking with a new complacency upon the White skin: there was something about a *Paleface*, was there not? that I had overlooked in my zeal for a non-national consciousness: I could scarcely understand how it had escaped my attention that all these familiar lightish masks held something for my eye, nevertheless (blunted by familiarity), that the varnished countenance of a quadroon or a "high yaller," or the sickly liverish ambers of an Hawaiian girl, did not contain. (*P*, 20)

Just as with Fanon's existential self-examination, Lewis presents his revelation in the mode of self-observation. "Flung" into affirming his racial identity, he "detects" the pride forming within himself. It is also a typically Lewisean posture—what Fredric Jameson identifies as an impulse to make of himself "the impersonal registering apparatus for forces which he means to record, beyond any whitewashing and liberal revisionism."[12] Lewis's purpose is to give articulation to a worldview, not to win an argument. Accordingly, we should approach the racism evident in the work as the result of willfully occupying a rhetorical structure rather than as a manifestation of personal prejudice. It is the logical requirement of his *esprit de peau*, placing it in dialectical relation to Fanon's desire to "lose [him]self in negritude."[13]

If Fanon wants to liberate negritude from the circumstances that compelled it into existence, what is Lewis's purpose in espousing *esprit de peau*? His named targets are Marxists and those sympathetic to colonized peoples. As far as he is concerned, though, the true enemy is a more pervasive European ideology. He provokes liberal outrage in order to sharpen his confrontation with Christian *ressentiment*.[14] With Lewis the insights and postures of Nietzschean antiprimitivism ripen. He uses the rhetoric of amoralism to trivialize colonial history, as well as the liberal response to it, just as national consciousness among the colonized was maturing. This leads Lewis to the perverse conclusion, which he knows is perverse, that having falsely set themselves up as an example for all humanity, white men must live positively as white Europeans lest Christian moralism infect the colonized by way of example:

> For, if all *Palefaces* in the world were so truly righteous that we as one man suc-cumbed, consequent upon the impossible burdens laid upon us by our puritan consciences (and I am perfectly ready to admit that if we sat down and thought comprehensively enough of all our sins and those of all our ancestors we should see no alternative but to succumb in that manner), why then all the Blacks, after us (who are even more emotional than we are and if anything better evangelists) would follow suit as one man, unable to bear the spectacle of this wholesale Tragedy of Conscience, in which they had been the innocent cause. . . . Let us draw back in time. Let us keep our noses well in the air. It is the White Man's Burden! (*P*, 22)[15]

It is a measure of the high self-consciousness of this work that Lewis never-theless issues the caveat that he would rather that white sentimentalism for nonwhites remain than "provoke in any way a reaction of intolerance" (*P*, 21). Unlike Nietzsche, he cannot quite bring himself to commit to his irony.

Lewis regards racial sentimentalism to be one form of appearance of a larger crisis in art and philosophy in the West that he had diagnosed two years earlier in the weightier volume *Time and Western Man* (1927). In that work he makes the following claims:

1. A "time-flux" philosophy recently has succeeded in establishing itself as the dominant paradigm in European arts and letters.

2. This "time-mind" insists on a "sensational" and "temporal" understand-ing of the world, as opposed to an "intelligible" and "spatial" one. It is anticonceptual and antipictorial.

3. "Sensational understanding" works by a process of "intensive abstrac-tion," whereby the temporal animation of subjective thought is attrib-uted to "dead" material things.

4. This liquidates the nonegoistic, objectivist tenets of secular Western thought that constitute its genius. It is hence an irrational, self-negating tendency within Western thought that perversely wishes to return to a "*primitive* condition."[16]

Positively, Lewis offers a fifth claim as a remedy to the time-flux worldview:

5. A neo-Berkeleyan philosophy of pure surface is required as a corrective. This would insist that nothing exists that cannot be perceived by the eye: a world of hollow mountains and humans without organs—an "extremist philosophy for *surface-creatures*."[17]

Paleface effectively is a variation on the theme of the fourth claim and takes as given the first three. Primitivism is the time-flux philosophy's cultural manifestation, performing, then disavowing, an abstraction whereby an idealized irrationalism is projected onto primitive entities that have been evacuated of substantive content. The postmodern critique of primitivism, it turns out, was patented by a reactionary.

Paleface is not simply an appendix to *Time and Western Man*, though. The engagement with the colonial context modifies and resituates the earlier study. For the most part, *Time and Western Man* appears simply to reiterate age-old binaries of the mind and the senses, the rational and the irrational, the civilized and the primitive, the West and the non-West, as well as the essentializing habits we now associate with these binaries. In a significant passage, though, Lewis makes it clear that the intellectual heritage that he defends is not the result of an inherent rationality but is actually a kind of sensibility: "It is in non-personal modes of feeling—that is in *thought*, or in feeling that is so dissociated from the hot, immediate egoism of sensational life that it becomes automatically intellectual—that the non-religious Western Man has always expressed himself, at his profoundest, at his purest."[18] Rational thought is one "mode of feeling" among others, whose peculiarity is to dissociate itself from itself as feeling. Accordingly, his study turns out not to be the paean to scientific thought that we might anticipate but a defense of those traditions of artistic expression that aim for sensual dissociation. It is, in other words, an argument about aesthetics. Lewis wants to show that bad philosophy and bad art feed off each other as they weaken the capacity for "non-personal modes of feeling."[19] Lewis is ready to admit that his conclusions, when considered discursively, are illogical because they really are a matter of position-taking within the artistic debates of the day. He is petitioning for an art of the "intellectual-object" and against dominance of the "time-object."

Primitivism, for Lewis, is the quintessential aesthetic of the "time-mind," combining subjectivist philosophy with a sentimental identification with those people that he believes have no history of objectifying thought; and D. H. Lawrence is the quintessential primitivist.[20] Having embraced all the tenets of time philosophy, Lawrence then "pumps" (*P*, 117) this into whichever hapless racial other comes to hand. His primitivism bestows "authority upon a hypothetical something or someone it has never seen, and would be [at] a loss to describe" (*P*, 103–4). As with the postmodern deconstruction of primitivism, Lewis leaves the matter there. Lawrence is using "primitives" as dummies to ventriloquize bad philosophy, so there is no need to think about those alternative social realities toward which his primitivism is drawn. Lewis cites as indicative the following passage from Lawrence's *Mornings in Mexico*: "There is no Onlooker. There is no Mind. There is no dominant idea. . . . The Indian is completely embedded in . . . his own drama. It is a drama that has no beginning and no end. . . . It can't be judged, because there is nothing outside it, to judge it" (cited in *P*, 184).

Curiously, though, Lewis confesses to taking pleasure in Lawrence's writing. Citing another passage, he comments, "I need not point out to the reader, probably, the virtues of this passage as a tour de force of literary art. It is reminiscent of the best manner of Anatole France only possessing greater freshness" (*P*, 190–91). Is it significant that he should indict Lawrence's primitivist ideology as part of making the case against the art of the "time-object" yet still relish the prose? The separation of artistic value and philosophical perspective is one that he has no qualms admitting to, stating his intention "to squeeze out all the essential meaning that there is in the works I select, and leave only the purely literary or artistic shells" (*P*, 111). This begs the question of whether his preferred "intellectual-object" would even need to be expressed as art, seeing as bad philosophy can exist within an otherwise compelling artistic shell. For once, Lewis seems unaware of the contradiction, which in itself is noteworthy. This could well be a deep-lying contradiction in the Hegelian sense of disclosing his argument's condition of possibility. The critique of the time-mind is an argument about affect—a struggle between "modes of feeling"—and yet the proof lies in separating out and targeting art's philosophical content.

Already we have seen that in his discursive writing, Lawrence acknowledges that reflexive consciousness can play an important role in identifying the truth of art's "pure passionate experience." This reflexive knowledge, he makes clear, serves ultimately to annul itself. It points the way and then should recede: "Knowledge is to consciousness what the signpost is to the traveller: just an indication of the way which had been travelled before . . . yet we *must* know, if only in order to learn not to know. The supreme lesson of human consciousness is to learn how not to know."[21] (As per Fanon, he needs *not to know*.) This is all grist for Lewis, but it does beg the question of what the work itself knows *as* literary expression. Lewis's blancitude is a riposte to Lawrence's signposts, as it were, not his literary work considered as stylistic and narrative constructions. Does the work do what the signposts say?

Techniques of Immediacy in *Women in Love*

The following passage is from a scene in the chapter "Moony" from *Women in Love*. Rupert Birkin and Ursula Brangwen are arguing about love.[22] Ursula wants joyful romantic love, but Rupert desires something more profound. As their disagreement intensifies, the representations of their thoughts and speech start to display typical features of Lawrence's heightened prose style at this time:

> "You don't even love me," she cried.
>
> "I do," he said angrily. "But I want—" His mind saw again the lovely golden light of spring transfused through her eyes, as through some wonderful window. And he wanted her to be with him *there*, in *this* world of proud indifference. But what was the good of telling her he wanted *this* company in proud indifference. What was the good of talking, any way? *It* must happen beyond the sound of words. *It* was merely ruinous to try to work her by conviction. *This* was a paradisal bird that could never be netted, *it* must fly by itself to the heart.
>
> "I always think I am going to be loved—and then I am let down. You *don't* love me, you know. You don't want to serve me. You only want yourself."
>
> A shiver of rage went over his veins, at this repeated: "You don't want to serve me." All the paradisal disappeared from him.
>
> "No," he said, irritated, "I don't want to serve you, because there is nothing there to serve. What you want me to serve, is nothing, mere nothing. It isn't even you, it is your mere female quality. And I wouldn't give a straw for your female ego—it's a rag doll."
>
> "Ha!" she laughed in mockery. "That's all you think of me, is it? And then you have the impudence to say you love me!"
>
> She rose in anger, to go home.
>
> "You want the paradisal unknowing," she said, turning round on him as he still sat half-visible in the shadow. "I know what that means, thank you. You want me to be your thing, never to criticise you or to have anything to say for myself. You want me to be a mere *thing* for you! No thank you! *If* you want that, there are plenty of women who will give it to you. There are plenty of women

who will lie down for you to walk over them—*go* to them then, if that's what you want—go to them."[23]

Tracking the word *paradisal* through this passage brings to the fore the peculiar way in which cognition is represented in this novel. The word occurs three times, and each is markedly different. To begin with, it is a metaphor: "This was a paradisal bird." Working out the identity of the demonstrative to which "paradisal bird" is metaphorically conjoined is not easy, though. It is hard to say for sure whether "*there*" is the "golden light of spring," whether "*this* company in proud indifference" is the possibility of Ursula joining Rupert "*there*," whether "*it*" "happen[ing]" is Ursula's coming to know that she needs to join Rupert "*there*," or, finally, whether "*this*" entity that is like a "paradisal bird" is the knowledge of the proud indifference of the company that would be kept in the golden light of spring that Rupert sees transfused in Ursula's eyes. Each might denote an undisclosed noun—an *x*—that Rupert is thinking but that the narration of his thoughts does not or cannot articulate. It is not even clear whether "paradisal bird" is a direct object of Rupert's consciousness, a comment from the narrator focalizing Rupert's consciousness indirectly, or if it is the narrator's own separate way of articulating Rupert's thoughts. As they accumulate, the demonstratives and pronouns increasingly detach from particular objects and attain a certain autonomy. They no longer feel like efficient placeholders for objects that have been or will be announced. What we have is more the narration of a consciousness continually reaching for half-cognized objects than a retrospective certainty about what those objects might be.

The charge that Lawrence's work is under the spell of the "time-mind" thus is not leveled without cause. One certainly would not characterize the presentation of Rupert's thoughts as *spatial*. We might contrast the ambiguities of the "paradisal bird" passage with the use of analogy in the following passage:

> "I'm sure she'll outlive *me*," Sir James grinned in bland repose, the death's head sweetened with the faintest irony. For a moment they grinned in each other's eyes—the animal, which has suddenly caught sight of its own person in a glass, and for a moment, before it thinks it has happened on another dog, perceives itself. The presence in their thoughts of the bitter matriarch whom he had just left, and under whom Sir James had suffered for half a century, conspired to compel their minds together in what was almost a caress.[24]

The analogy with the dog in this passage from Lewis's *Apes of God* (1929) serves to isolate a specific duration of cognition and give it quantity, at once giving the "flicker" of collusion between Sir James and Dick temporal substance and slowing the moment down so that we can look at it from all sides. Their snickering is heightened with the implied anagrammatic euphemism: "bit[ter matriar]ch." (Lewis has just spent seventeen pages describing the ritual grooming of Lady Fredigonde, the object of their derision—an extended passage that both minutely defines the physical image of the woman and establishes her tart character.) Where Lewis's dog analogy helps to ensure that no detail is missed, Lawrence keeps us moving from sentence to sentence, waiting for the consolidation of meaning that metaphor only suspends further.

The fluidity of thought in the "Moony" scene is not a matter of cognitive mode only; it also serves a narrative function. As Rupert pursues the object of his intuition about the light in her eyes, he trails off from speaking, and Ursula has a chance to cut in. She will not go along with his "proud indifference." This irritates and deflates Rupert, and the object of the modifier *paradisal* accordingly is withdrawn ("all the paradisal disappeared from him"). When Ursula responds to his irritation, she comes out and says the word aloud: "You want the paradisal unknowing. . . . I know what that means." She is entirely aware of where Rupert is going, and she calls this out as the attempt to make her the testing ground for his speculations. His abstractly conceived love has no relation to any particular characteristic of hers that might inspire love.

To enable Ursula to break the spell cast by Rupert's relentless idealizing, Lawrence allows the narrator to break the spell of cognitive literalism. Rupert evidently does not explicitly think the word *paradisal*, or else we would expect him to react with surprise when Ursula utters it aloud. Yet this does not jar because, by this point, the reader is well accustomed to the reckless quality of the novel's narration. Lawrence does not seek to differentiate the elements of his description to give specificity to each event of thought and speech. The effect is counterdialogic: the boundaries between individual consciousnesses become blurry, and their interactions can seem at times like an internal monologue.

This counterdialogic repetition is most marked when Lawrence's techniques of cognitive immediacy intensify. At such moments the narrative voice fixates on particular words, repeating them, and sometimes elements of the syntax in which they are set, to create a mantra-like effect. At times this produces parallelism, but more often there are syntactic variations with interlocking repetitions. This is a description of Gerald Crich and Rupert wrestling:

> They seemed to drive their *white* flesh deeper and deeper against each other, as if
> they would break into a *oneness*. . . . Both were *white* and clear. . . . They wrestled

swiftly, rapturously, intent and mindless at last, two essential *white* figures ever working into a tighter, closer *oneness* of struggle, with a strange, octopus-like *knotting* and flashing of limbs . . . a tense *white knot* of flesh gripped in silence. . . . Often, in the *white*, interlaced *knot* of violent living being that swayed silently, there was no head to be seen, only the swift, tight limbs, the solid *white* backs, the physical junction of two bodies clinched into *oneness*. (*WL*, 270; my emphasis)

This is Rupert and Ursula making love:

She recalled again the old magic of the Book of Genesis, where the *Sons of God* saw the *daughters of men*. . . . It was here she discovered him one of the *Sons of God* such as were *in the beginning* of the world. . . . It was the *daughters of men* coming back to the *Sons of God*, the strange inhuman *Sons of God* who are *in the beginning*. . . . She had found one of the *Sons of God* from *the Beginning*, and he had found one of the first most luminous *daughters of men*. . . . He stood there in his strange, whole body, that had its marvellous fountains, like the bodies of the *Sons of God* who were *in the beginning*. (*WL*, 312–14; my emphasis)

The narrative voice displays no self-consciousness when making these repetitions. Each iteration of the word is as though it were the first impression made all over again. Repetition provides no new detail, and the descriptions do not accrue to form a nuanced composite picture. Rather, it produces the effect of a continual thrusting forward of narratorial perception.

The same sense of a driving and forceful narrative consciousness is also achieved by the opposite means. In "Moony," just before the excerpt discussed above, Lawrence extravagantly varies the use of metaphor to describe a single repeated action. Four times in succession Rupert throws a stone into the center of a reflected image of a moon on the surface of the pond. The disturbance of the surface is described successively as "cuttlefish shooting out fire," "luminous polyp," "flakes of white and dangerous fire," "white birds . . . fleeing in clamorous confusion," "darts of bright light," "a battlefield of broken lights and shadows," "white fragments" like "petals of a rose that a wind has blown far and wide," a "few broken flakes tangled and glittering," and "a black and white kaleidoscope tossed at random" (*WL*, 246–48). Where repetition makes tangible the presence of narratorial perception, the variation of metaphor subjectifies the objective event. The image of light scattering on a liquid surface is easily brought to mind, so the narrator works all the harder to compel his readers to see in their mind's eye *this* disruption of the surface, and then *that* disruption, and then the other, and so on.

These techniques of immediacy aim to bring the reader into direct contact with the movement of consciousness as it encounters and makes sense of phenomena in the world without at the same time abstracting those phenomena or drawing attention to signification in a way that decisively punctures the illusion of the fictional world. Such moments are frequent but not all-pervasive. They are propelled by an urgency to sustain and draw out immediate experience for as long as possible before lapsing back into a more familiar world of objective surfaces and social relations. This rightly can be considered a kind of "time-flux" narration. Had Lewis wanted to, he could have integrated questions of prose style into his criticism of Lawrence's time-flux philosophy. This leaves open the question, though, of the connection between the techniques of immediacy and those moments that Lewis does highlight in which a non-European "other" seemingly is idealized. In the terms of this study, we are concerned to explore the connection between Lawrence's techniques of immediacy and those "primitive" remnants that seem to give this immediacy its animating purpose. Does the immediacy of the prose style have a primitivist telos? Is Rupert heading in the direction of, say, the "Indian" consumed unselfconsciously with his own "drama"? This, then, becomes a question of narrative form. Were the techniques of immediacy sufficient in themselves, Lawrence might have stuck to writing short fiction and free verse. The choice in this case of a long, chronologically structured narrative suggests that the local means for presenting preconscious thought might not be sufficient in themselves.

Blancitude and Narrative Primitivism

The following passage from a scene toward the beginning of *Women in Love* is often cited as a straightforward statement of Lawrence's primitivism. Rupert and Gerald Crich, the son of an industrial magnate, are staying with the bohemian Julius Halliday in his London flat. Rupert, Julius, and a Russian man stand naked around a West African carving owned by Julius:

> Birkin, white and strangely present, went over to the carved figure of the negro woman in labour. Her nude, protuberant body crouched in a strange clutching posture, her hands gripping the ends of the band, above her breast.
>
> "It is art," said Birkin.
>
> "Very beautiful, it's very beautiful," said the Russian.
>
> They all drew near to look. Gerald looked at the group of naked men, the Russian golden and like a water-plant, Halliday tall and heavily, brokenly beauti-

ful, Birkin very white and immediate, not to be defined, as he looked closely at the carven woman. Strangely elated, Gerald also lifted his eyes to the face of the wooden figure. And his heart contracted.

He saw vividly, with his spirit, the grey, forward-stretching face of the negro woman, African and tense, abstracted in utter physical stress. It was a terrible face, void, peaked, abstracted almost into meaninglessness by the weight of sensation beneath. He saw the Pussum in it. As in a dream, he knew her.

"Why is it art?" Gerald asked, shocked, resentful.

"It conveys a complete truth," said Birkin. "It contains the whole truth of that state, whatever you feel about it."

"But you can't call it *high* art," said Gerald.

"High! There are centuries and hundreds of centuries of development in a straight line, behind that carving; it is an awful pitch of culture, of a definite sort." (*WL*, 78–79)

The orthodox critique of primitivism understands the carving to be a thematization of the narrative's primitive ideal.[25] The novel's primitivism consists, thus, in the movement from this alienated condition here in civilized Europe toward that ideal state of sensual-knowledge over there in primitive Africa. Insofar as this ideal rests on a series of binary oppositions, it is revealed to be another kind of manifestation of the self/other ur-structure of colonial discourse. The question I want to pose is whether the carving indeed encapsulates the objective of the novel's primitivism. We need to look at the programmatic place of this scene, and the role of African carvings more generally, within the unfolding narrative.

This takes us back to "Moony" and the moment following the "paradisal" passage. Following the confrontation at the pond, Rupert is wistful. He had refused Ursula's advances but now feels a physical yearning. In the extended passage of thought that follows, Rupert puzzles over the contradictions between physical desire and spiritual love. At three pivotal moments in the course of these reflections he makes a concatenation between disparate memories and objects, sending his thoughts in a new direction. The sequence begins with self-interrogation. Rupert sees that there is a contradiction between his constant ruminations on sensual fulfillment and his hesitation about acting on his desires. He has a flash of insight: "he found himself face to face with a situation. It was as simple as this: fatally simple" (*WL*, 252). The thoughts that follow set out with the intention of making explicit the "fatally simple" "this" that has flashed up in his mind: "On the one hand, he knew he did not want a further sensual experience—something deeper, darker than ordinary life could give. He remembered the African fetishes he had seen at Halliday's so often. There came back to him one, a statuette about two feet high, a tall, slim, elegant figure from West Africa, in dark wood, glossy and suave" (*WL*, 252–53).

This first concatenation is prompted when he sets out to solve his predicament in classic dialectical fashion, weighing something "on the one hand" against the other. The carving embodies one of his two opposing theses. Rupert vividly recalls the "fetish," with several lines given to outlining its features: her "beetle" face, her long body, short legs, and "heavy buttocks." He then speculates on the kind of knowledge that the figure embodies. It is "mindless" knowledge that actively dissolves and disintegrates the knowledge of the mind, working through and ending in the senses. He perceives this "disintegration and dissolution" to be "imminent in himself" (*WL*, 253). At the same time, he believes that it would take centuries for this state to be realized as a general social condition in Europe.

We might expect next to hear "the other hand," but Rupert's thoughts run on to speculate about what the "awful African process" would entail for Europe writ large: "There remained this way, this awful African process, to be fulfilled. It would be done differently by the white races. The white races, having the arctic north behind them, the vast abstraction of ice and snow, would fulfil a mystery of ice destructive knowledge, snow-abstract annihilation. Whereas the West Africans, controlled by the burning death-abstraction of the Sahara, had been fulfilled in sun-destruction, the putrescent mystery of sun-rays" (*WL*, 254). There is no direct identity, it turns out, between that which is "imminent" in Rupert and the form of knowledge he perceives in the carving. It serves as a *remnant*, allowing Rupert to reflect on what the pursuit of "sense knowledge" would mean for those belonging to a race formed within a different geology and history. The remnant is sublimated into the process of imagining what it would take for the "white races" to achieve a primitive state.

This brings Rupert to make a second concatenation: "Birkin thought of Gerald. He was one of these strange white wonderful demons from the north, fulfilled in the destructive frost mystery. And was he fated to pass away in this knowledge, this one process of frost-knowledge, death by perfect cold? Was he a messenger, an omen of the universal dissolution into whiteness and snow?" (*WL*, 254). Rupert here prophesies the novel's denouement. The carving has led him, *by analogy*, to identify the logic of the process that leads Gerald spontaneously to attack Gudrun before wandering off to his icy death in the Alps. Rupert has given a name, "frost-knowledge," to the death-drive that is associated with spontaneous activity by white characters throughout the novel. When she learns that Gerald had killed his brother accidentally as a child, Ursula wonders if "this playing at killing has some primitive desire for killing in it" (*WL*, 49); Gerald comments that Rupert's notion of individuals acting individually and instinctively "should have everybody cutting everybody else's throat in five minutes" (*WL*, 33); as she drowns, Gerald's younger sister Diana also kills her would-be savior by wrapping her arms tight around his neck (*WL*, 189), and Rupert sees this as typical of a "life that belongs to death—our kind of life" (*WL*, 186); Gerald muses that if people in England were to act collectively on their impulses, it would be "like bringing the light a little too near the powder-magazine, to let go altogether in England. One is afraid what might happen, if *everybody else* let go" (*WL*, 395).

A parallel with Fanon's essay on the lived experience of blackness again is suggestive. When Fanon abandons himself to negritude, it brings to the surface in its immediacy the reified subjectivity "Negro." He cites Bigger Thomas's exultation after he accidentally suffocates a white girl in Wright's *Native Son*. Bigger experiences catharsis by externalizing the death that he carries inside himself. Strangling Gudrun also gives Gerald a heightened sense of himself, as he thinks: "What bliss! Oh what bliss, at last, what satisfaction, at last! The pure zest of satisfaction filled his soul. He was watching the unconsciousness come unto her swollen face, watching the eyes roll back. How ugly she was! What a fulfillment, what a satisfaction!" (*WL*, 471–72). In their immediacy, negritude and blancitude are manifest as gendered violence. This is not to imply an equivalence, but it does register the ways in which racial thinking had damaged immediacy in the world created by imperialism. If anticolonial righteousness colors Fanon's comments on *Native Son*, with Bigger Thomas presaging his later analysis of violence and decolonization, Gerald's blancitude allows us to see how Lawrence plots the predatory civilizational logic of imperialist Europe.

The whiteness of several characters is remarked on in the novel. Gerald, however, possesses a whiteness that is more than physical bearing, such as we find in the following descriptions: "a sort of soft white magnetic domination from the loins and thighs and calves, enclosing and encompassing the mare" (*WL*, 113); "She saw his back, the movement of his white loins. But not that—it was the whiteness he seemed to enclose as he bent forwards, rowing" (*WL*, 120); "There seemed a faint, white light emitted from him, a white aura, as if he were [a] visitor from the unseen" (*WL*, 331). Set against the passages on the African carvings, we might consider what historical forces have given shape to Gerald's whiteness and how it has come to have such a morbid trajectory.

In another of his speculative monologues, Rupert, ever the narrative's clairvoyant, divines the destructive arc of Gudrun and Gerald's relationship. Again, human relations are cast as part of epochal civilizational shifts: "When the stream of synthetic creation lapses, we find ourselves part of the inverse process, the flood of destructive creation. Aphrodite is born in the first spasm of universal dissolution—then the snakes and swans and lotus—marshflowers—and Gudrun and Gerald—born in the process of destructive creation" (*WL*, 172). At first sight "synthetic creation" presents a tautology; is not all creation in a sense synthetic? Set against "destructive creation," though, we see that he is distinguishing different modes of creation, with the modifier indicating the telos of the creativity concerned. The oxymoron brings me to a concatenation of my own, one that might help to explain why there is a "flowering mystery" in the "death-process." Two decades after *Women in Love*, Joseph Schumpeter stamped his survival-of-the-fittest, evolutionary conception of capitalism with the concept of "Creative Destruction." The innovation of this idea within economic debates at the time was to direct attention to the effect on market structures of the continual introduction of new consumers, commodities, technologies, methods of organization and transportation, and the manner in which these forces were wielded creatively by risk-taking entrepreneurs. The disruptive effects of entrepreneurs are not, for Schumpeter, only a matter of winning customers from competing firms but of changing the very economic environment in which profits are sought and gained. Schumpeter self-consciously uses the biological term *industrial mutation* to describe the immanence of a process that "incessantly revolutionizes the economic structure *from within*, incessantly destroying the old one, incessantly creating a new one. This process of Creative Destruction is the essential fact about capitalism."[26] This quasi-Darwinian theory emphasizes individual human actors above Marxian concerns with surplus value or the focus in classical economics on the relation between seller and buyer. Schumpeter's catchphrase is about shifting the criteria for success in mature capitalism. Rather than being a question, say, of the inventiveness required to conceive of a new product or method of distribution, creativity is to be measured by the magnitude of disruption it causes to received ways of conducting business.

"Creative Destruction" cuts to the core of Gerald's story. The convulsive environment of industrial capitalism is the natural habitat for his blancitude.

His backstory, which is sketched in a chapter called "The Industrial Magnate," is textbook Schumpeter. Gerald tries out careers as a soldier and explorer (to "savage regions" [*WL*, 222] no less) before realizing that he best can fulfill his inner drives by succeeding his father as a "Napoleon of industry" (*WL*, 64). As an explorer he had found "humanity very much alike everywhere, and to a mind like his, curious and cold, the savage was duller, less exciting than the European" (*WL*, 222). Returning to the colliery towns of the Midlands is his shot at a "a real adventure" (*WL*, 222).

Gerald's assumption and transformation of his father's business exemplifies the immanent character of Creative Destruction. He aggressively restructures the business according to hard economic principles. He expunges the Christian-paternalist worker's welfare provided by his father, introduces new technologies and specialists, and pares down management. Creative Destruction, Gerald's story shows us, does not only apply to competition between established and new players but is part of the internal progression of individual firms: "As soon as Gerald entered the firm, the convulsion of death ran through the old system. He had all his life been tortured by a furious and destructive demon, which possessed him sometimes like an insanity. This temper now entered like a virus into the firm, and there were cruel eruptions" (*WL*, 229). His new order may be brutal, but the workers who survive the convulsions feel that they belong to it: "His father was forgotten already. There was a new world, a new order, strict, terrible, inhuman, but satisfying in its very destructiveness" (*WL*, 231). Their acquiescence is gained by being a part of the, as it were, "flowering mystery" of Gerald's blancitude. In Gerald race and capitalism are locked in uneasy tautology. His white primitive drive evidently is at home in the industrial system, but it cannot be determined whether it is the whiteness of the race that drives the logic of the system, or the other way round.

The manifest contradictions of Gerald's deathward trajectory throw into doubt the whole aesthetic project of immediacy to which Rupert gives impetus throughout the novel. This is a matter of both style and content. If passages of prose immediacy appear implicitly to affirm an art of the absolute present, the novel's plotting, which is hardly unconventional in its linear chronology and division into scene-based chapters, points to the disastrous consequences of presentism. In his essay "The Poetry of the Present" Lawrence recommends a free verse unconstrained by form in terms that could just as well apply to his prose techniques of immediacy: "This is the immanence"; "The law must come new each time from within."[27] In *Women in Love* the law of immanence is also capitalist upheaval. If Rupert so often pauses before abandonment to his impulses, it is because he intuits that the expression of essence under capitalism is that of a morbid subjectivity.

Returning to his second concatenation in "Moony," it is apparent now that the memory of the African carving *qua* remnant of a social reality in which instinct and knowledge are reconciled allows him to see the horrendous consequences that would come with abandoning oneself to instinct in the European context. It is not a surprise, therefore, to find that his apparent negrophilia turns to negrophobia later in the novel.[28] Not only does Rupert see that abandonment to blancitude is an abandonment to Creative Destruction, but that "the Savage," as well, burns with destructive will; a premonition of the pressures of anticolonialism that will become the subject of *The Plumed Serpent*.

This brings him to his third and final concatenation. Rupert's "strange, strained attention" gives way, and the answer to his crisis comes to him: "There was another way, the way of freedom. There was the Paradisal entry into pure, single being" (*WL*, 254). He decides at once that he must marry Ursula. The carving and Gerald are left behind, and the pledge of an absolute heterosexual union appears as the alternative path. If this seems terribly conventional, it turns out that marriage, for Rupert, is really a pledge to pursue social renewal. The terms by which he idealizes marriage take us back to abstractions of the final passage of the *Rainbow*. Rupert explains to Ursula that they must leave England in order to pursue his marriage ideal:

> "But where can one go?" she asked anxiously. "After all, there is only the world, and none of it is very distant."
>
> "Still," he said, "I should like to go with you—nowhere. It would be rather wandering just to nowhere. That's the place to get to—nowhere. One wants to wander away from the world's somewheres, into our own nowhere."
>
> Still she meditated.
>
> "You see, my love," she said, "I'm so afraid that while we are only people, we've got to take the world that's given—because there isn't any other."
>
> "Yes there is," he said. "There's somewhere where we can be free—somewhere where one needn't wear much clothes—none even—where one meets a few people who have gone through enough, and can take things for granted—where you be yourself, without bothering. There is somewhere—there are one or two people—" (*WL*, 315–16).

Rainbows and marriage: the primitivist response to capitalist alienation at the moment of Imperialism turns out to be entirely quaint. The tendency toward the contentless abstraction of the rainbow and a married life lived "nakedly" in a "nowhere" holds over the course of the two novels. The narrative logic shows with precision how primitivism is forced to abandon the concrete.

In Ursula's mind the frontier of civilization no longer exists: "there is only the world, and none of it is very distant." There is no existing place in which a perfect form of reconciled sensuous knowledge could be imagined. Lewis is wrong, thus, to characterize Lawrence's primitivism as the sentimental attempt to emulate an idealized primitive (as are Lawrence's recent critics). If anything, the primitivist project pushes Rupert back into the mode of reflective knowledge in order that he be in a position to imagine a good immediacy beyond the spatiotemporal saturation of the imperialist world-system. Nevertheless, Rupert and Ursula *do* set off at the novel's end on a journey. It seems there is a lingering hope that "nowhere" might be an actual place.

Here! Blood!

The Plumed Serpent is a turgid and tedious novel but a fascinating document in the history of literary primitivism. Its evident failures as a work of art are at least partly the result of the attempt to transmute primitivism from potentiality to actuality, a claim that I follow Michael Bell in making. The urgent yet latent power of the Ursula novels, in which intensifying despair and the compulsive urge toward the primitive give prose, character, and scene a compelling volatility, becomes a garish yet flat surface as Lawrence seeks to narrate, here-and-now, the incarnation of the primitive. Bell perceptively observes that *The Plumed Serpent* does not narrate transformation as the development of a sensibility but as "an objective quality in the world itself."[29] The narrative pacing is much slower as the work continually asks the reader to imagine visual details in a manner that leans toward the exoticism and lists of travel writing: "Baskets of spring guavas, baskets of sweet lemons called *limas*, baskets of tiny green and yellow lemons, big as walnuts; orange-red and greenish mangoes, oranges, carrots, cactus fruits in great abundance, a few knobbly potatoes, flat, pearl-white onions, little *calabazitas* and speckled green *calabazitas* like frogs, *camotes* cooked and raw—she loved to watch the baskets trotting up the beach past the church."[30] The analogies are somewhat animated by Kate Leslie's concatenating perception, but this only strengthens the effect of realism. Reality is not subordinated to the project of the subject but subjectivity given over to externals. Even as she is drawn into a monumental tale of primitive-nationalist insurrection Kate still finds time for the restful contemplation of a tourist.

The novel is set in Mexico and follows Kate, a middle-aged Anglo-Irish woman, as she is seduced into a neo-Aztec national movement by the anthropologist Don Ramón Carrasco (a.k.a. "Quetzalcoatl") and the military leader General Cipriano Viedma (a.k.a. "Huitzilopochtli"). The novel tests whether Kate's "old" European individuated consciousness can willingly give itself over to a resurgent Mexican "blood-consciousness." Lawrence's Mexico holds both highly visible remnants of precolonial Aztec society and a brooding energy of resentment at its subsequent colonial history. Beating a path to the primitive through the novel form takes Lawrence from a modernist psychologism to something akin to what has recently been called "peripheral realism."[31] He may not be a writer *of* the colonial periphery, but the periphery—primitivism's center of gravity—pulls him inexorably toward it. The novel's tedium arises in part from a confusion about whether Mexico *is* primitive or must again become primitive. It gets caught halfway between describing the current "primitiveness" of Mexico and the need to narrate a political upheaval that will resurrect the primitive.

This confusion extends to narrative technique. There are passages in which Lawrence makes full use of his techniques of immediacy, such as when Kate falls under the spell of Cipriano's "phallic" presence,[32] but these moments tend to be exceptional rather than a constant feature of the prose. Primitivist becoming is relegated almost entirely to the level of plotting. If Lawrence can convincingly render the events of the novel, then he might convince the reader that the rebirth of Quetzalcoatl as a national theology is an actually happening transformation of spirit—primitivism arriving at the primitive.[33]

This turn outward accompanies an unremitting emphasis on "blood." The shift from *Women in Love*'s preoccupation with knowledge, and especially "sense knowledge," to blood and "blood consciousness" can be gauged numerically: there is a nine-fold reduction in references to "knowledge" (from 116 to 13) and a five-fold increase in references to "blood" (from 53 to 241). This reflects the stylistic shift from the abstract to the concrete. The general is now carried in the physical material of blood, and, as a consequence, Rupert's speculative premonitions are replaced by a speculative plotting of the emergence of blood consciousness as a political movement.

Blood also reorients the language around race. The following comments of J. M. Coetzee regarding the "poetics of blood" in the work of Sarah Gertrude

Millin, born four years after Lawrence, also ring true for *The Plumed Serpent*: "unlike the abstraction of race, Millin's blood is also a fluid that can be thick or thin, hot or cold, healthy or diseased; a quintessence of blood flows from man to woman in sexual intercourse. . . . It is the poetics of blood rather than the politics of race that sets off Millin's imagination."[34] Ruminations on race in *Women in Love* are conducted at the level of geological epochs and civilizational ages, which makes uncertain the relation between race and specific individual decisions.[35] In *The Plumed Serpent* action follows from the impulsions of blood-consciousness, implicating race more directly in the drama. The determinations of race affect the course of the action, and, conversely, the demands of narrative form affect the ways in which race makes its presence felt. If dramatic tension and narrative momentum typically require the suspension of uncertainty, then racial determinism is a weak narrative theme. Eugenic narratives thus typically introduce miscegenation. We only discover the influence of the general once the drama of the mixed-race individual has played itself out. Coetzee argues that in the case of Millin the poetics of blood plays out in the form of tragedy. The tragic surfacing of the "flaw of *black blood*" through the generations of coloreds in *God's Step-Children* supplies the novel with its tension and pathos.[36]

In *The Plumed Serpent* miscegenation is introduced as the theme by Ramón's friend Julio Toussaint, "an elderly man in a black cravat" (*PS*, 53). At a dinner party, Toussaint steers the conversation toward what he regards to be the racial underpinnings of recent political conflict in Mexico:

> "I myself have French, Spanish, Austrian, and Indian blood. Very well! Now you mix blood of the same race, and it may be all right. Europeans are all Aryan stock, the race is the same. But when you mix European and American Indian, you mix different blood races, and you produce the half-breed. Now, the half breed is a calamity. For why? He is neither one thing nor another, he is divided against himself. His blood of one race tells him one thing. His blood of another race tells him another." (*PS*, 56–57)

Coetzee actually references this passage in a note to his essay on Millin. From it he infers the racial ideology of Lawrence's novel as a whole: "the spirit of the 'moment of coition' between Spanish man and Indian woman is similarly 'abject' and their progeny therefore abject-spirited too."[37] It is notable, though, that Kate challenges Toussaint, exclaiming, "But what sort of a spirit is there between white men and white women!" (*PS*, 56). Lawrence's critiques of Europeans and their "civilization" hover in the background here. It is not at all clear that the narrative values racial purity above miscegenation. Lawrence's poetics of blood will not necessarily play out as tragedy.

There is a range of ethnoracial mixtures among *The Plumed Serpent*'s central characters: the Anglo-Irish Kate, the Spanish-Mexican Ramón and Carlota, the indigenous Cipriano, and Kate's indigenous and mestizo servants. Comments on the effects of miscegenation occur throughout the novel, in the thoughts and dialogues of characters, as well as the narrative voice. Blood consciousness emerges as a *political* contest within and between characters. Mestizo Mexican blood does not internally consolidate itself but has an appropriative impulse. When Kate reflects toward the end of the novel on whether she will stay and fulfill her role as "Malintzi" in Ramón's neo-Aztec pantheon, she fears above all appropriation into the collectivizing instinct of Mexican blood:

> Kate was of a proud old family. She had been brought up with the English-Germanic idea of the intrinsic superiority of the hereditary aristocrat. Her blood was different from the common blood, another, finer fluid.
>
> But in Mexico, none of this. Her *criada* Juana, the *aguador* who carried the water, the boatman who rowed her on the lake, all looked at her with one look in their eyes. *The blood is one blood. In the blood, you and I are undifferentiated.* . . . It made her physically sick: this overbearing blood-familiarity. (*PS*, 378–79)

The Indian blood calls for absolute communality regardless of race. To satisfy its urges, it exceeds its own racial boundaries. Kate's European blood, for its part, tries to distinguish and separate-out the Indian mass into distinct subjectivities. Race as blood plays out as a contest between modes of intersubjectivity.

The politics of blood also raise questions of motive. Why is the collectivizing indigenous instinct not content to rest within its racial boundary? Why is Cipriano so keen from the first to marry Kate and integrate her into Ramón's order? Kate does not experience the blood familiarity as a disinterested quality of the Indian race. She senses that the demand "*The blood is one blood*" calls for something "worse than death to the white individual." Throughout the novel there is an atmosphere of simmering resentment and perverse attraction that surrounds the indigenous proletarians and peasants: "men, some of them scaly with dirt, who looked at you with a cold, mud-like antagonism as they stepped cattishly past" (*PS*, 67); "the peon men only emitting from their souls the black vapour of negation, that was perhaps hate. They seemed, the natives, to have the power of blighting the air with their black, rock-bottom resistance" (*PS*,

209–10); "the people went away in sensuous looseness, which soon turned, in the market, to hate, the old, unfathomable hate which lies at the bottom of the Indian heart" (*PS*, 250).[38] If Indian blood has a substantive content, it is this characteristic of antagonism and resistance.

In *Studies in Classic American Literature* Lawrence discusses without ambiguity the historical nature of the indigenous resentment of whites in North America: "The Red Man died hating the white man. What remnant of him lives, lives hating the white man. . . . He doesn't believe in us and our civilization, and so is our mystic enemy, for we push him off the face of the earth."[39] The precolonial remnant lives on in the mode of ressentiment, not as positive identity. This is not conveyed in such blunt terms in *The Plumed Serpent*, where the speculations on the spiritual orientation of Indians are focalized mostly through Kate's consciousness. As far as she is concerned, the Indian is unremittingly diabolic, and she does not think to historicize this conviction. But this blindness may well be a function of narrative, as her entanglement in the neo-Aztec movement relies on her being only partially conscious of its deep-rooted motivation. She feels that the vengeful indigenous blood wants to claim her, but she is only peripherally aware that this could relate to the colonial past. If her servants repulse her, why is she drawn to the "blood-consciousness" of Ramón and Cipriano? Cipriano, whose "blood" is entirely indigenous, carries the same dark appropriative impulse:

> She could see how different his blood was from hers, dark, blackish, like the blood of lizards among hot black rocks. She could feel its changeless surge, holding up his light, bluey-black head as on a fountain. And she would feel her own pride dissolving, going.
>
> She felt he wanted his bloodstream to envelop hers. (*PS*, 287)

The crucial difference is the role Cipriano plays in the novel's political narrative. Kate is attracted to his proactive strength and clarity of purpose. He wants to possess her as part of the larger project of seizing political power over the colonial state.

It is conventional to read *The Plumed Serpent* in the terms of European fascism.[40] Critics focus on Ramón's charismatic leadership and the fascist iconography and rituals of command of his movement.[41] Ramón's vision of a "Natural Aristocracy of the World," in which the "First Men" of each race would head a new international order, sounds like a Fascist International. Its political mode may be authoritarian, but the galvanizing motive for his populism is explicitly anticolonial. When Ramón and Cipriano appeal to the Mexican masses in their propaganda and military speeches, they continually refer to the ruinous effects of colonial conquest. Ramón's fourth "hymn," conveyed to the people as though it were a transcription of the voice of Quetzalcoatl, speaks of "the greedy ones," "the paleface masters," who have spoiled and robbed Mexico with their "machines of iron." He warns that all those Mexicans who have become weak and submitted to the ways of the white masters shall be destroyed by the dragon of the "Morning Star" unless they join the Aztec revival (*PS*, 232–35). Their duty is to reestablish the "blood of America" (*PS*, 328–30).

Tracking "blood" in the novel, then, takes us away from racial determinism and toward anticolonial violence. Blood becomes that which is spilt in conflict. There is a relish in detail of violent acts throughout the novel, particularly as perpetrated with knives—the puncturing of flesh and pouring forth of blood: "And came the *thud! thud! thud!* Of a machete striking with lust in a human body" (89); "the instriking thud of a heavy knife, stabbing into a living body, this is the best . . . the knife strikes in and the blood spurts out!" (*PS*, 122); "she saw Ramón . . . holding down the head of the bandit by the hair and stabbing him with short stabs in the throat, one, two, while blood shot out like a red projectile" (*PS*, 267). This culminates with the incorporation of ceremonial stabbing into Ramón's neo-Aztec rituals. Traitors of the movement are stabbed with a thin dagger and their blood placed in a bowl to be used as part of a prayer to Quetzalcoatl.

Ultimately, it is not important for this discussion whether we regard the Quetzalcoatl movement to be protofascist, protoanticolonial, or both, as we are not making a judgment about the novel's putative political philosophy. What is significant is that the attempt to narrate the primitive as here and now (the final chapter fittingly is titled "Here!") cannot take the form of a description of an established social order. The utopian primitive exists "nowhere" in the imperial world—there are none left whose "blood" is uncontaminated by imperialism. The result is a gaudy mix of the Third Reich and philo-primitivist stereotypes:

> All the interior was hung with red and black banners. At the side of the chancel was a new idol: a heavy, seated figure of Huitzilopochtli; done in black lava stone. And round him burned twelve red candles. The idol held the bunch of black strips, or leaves, in his hand. And at his feet lay the five dead bodies. . . . Cipriano had his face painted with a white jaw, a thin band of green stretched from his mouth, a band of black across his nose, yellow from his eyes, and scarlet on his brow. One green feather rose from his forehead, and behind his head a beautiful headdress of scarlet feathers. (*PS*, 346)

There is no good reason why the idol should be in black lava stone, why the face paint should be these particular colors with scarlet feathers, why the predicate should precede the subject in the "hymn," and so forth. These just seem to be the sort of things that would constitute a neo-primitive movement. They bear no meaningful relation to a current or prior form of life, and it is wearying to read through countless similar descriptions over the course of the novel. The harder Lawrence works to specify the primitive form of worship, the harder it is to suspend belief. That which the blood knows is better kept latent.

Chapter 7

CLAUDE MCKAY'S PRIMITIVIST NARRATION

Among the authors whose work is considered in this book, Claude McKay's primitivist novels conform most closely to the abstract morphology of primitivism that I have identified, at least outwardly. If literary primitivism were an equation, McKay's *Banjo* could occupy the other side of the equals sign:

$$\text{literary primitivism} = \frac{\substack{\text{utopian primitive narrative} \\ \text{(immediate style–reflexive cognition)}}}{\substack{\text{despair at colonial civilization} \\ \text{(primitive remnant–racial mediation)}}} = \text{McKay's } Banjo$$

In his work primitivism is pursued with an earnestness that the other writers either ultimately pull back from or rhetorically finesse. With McKay there is an abiding sense that authentic primitive experience is still within reach, so in both style and form the contradictions of primitivism are manifest all the more directly. We glimpse simultaneously *that* which is supposed to be primitive and perceive more acutely its present impossibility as a social reality.

In his work there is also something of a convergence of the authorships considered in this study, giving us an opportunity to think about some of the direct historical connections between otherwise disparate primitivist practices. Most conspicuously, McKay was an enthusiastic reader of Lawrence, with whom he declared a spiritual kinship, and would become a catalyzing influence for the poets of negritude. If a discussion of McKay promises neatly to tie together the threads of this study, though, reading his fiction serves only to underline literary primitivism's instability. His primitivist plunge involved taking real artistic risks, the results of which have not always aged well. It also puts into relief the achievement of Césaire, who absorbed these risks into the style and form of his work. McKay's work, and particularly *Banjo*, his novel about dock life in Marseille, brings out the world-historical character of primitivism, an aspect that several critics have discussed in terms of "transnationalism." Deeply conscious of the totality of the imperial world-system, McKay's narratives gravitate not to some notional unmediated primitive beyond the vanishing colonial frontier but rather the lumpenproletarians, the vagabonds, and the drifters who have no place or stake in the system other than the pleasures that can be gained from it. In their pursuit of pleasure, and the deep-seated instincts that McKay believes drives this pursuit, the chimera of the primitive fleetingly attains presence. His unrelenting pursuit of immediacy pushes him to primitivize the substance of narration itself.

McKay and Negritude

In September 1937 Léopold Senghor addressed Dakar's Chamber of Commerce on the subject of "The Cultural Problem in French West Africa." He presented to his audience as the model "native intellectual": a graduate of an *école normale supérieure* and the first black francophone recipient of the *Agrégation*. He chose the subject of literature and assimilation, asking his audience: "Can we conceive of an indigenous literature which is not written in an indigenous language?"[1] His answer was a qualified yes. Whether on the African continent or throughout the global diaspora, Africans express themselves with "a certain savour, a certain odour, a certain accent, a certain timbre, inexpressible by European instruments."[2] He moved to a discussion of the literary efforts of some of his Caribbean contemporaries before closing with a citation of a comment from *Banjo*'s protagonist, Ray: "Plonger jusqu'aux racines de notre race et bâtir sur notre profond fond, ce n'est pas retourner à l'état sauvage: c'est la culture même" (Plunging down to the roots of our race and building on our deep reserves is not returning to a savage state: it is culture itself).[3]

Senghor was quoting from the French translation of *Banjo*, which appeared in 1931.[4] It seems hard to overstate the impact of this publishing event for black francophone writers living in Paris in the 1930s, particularly those who would form the hub of the negritude movement. We have the following testimonies from the leading triumvirate of negritude poets: "Claude McKay can be considered, deservedly, as the veritable inventor of negritude. I don't mean of the word, but of the values of negritude" (Senghor);[5] "McKay's novel, *Banjo*—describing the life of dockworkers in Marseille—was published in 1930. This was really one of the first works in which an author spoke of the Negro and gave him a certain literary dignity" (Césaire);[6] "[*Banjo* was] the favourite book of our generation" (Léon Damas).[7] Damas spoke of the eagerness with which he and his comrades circulated the novel. Excerpts appeared in two important periodicals: Paulette and Jeanne Nardal's bilingual magazine *La revue du monde noir/The Review of the Black World* in 1930 and the single issue of *Légitime défense* in 1932, the inaugurating manifesto of what would soon become known as *Négritude*.[8] (The excerpt in the latter includes the passage read out by Senghor in Dakar.)[9]

McKay's relocation of Ray, his fictional alter ego, from Harlem to Marseille justifiably can be called a seminal moment in pan-Africanism.[10] Harlem's New Negro movement had been closely followed by francophone writers, but McKay's novel showed them that the transvaluation of black experience could just as well be undertaken across the Atlantic.[11] It also allowed the negritude writers to clarify their relationship to surrealism.[12] They were not black surrealists, as Breton would later claim, but rather surrealism supplied literary resources for that "plunging down to the roots" that McKay's work had exemplified.

If the evidence of influence is indisputable, it is less clear how this played out in the stylistic and formal choices made by the negritude writers. They were excited by McKay's narrative fiction but themselves looked to the medium of poetry during negritude's formative period. Where there is evidence of direct influence, particularly in the work of Damas, the connection is thematic. Insofar as we seek in McKay's work the stirrings of the cultural politics of negritude, and this is where scholars largely have concentrated their efforts, the connective tissue cannot be disputed.[13] It is not so straightforward when we start to look at such utterances in the context of the narrative logic of *Banjo*. For instance, Ray holds a paradoxical position in the novel as the spokesperson for a form of experience that he himself is unable fully to enter into. For this study of literary primitivism, in which we are trying to seize on the aesthetic agency of the works themselves, such aspects of characterization are crucial. I will argue that, *qua* primitivism, negritude's relationship to McKay was more a matter of negation than continuity or fulfillment. For Césaire in particular, the capacity to play with voice, rhetoric, and syntax in dense poetic forms is essential to his aesthetic. In McKay the paradoxes of negritude play out in contortions of plot and character that are at times exhilarating, at others awkward.

With respect to *literary* primitivism, a more immediate point of comparison perhaps presents itself on the other side of the equation, as it were. McKay follows Lawrence in looking to the novel to set in motion the interplay of immediacy and mediation that is so central to the primitivist mode. McKay, we will see, has his own peculiar techniques of immediacy, which, as with Lawrence, often exist in tension with his narrative structures. If the mode is similar, the valency and trajectory of his primitivism are profoundly different, and not only because McKay occupied such a dramatically different position within the imperial world-system. To explore these differences, I will compare the ways in which both authors set about writing *musical* novels. I will begin, though, with the question of literary influence in order to clarify the basis for the comparison.

Style and Character

McKay wrote frequently of his admiration for Lawrence's work. In his autobiography, he records that "D. H. Lawrence was the modern writer I preferred above any. . . . In D. H. Lawrence I found confusion—all the ferment and torment and turmoil, the hesitation and hate and alarm, the sexual inquietude and the incertitude of this age, and the psychic and romantic groping for a way out. . . . What I loved was the Laurentian language, which to me is the ripest and most voluptuous expression of English since Shakespeare."[14] He admires both the spiritual disposition of Lawrence's work and his ability to find the language to express it. Ray expresses a similar enthusiasm in *Home to Harlem*, written a decade earlier: "He had read, fascinated, all that D. H. Lawrence published. And wondered if there was not a great Lawrence reservoir of words too terrible and too terrifying for nice printing."[15] When he learned of Lawrence's death in 1930, McKay told his agent that "although I never met him, it was like losing a close friend."[16]

Nowhere does McKay speak of directly emulating Lawrence's style, though, and reading across the corpora of these two writers, one sees little evidence of it. Perhaps the closest he comes is the following description of sex between Ray and Latnah toward the end of *Banjo*:

> Warm brown body and restless dark body like a black root growing down in the soft brown earth. Deep dark passion of bodies close to the earth understanding each other. Dark brown bodies of the earth, earthy. Dark . . . brown . . . rich colors of the nourishing earth. The pinks bring trouble and tumult and riot into

dark lives. Leave them alone in their vanity and tigerish ambitions to fret and fume in their own hell, for terrible is their world that creates disasters and catastrophes from simple natural incidents. (*B*, 283–84)

There are several aspects that might attest to Lawrence's influence: the characters do not come together as named subjects but as bodies bearing essential forces; lexical repetition intensifies the magnitude of the encounter, and fully spiritualized sex is attributed a political significance. There is, though, nothing like the drawn-out persistence of Lawrence and the mantra-like repetitions that envelop his descriptions of sexual intercourse (cf. the "Sons of Men" sequence cited in Chapter 6). The prose also shows the proclivities of what we will identify as McKay's jazz style: the use of ellipsis to give temporality an explicit representation, the use of the present participle to suggest continuous animation, and the introduction of Harlem slang through free indirect discourse, hinting at a different relationship between narrator and protagonist than that found in Lawrence.

The passage seems to point more to the transference of a primitivist attitude from one writer to the other rather than a stylistic means with which to realize it. In the period leading up to the composition of *Home to Harlem* and *Banjo*, and especially as he distanced himself from communism following his Soviet tour in 1923, McKay increasingly espoused Lawrentian attitudes, especially with respect to education and knowledge. Communism had given him a language to think about the structural nature of inequality, but in Lawrence he found a more extreme critique of the state of the world, something that would help him to negotiate his double consciousness as a "conscript of modernity." If the colonial relation had rendered him the racial object of "civilization," he would emphasize the power of his discrepant ontology in order to break from that system. For McKay, to eschew "civilized" education increasingly became a matter of exorcism. In the following argument in *Home to Harlem*, Ray plays the Rupert Birkin role, expounding to Jake on the need to undo the damage of education:

"Can't a Negro have fine feelings about life?"

"Yes, but not the old false-fine feelings that used to be monopolized by educated and cultivated people. You should educate yourself away from that sort of thing."

"But education is something to make you fine!"

"No, modern education is planned to make you a sharp, snouty, rooting hog. A Negro getting it is an anachronism. . . . Keep your fine feelings, indeed, but don't try to make a virtue of them. You will lose them, then. They'll become all hollow inside, false and dry as civilization itself. And civilization is rotten. We are all rotten who are touched by it." (*HH*, 242)

In the vein of Lawrence's "learning not to know," Ray moves to devalue reflexive knowledge and the life-form of which it supposedly is an expression. He speaks as someone wrestling with his own detached perspective onto experience and who at times despairs of the gap between his introversion and the extroverted abundance of the drifters that he runs with. I will argue that this relation is constitutive for the two "Ray" novels (*Home to Harlem* and *Banjo*). The crisis of reflexivity and the ambition to get down to the roots of the race bring together the loosely plotted episodes. This needs to be worked through patiently if we are to get beyond the bad choice between criticizing McKay for racial essentialism and lauding him for an implicit deconstruction of the same.[17] Ray's desire to reach a profound self needs to be understood as part of his attempt to escape from conventions of knowledge that he himself inhabits. The significant difference between Lawrence and McKay is that the hope for a life reconciled with nature and knowledge in sensual immediacy is cast as self-realization rather than as self-transformation. It is just as clear to McKay, however, that it is no longer possible to imagine that one can circumvent the mediations of a corrupt civilization:

> Whatever may be the criticism implied in my writing of Western Civilization I do not regard myself as a stranger but as a child of it, even though I have become so by the comparatively recent process of grafting. I am as conscious of my new-world birthright as my African origin, being aware of the one and its significance in my development as much as I feel the other emotionally.
>
> One of my most considerate critics suggested that I might make a trip to Africa and there write about Negro life in its pure state. But I don't believe that any such place exists anywhere upon the earth today, since modern civilization has touched and stirred the remote corners.[18]

The quest for a "pure" African state may seem futile at a moment when capitalism has reached global saturation, but this does not mean McKay affirms the process of being "grafted" onto it. It is important for McKay that the African diaspora stay open to the possibility of gaining "spiritual benefits by returning in *spirit* to this African origin," a phrase that is very similar to the comment by Alain Locke that was discussed in Chapter 3.[19] It is a question, that is, of believing that the remnant of a precolonial self yet can be reanimated. Unable to give direct representation to an unmediated African origin, McKay seeks out the embers of it in the colonized lumpenproletariat. This is romantic anticapitalism, but it does not rest on a romance of oppression. The black drifters of McKay's novels are idealized not because they are the most oppressed and therefore structurally privileged actors in history. It is because they have been able to resist assimilation by "civilization" and so have preserved the capacity for what McKay portrays as healthy spontaneity.

Brent Hayes Edwards has commented astutely on the significance of the social position of McKay's vagabonds: "The black vagabonds in *Banjo* cannot be understood simply as an emerging proletariat. . . . In rejecting the principle of wage labor, they challenge the very logic of civilization itself and, moreover, expose its underbelly, its elusive escape hatch—precisely by proving with 'happy irresponsibility' that civilization can be defied."[20] In seeking a safe-haven for spirit, McKay circumvents the framework of alienation that would render the industrial working class as the inevitable protagonist in the dialectic of capital and labor. The totalization of the capitalist world-system does not mean that all subjectivities within it have been determined through and through by capital. The Ray novels do not play out as an allegory of class conflict but in the utopian mode of the primitivist project. The life of the vagabonds is celebrated insofar as it is nonsynchronous with "civilization."

The central stylistic and narratorial conduit for this regeneration is music. The spirit of the vagabonds in *Home to Harlem* and *Banjo* flourishes most abundantly in scenes of musical performance and dancing. It is for such moments of abandonment that they live, and, in turn, they give impetus to the novels' literary style. As their living conditions are so tenuous, these moments of full musical life sit in direct opposition to the near deathliness of their day-to-day existence. This is reflected in shifts in character and prose style. Musical immediacy stands against a language that can only reflect that immediacy after the fact. This division extends into the structure and characterization of both novels. Each has a picaresque opening, as we follow Jake and Banjo respectively through the nightspots of Harlem and Marseille. Once established as forces in their own right, McKay introduces Ray, who is able to articulate to the reader their social and political significance. It is in the split between "musical" characters who exist in the desired state of immediacy, albeit blindly, and the reflexive, politically conscious writer Ray that we find the closest affinity with one of Lawrence's works.

Banjo is similar enough to Lawrence's *Aaron's Rod*, written eight years earlier, to invite considerations of direct influence.[21] There are no intertextual clues to ground this hypothesis, but the central conceit of a musician protagonist who meets and becomes intimate with a writer figure suggests, if nothing else, that the primitivist zeitgeist produced similar narrative conceits. There are several direct parallels. In both, the title names the musician hero and his instrument, the hero supports himself by selling his musical talents, the writer figure at some point nurses the musician to health, and the loss of the musical instrument breaks the hero's spirit. It is thus *characterization*, rather than style, that gives a comparison of the two authors' primitivism its point of focus.

By structuring the narrative around the relationship between a musician and a writer, the two novels attempt to address a crisis of immediate experience. Writer and musician serve as allegorical figures in a kind of primitivist morality play. The musician appears as the impulsive ideal, at one with his sensual self, but at odds with the world. The writer comes along to make explicit to the audience the spiritual value of this mode of existence, before, it is hoped, he rids himself of his own reflexive nature and joins the musician in the realm of spontaneous intuition. Neither narrative is so simple, but writer and musician, language and music, constitute distinct poles whose forces of attraction and repulsion generate the trajectory of the works. Music promises to deliver language its sensuous, sounding body, and, in return, language pledges to relieve music of its semantic deafness.

Musical Consciousness in *Aaron's Rod*

Music assumes the role in *Aaron's Rod* respectively assigned to "sense knowledge" and "blood-consciousness" in *Women in Love* and *The Plumed Serpent*. Aaron's musicality is not restricted to his skill as a flautist. He is "musical" through and through. He cognizes language, people, and events with the same immediacy as when he plunges into musical performance.[22] The following excerpt comes at the very end of the novel as Aaron endures a "harangue" from Lilly, the novel's Lawrentian alter ego, that runs to eight pages: "Aaron listened more to the voice than the words. It was more the sound value which entered his soul, the tone, the strange speech-music which sank into him. The sense he hardly heeded. And yet he understood, he knew. He understood, oh, so much more deeply than if he had listened with his head."[23] Aaron's musicality allows him to cut out the semantic middleman. Music, though, is an art form with its own quasi-semantic systems of organization. It is perhaps for this reason that Lawrence does not give anywhere near as much space to music in *Aaron's Rod* as he does to "knowledge in the senses" and "blood" and in the novels discussed in Chapter 6. It might only highlight the mediations of consciousness that music is supposed to be able to evade. Having described Aaron's "mindless" (20) absorption when playing the flute in the novel's opening scene, it is not until the novel's final section that we are presented with another extended description of his playing. It comes when he initiates a brief, but intense affair with a Marchese in Florence:

> It was [a] clear, sharp, lilted run-and-fall of notes, not a tune in any sense of the word, and yet a melody: a bright, quick sound of pure animation: a bright, quick, animate noise, running and pausing. It was like a bird's singing, in that it had no human emotion or passion or intention or meaning—a ripple and poise of animate sound. But it was unlike a bird's singing, in that the notes followed clear and single one after the other, in their subtle gallop. A nightingale is rather like that—a wild sound. To read all the human pathos into a nightingale's singing is nonsense. A wild, savage, non-human lurch and squander of sound, beautiful, but entirely unaesthetic. (*AR*, 271)

Here, again, are Lawrence's techniques of immediacy. Each sentence builds on the lexicon of the previous sentence either by repetition or synonym. Yet the narrator is reluctant to commit to analogies. It is "like a bird's singing." "But . . . unlike a bird's singing," it is "beautiful" but "entirely unaesthetic." The narrator does not want the reader to imagine that his playing is consciously deliberated, but nor can he hold to analogies with sheer nature. He brings to the reader's mind certain images of nonintentional nature to convey the sense of the mindlessness of Aaron's playing, but each image risks giving the wrong impression as the musical line is not altogether without conscious effect.

This space between conscious and unconscious activity is also apparent in the representation of Aaron's thoughts. Particularly notable is the chapter "Wie es Ihnen gefällt" (As You Please), in which eleven pages are given to memories of his abandonment of his wife and reflections on relationships in general. The passage employs a complex, perhaps convoluted, free indirect discourse, oscillating between Aaron's perspective and that of wife, though as putatively embedded in his memory, with some short passages contributed by the omniscient narrator. The representation of Aaron's thoughts opens the narrative to the psychoemotional world of his relationship beyond his experiences and, we would assume, his literal thoughts. The omniscient narrator feels it necessary nevertheless to clarify: "Thoughts something in this manner ran through Aaron's subconscious mind as he sat still in the strange house. He could not have fired it all off at any listener, as these pages are fired off at any chance reader" (*AR*, 197). As with Aaron's performance, it is like *x* but not actually *x*. The narrator continues: "If I . . . must translate his deep conscious vibrations into finite words, that is my own business. I do but make a translation of the man. He would speak in music. I speak with words" (*AR*, 199). Here we have music as unobjectifiable flux, a notion popular in Europe at least since Arthur Schopenhauer's *The World as Will and Representation*. Yet, unlike a great deal of the modernist literature that uses musical expression as a benchmark, there is no pretense that the literary medium could emulate the musical one. One is deep vibration, the other finite object, and it is the task of the narrator to make the inadequate gesture of "translation." Rather than use the music/language analogy to draw language onto the privileged terrain of musical cognition, the narrator maintains the separation. If the pretense cannot be upheld that the representation of musical thinking is the thought itself, then the agency of the narrator stands revealed. As a consequence, this discrete narrative consciousness appears regularly throughout the novel, at times speaking from the singular first-person "I" but more often from the collective first person.[24]

This also establishes a relation of power between narrator and the narrated musical character. The narrator is privy both to Aaron's invisible thought-vibrations and the objectified prose world of signifier and signified. The narrator's professed humility is false because s/he forms a master consciousness that encompasses both kinds of knowledge. This makes for a one-sided relation in which Aaron's "musical" soul can be known, if inadequately represented, but Aaron himself is unable to know things explicitly. His subordinate position plays out in the events in the novel. When he leaves his wife and mining job, Aaron gives his fate and material circumstance over to chance acquaintances and becomes reliant on his musical talents to subsist. The destruction of his flute at the end of the novel by a random act of political violence exposes his vulnerability. In the final chapter, ominously titled "Words," he realizes this. His only recourse is to the "thread of destiny" (*AR*, 335) that connects him to Lilly. We might expect this to prepare us for a decisive reconciliation between the writer and the musician. Instead, Lilly subjects Aaron to the long "harangue" mentioned earlier. Over the course of this monologue he instructs Aaron on the meaning of his life and the nature of the problems he has sensed but cannot control. Lilly assumes power of explicit cognition for both of them. In the final lines of the novel he tells Aaron that he (Aaron) has "needed livingly to yield to a more heroic soul, to give yourself" (*AR*, 347). Aaron does not resist; he only asks, "And whom shall I submit to?" Lilly replies, "Your soul will tell you." Musical thinking may be more powerful than prose thinking, but it is nevertheless blind and easily loses control of its destiny.

Mckay's Techniques of Immediacy

In the Ray novels McKay approaches the task of representing musical experience in a very different way. There is no sense that the gap between music and language is unbridgeable. McKay strives throughout both novels to convey one by means of the other. At moments of musical climax, the prose reaches its mimetic limit and spills over into transcriptions of musical sounds. It seems reasonable to ask, therefore, why McKay would need the novel form at all. When he began writing narrative fiction in the mid-1920s, he was already well known for his poetry, both his earlier Jamaican Creole ballads and his lyric work, mostly in Standard English, written after arriving in Harlem. As he explains in his autobiography, though, he did not feel that he would be able to present the unvarnished truth of his vagabonds in the medium of poetic thinking: "I told her [Louise Bryant] of my great desire to do some Negro stories, straight and unpolished, but that Max Eastman had discouraged me and said I should write my stories in verse. But my thinking in poetry was so lyric-emotional that I could not feel like writing stories in that vein."[25] If poetry is usually considered the best medium for exploring language's musicality, for McKay it is prose that will represent the world of black musical experience without distortion.

The musical scenes in the Ray novels are the culmination of a prose style that consistently pursues immediacy through acts of signification. The device that McKay calls on most frequently is the list. Whether detailing a series of actions, people, or objects, he wants to impress on the reader the thingness of things by massing them up. The following is only a representative selection of such moments:

> Cream tomato soup. Ragout of chicken giblets. Southern fried chicken. Candied sweet potatoes. Stewed corn. Rum-flavored fruit salad waiting in the ice-box. (*HH*, 78)

dim brown, clear brown, rich brown, chestnut, copper, yellow, near-white, mahogany, and gleaming anthracite. Charming brown matrons, proud yellow matrons, dark nursemaids pulled a zigzag course by their restive little charges ... (*HH*, 289–90)

European, African, Asiatic. Contemporary feminine styles competed with old and forgotten. Rose-petal pajamas, knee-length frocks, silken shifts, the nude, the boyish bob contrasted with shimmering princess gowns, country-girl dresses of striking freshness, severe glove-fitting black setting off a demure lady with Italian-rich, thick, long hair, the piquant semi-nude and Spanish-shawled shoulders. (*B*, 52)

The Caribbean, the Gulf of Guinea, the Persian Gulf, the Bay of Bengal, the China Seas, the Indian Archipelago. And, oh, the earthly mingled smells of the docks! Grain from Canada, rice from India, rubber from Congo, tea from China, brown sugar from Cuba, bananas from Guinea, lumber from the Soudan, coffee from Brazil, skins from the Argentine, palm-oil from Nigeria, pimento from Jamaica, wool from Australia, oranges from Spain and oranges from Jerusalem. (*B*, 67)

Often, and especially in *Banjo*, these lists stress the diversity of human types, whether defined racially, nationally, or by other characteristics. It is as though the bewildering reality of accelerated global commodity exchange, and the multicolored class of cosmopolitan proletarians created in the process of trans-porting goods around the world, could be made concrete by cataloguing their accumulation.

In musical scenes the lists extend to the actions of the dancers, creating syntactic parallelism: "Senegalese in blue overalls, Madagascan soldiers in khaki, dancing together. A Martiniquan with his mulatress flashing her gold teeth. A Senegalese sergeant goes round with his fair blonde. A Congo boxer struts it with his Marguerite. And Banjo, grinning, singing, white teeth, great mouth, leads the band. . . . Shake that Thing" (*B*, 48–49). Each sentence or sentence fragment immediately is matched with another in kind (two times men in types of clothes dancing, three times men dancing with women, two times Banjo's actions, two times Banjo's features). In the final sentence parallelism becomes quasi metrical, with three trochees and then two spondees creating jazz-like cross-rhythms. Listing things becomes musical in its own right.

Both novels feature a climactic musical scene in which the full cast assembles in one place. In both cases these spark key moments of conflict and resolution.

The structural burden shows in the variety and complexity of prose techniques McKay uses to convey their energy. I will focus on the chapter "Jelly Roll," from the conclusion of the first part of *Banjo*, which represents McKay's most sustained attempt to create a jazz aesthetic in prose. His musical scenes typically begin with inset lyrics from a jazz or blues hit. In this case it is "Shake That Thing!," an adaptation of Jelly Roll Morton's then ubiquitous "Jelly-Roll Blues":[26]

Old Uncle Jack, the jelly-roll king,
Just got back from shaking that thing!
    He can shake that thing, he can shake that thing
    For he's a jelly-roll king. Oh, shake that thing! (*B*, 47)

Following this, fragments from the song of equal or shorter length are distributed throughout the scene, serving to remind us of the diegetic presence of music and to give the events an acoustic realism.

The lyrics are also woven into the narrative voice. This nondiegetic quotation serves to punctuate and organize the sequence of actions in the scene. The refrain, "shake that thing!," is repeated eleven times by the narrator, nine times at the end of a paragraph. At one point the narrator becomes an actor in the scene, egging Banjo on: "Sing, Banjo! Play, Banjo! Here I is, Big Boss, keeping step, sure step, right long with you in some sort a ways. He-ho, Banjo! Play that thing. Shake that thing!" (*B*, 49). The impulse to bring the narrative right into the action prompts the voice to abandon a detached omniscient perspective and notionally occupy a physical body in the scene. In *Aaron's Rod* it is because Aaron does not think in language that the narrator steps in as "I." Here the intensification of the immediacy of the musical scene leads to the narrator's embodied participation.

It would be disjunctive if these diegetic and nondiegetic musical cues were part of an otherwise unreceptive narratorial fabric. The compressed "jazz" syntax McKay devises to narrate the musical scenes is the most distinctive of his techniques of immediacy. In "Jelly Roll" he uses the second break in the text made by the inset lyrics to shift tense from the past simple to a mixture of the present simple and present participle. From here diegetic interludes are used to switch among tenses, moving the perspective into and then away from the action. When the atmosphere on the dance floor comes to a climax, McKay intensifies the mood of the present participle by suppressing the possessive pronoun and auxiliary verb: "A coffee-black boy from Cameroon and a chocolate-brown from Dakar stand up to each other to dance a native sex-symbol dance. Bending knee and nodding head, they dance up to each other. . . . Black skin itching, black flesh warm with the wine of life" (*B*, 50). The effect is to give autonomy to the dancing body. It is the knee itself that bends, the head that nods, the body as a body that generates the heat of the dance. The clipped prose wants to be the physical animation of the music. In an early scene in *Home to Harlem* McKay uses a sequence of gerunds to the same effect: "Black-framed white grinning. Finger-snapping. Undertone singing" (*HH*, 54). As there is no identifiable subject coordinating the movements, they become part of the texture of the atmosphere; an aesthetic akin to the jazz cubism popular at that time. The dancers in such scenes are usually anonymous, identified only by race, nation, and/or skin color.

Detached from specific subjects, music starts to become a generalized metaphysical racial force: "Yellow balancing between black and white. Black reaching out beyond yellow. Almost-white on the brink of a change. Sucked back down into the current of black by the terrible sweet rhythm of black blood" (*HH*, 57–58). The music and the dance manifest a black spirit that moves in the blood itself. Is this akin to *The Plumed Serpent*'s "blood-consciousness"? If anything, the stylistic logic that leads description beyond distinct subjects makes more pronounced the blood's racial character. The jazz style wants to be the immediate manifestation of that ancestral force that otherwise is consumed by white "civilization." What is at stake in McKay's musical style is the capacity to make the identity of profound being and the hedonist atmosphere of the jazz salon complete. At these moments the novels tilt into the kind of philo-primitivism that Langston Hughes would satirize in *The Ways of White Folks*: "Tum-tum . . . tum-tum . . . tum-tum . . . tum-tum . . . Simple-clear and quivering. Like a primitive dance of war or love . . . the marshaling of spears or the sacred frenzy of a phallic celebration" (*HH*, 197).[27] It is as though the primitive realizes itself in sound alone, only for the narrator to step in and make the significance explicit by means of ethnographic analogy.

It is interesting to contrast briefly McKay's musical prose with another contemporaneous attempt to write in a jazz style. The following is excerpted from the final chapter of Carl Van Vechten's *Nigger Heaven*, published two years earlier:[28] "The music shivered and broke, cracked and smashed. Jungle land. Hottentots and Bantus swaying under the amber moon. Love, sex, passion . . . hate. Lef' side, right side! Git off dat dime. . . . The dancers swayed from one side to the other like sailors heaving an anchor. Black, green, blue, purple, brown, tan, yellow, white: coloured people!"[29] There are several stylistic features that are similar to McKay: the personification of music, the use of the present participle and ellipses, the phonetic representation of dialect, the use of lists and emphatic punctuation. Van Vechten does not, however, dwell extensively on the details of the cabaret scene or focus on particular exchanges or actions but uses this style to create an atmosphere of licentiousness and abandon. The passage comes at the novel's denouement. Byron Kasson, the novel's hero, has decided in a fit of hysteria to kill his would-be lover Lasca Sartoris. The wildness of the cabaret scene increases his hysteria. It brings on his tragic decision to fire into the already gunned-down body of Lasca's new lover, Randolph Pettijohn, leading to his arrest for the murder. In other words, the jazz style serves the plot; it is not the manifestation of an ontology. This comes out in the final exclamation: "coloured people!" The dancing bodies are part of the kaleidoscope of sensations impelling Byron to his destiny rather than beings brought together by a common "rhythm of black blood." It is an aesthetics of titillation, a philoprimitivism for which race is an atmospherics.

Like Lawrence, McKay aspires to an immediacy that responds to a sense of necessity that is profoundly at odds with the world. In the jazz scenes his vagabonds *are* the remnant; they do not need to become it. The problem is that this profundity is either ignored or stifled by a wrongheaded social order. The appeal to music is therefore of a different order from that in *Aaron's Rod*. For Lawrence, mimicking music is out of the question. The rift between Aaron's unhappy consciousness and the world is not one that the prose imagines it can heal. McKay's approach is ingenuous, and decidedly so. At the end of "Jelly Roll" his techniques of immediacy converge into a kind of short jazz essay on the nonsynchronous vitalism of black vagabond life:

> Strong surging flux of profound currents forced into shallow channels. Play that thing! One movement of the thousand movements of the eternal life-flow. Shake that thing! In the face of the shadow of Death. Treacherous hand of murderous Death, lurking in sinister alleys, where shadows of life dance, nevertheless, to their music of life. Death over there! Life over here! Shake down Death and forget his commerce, his purpose, his haunting presence in a great shaking orgy. Dance down the death of these days, the Death of these ways in shaking that thing. Jungle jazzing, Orient wriggling, civilized stepping. Shake that thing! Sweet dancing thing of primitive joy, perverse pleasure, prostitute ways. Many-colored variations of the rhythm, savage, barbaric, refined—eternal rhythm of the mysterious, magical, magnificent—the dance divine of life. . . . Oh, Shake That Thing! (*B*, 57–58)

The prose rhythms are notably heightened. The parallelisms now become insistent and create overlapping metrical clusters. It is as close as McKay comes to embodying a jazz rhythm in the organization of phrases, and it is a more convincing form of mimesis than "tum-tum." The climactic expression of the techniques of immediacy for this jazz prose becomes the basis for the explicit articulation of its nonsynchronous primitive spirit.

Life and Ideology

Even in the midst of declaring the instantiation of the primitive here and now, the narrative voice indicates that the music's positive charge might nevertheless be impelled by a negation. It is the "eternal life-flow" and yet driven by the need to "Shake down Death and forget his commerce." Frequently, McKay's musical scenes are punctuated by, and often dissolve into, violence. In "Jelly Roll" a Senegalese man leaps through the crowd of jazzers and knocks out an enemy (B, 50). Soon after, a local gangster shoots and kills a woman just as the musicians get things humming again (B, 54–55).[30] In *Home to Harlem* a woman rushes and attacks a cabaret singer (*HH*, 33), there is a fight between two West Indian girls (*HH*, 96–97), a man punches and head-butts a boy over a poker game (*HH*, 72), and Zeddy and Jake have a standoff with knives and guns (*HH*, 326). The narrator observes of a dancing pair late in *Home to Harlem*, "that gorilla type wriggling there with his hands so strangely hugging his mate, may strangle her tonight" (*HH*, 337), before remarking that this is evidence of "simple, raw emotions and real" (*HH*, 338). In another scene a man accidently steps on Zeddy's toes, things get out of hand, and only Banjo's intervention halts the descent of Zeddy's knife. They are soon back playing and dancing, and the narrator comments: "Zeddy's gorilla feet dancing down the dark death lurking in his heart" (*HH*, 54). The possibility lingers that the language of nonsynchronicity, "the simple raw emotions," might serve more to highlight the nature of the vagabond's position within the social logic of the imperial world-system than to mark them as discrepant from it. This possibility is strengthened when we observe that there is a symmetry between the energetic abandon of the vagabonds and the frenetic movement of goods, capital, and labor between the colonies and metropolises. The same techniques of immediacy employed for the cabaret scenes are used to characterize the energy of global trade converging on the Marseille port. In one scene Ray looks on as agricultural commodities are unloaded, and he imagines the labor of the men who had produced them:

> Brown men half-clothed, with baskets on their backs, bending low down to the ancient tilled fields under the tropical sun. Eternal creatures of the warm soil, digging, plucking for the Occident world its exotic nourishment of life, under the whip, under the terror. Barrels . . . bags . . . boxes. . . . Full of the wonderful things of life.
>
> Ray loved the life of the docks more than the life of the sea. (*B*, 67)

The knowledge of the oppressive conditions in which the goods have been produced does not stop Ray from marveling at a life entwined in the grandeur of global commerce. The lists, anonymous bodies, present participle, and ellipses create a romance of labor, which likewise is set against the deathliness of their conditions. At the close of this scene he thinks with particular awe of the United States. It excites "a great fever in his brain, a rhythm of a pattern with the time-beat of his life, a burning, throbbing romance in his blood" (*B*, 69). Later in the novel he remarks to himself that "commerce" is "of all words the most magical. The timbre, color, form, the strength and grandeur of it . . . sublime yet forever going hand in hand with the bitch" (*B*, 307).

The symmetry of the peripheral sphere of colonial commodity production and the lives of the urbanized vagabonds is compounded by the creeping commodification of their culture in the mode of philo-primitivism. The passage at the end of "Jelly Roll" comes after a white soldier of high rank solicits Banjo and company: "Please play. You American? I like much *les Negres* play the jazz American" (*B*, 57). There is the troubling sense that the primitive, far from providing the escape-hatch of nonsynchronicity, is something that this "civilization" is as eager to appropriate as the surplus value of colonial labor. If the manifestation of the primitive here and now actually turns out to be an embrace of a precarious position within global industry, which is itself subject to commodification, it threatens to cast the "eternal life flow" as an ideological veil.

To take this further we can scrutinize the terms of nonsynchronicity employed in the novels—not with the expectation of conceptual consistency but to identify the different registers and rhetorics of primitivity. At various points anthropological terms are used in such a way as to suggest direct continuities with precolonial Africa: "native sex-symbol dance" (*B*, 50), "gorgeous sublimation of the primitive African sex feeling" (*B*, 105), "sacred frenzy of phallic celebration" (*HH*, 197). Rhetorically, such descriptions appear sincere; they certainly do not have the double-edged quality that such representational frames acquire in the hands of Césaire. Yet they are not necessarily literal, something that seems to be confirmed when Ray contrasts the new-world vagabonds with Africans: "Not so the Africans, who were closer to the bush, the jungle, where their primitive sex life had been controlled by ancient tribal taboos. . . . And so it was not natural for them, so close to the tradition of paying in cash or kind or hard labor for the joy of a woman, to live the life of the excrescences attaching like mushrooms to the sexual life of civilization" (*B*, 212). There is a difference between this sense of the "primitive" as a form of life constrained within a radically different set of social norms and the "sweet thing of primitive joy" that can make the most of the environment around the docks. The crucial word, perhaps, is *sublimation*, which, read in the context of the passage, refers to the various ways in which a common African sensibility has been transferred into diasporic forms of dance. There is a sense, though, that it is not the social norms that are sublimated, those "ancient tribal taboos," but a more nebulous capacity to be reconciled with one's environment in such a way as to be able to live spontaneously within it—to act "naturally," even where the environment is not natural.

The word *primitive* is used nineteen times in *Banjo*, sometimes positively, sometimes neutrally, but never negatively. (The latter is not true of *savage* or *barbaric*.) In one scene Ray observes that Africans are "less 'savage' and more 'primitive'" than "New World Negroes" when drunk and are, in this respect, "finer" (*B*, 202). This is the only time in either novel that either of these terms appears in quotation marks. Without a point of comparison the intention informing the quotation marks is not easy to determine. They might indicate a wariness about stereotypes, which we would readily assume today, or simply mark a conceptual distinction. Either way, Ray, and the novel by means of his distinctions and judgments, is trying to delimit a sphere of primitivity that is neither an expression of the ideology of the commodity nor unmediated nonsynchronous "African" instincts. Yet it seems he is forced to play these two frames against each other in order to specify it—like *x* but not *x*. For all the apparent confidence that the primitive can be instantiated by stylistic means and named as such, the Ray novels continually undermine the basis by which this could positively be affirmed. On the one side, it might only be a fleeting pleasure in a degraded environment, on the other, a form of distinction whose social basis has collapsed. As a consequence the novels vacillate between a neo-

African philo-primitivism (which we might call a naive negritude) and primitivism proper (i.e., primitivism as a project of renewing the primitive).

Primitivist Narration

As with Lawrence, McKay hopes to bring the reader into contact with raw experience through the immediacy of his prose, but it is a fleeting contact whose condition of possibility is not secure. Jake and Banjo both fall into apparent terminal illness from their hard living, only to be saved by Ray. Just as Lilly nurses Aaron to health in *Aaron's Rod*, Ray heals these avatars of immediacy. His role in the respective novels is quite different, though. *Home to Harlem* and *Banjo* share a basic three-part structure, but when we look more closely at the plotting, we find substantial, perhaps even generic, differences between them. Each opens with a picaresque episode centered on Jake/Banjo, has a middle section centered on the relationship between Ray and the respective protagonists, and ends with the characters moving on from Harlem/Marseille. The first two parts of *Home to Harlem* are of almost equal length, giving Ray less prominence, especially as he exits the novel at the end of the second part. Thematically, the interactions between Jake and Ray are central, but the larger part of the narrative concerns the relationship between Jake and his lover, Felice. They meet in the novel's opening scene and are set to marry at its end. In this regard the novel perhaps reveals its origin as a short story—it is a love story with a reflexive interlude.[31]

Lacking Ray's presence for long stretches, the ethical and political significance of the vagabonds' musical spirit in *Home to Harlem* is left largely implicit. Ray's affirmations of the primitive are not something on which the fate of any character other than himself turns. When Jake leaves for Chicago with Felice, it seems he will give up his hard living and settle down within the given social conditions. Monogamous commitment supplies closure to the inchoate energies of the Harlem music scene that threaten to destroy him.

When Ray leaves Harlem, and the novel, he makes this final comment to Jake: "I don't know what I'll do with my little education. I wonder sometimes if I could get rid of it and go and lose myself in some savage culture in the jungles of Africa. I am a misfit. . . . You're happier than I as you are. The more I learn the less I understand and love life" (*HH*, 274). Ray is on a parallel trajectory to Birkin in *Women in Love*. Unable to realize his primitivism in Harlem, he is drawn to a notional space beyond imperial reality where he might be able to

abandon his reflexive consciousness and lose himself in a culture still reconciled with nature. In his case it would also allow for a reconciliation with his
ancestral being. At the same time, he defers to Jake as someone who can live
with authenticity in civilization in a way that he is unable. Though Ray recognizes the aesthetic and moral value of Jake's unreflective spontaneity, he does
not hitch his own fate to Jake's. The environment itself, "civilization," remains a
static background to each characters' quest for self-realization.

Banjo's picaresque opening is both shorter and more frenetic and the second, Ray-centric section much longer. There is no great importance attached
to the novel's (explicit) love story, that between Banjo and Latnah, which is
subordinated to his relationship to Ray. The novel ends with the reunification
of the two men and their pledge to pursue itinerant lives together. Ray actually
displaces Banjo as the novel's protagonist in the final section. The narrative remains with him after he and Banjo separate at the end of part 2. His thoughts
on the lives of the vagabonds, art, politics, and the condition of "civilization"
in general now acquire plot significance. With his reflections, the novel's epi-
sodic character gains a unifying thread, and it could almost be called a philosophical novel.

Over the course of the narrative there are three means by which Ray's reflections find articulation: in arguments with strangers, through his interactions
with the beach boys, and in his interior monologues. In one scene he argues
with a Martinican student. (It is from this exchange that Senghor later would
quote at his address in Dakar.) The student's idea of a "racial renaissance" is
to attain respectability according to white metropolitan standards. This gives
Ray the opportunity to discourse on the need to jettison white education in
the process of "getting down to our native roots" (*B*, 200): "You're a lost crowd
you educated Negroes, and you will only find yourself in the roots of your own
people" (*B*, 201). He makes a similar argument with respect to education to a
white bohemian American poet later in the novel (*B*, 271–72). In his conversa-
tions with Banjo and his crew, Ray speaks as an insider who nevertheless has
the capacity to give their form of life an ethical rationale. In their turn the boys,
and particularly Banjo, acknowledge him as their mouthpiece. In one scene
Banjo defers to Ray to explain to a group of white bohemians the language of
"black freemasonry" (*B*, 217).

His ideas are given their lengthiest expositions in his private reflections.
These passages also contain some of the novel's most pedestrian and didactic
passages. Just as there is willfulness apparent in the desire to make the music

happen in the medium of words, so McKay sometimes overstretches when delivering the lesson:

> He hated civilization. Once in a moment of bitterness he said in Harlem, "civilization is rotten." And the more he travelled and knew of it, the more he felt the truth of that bitter outburst.
>
> He hated civilization because its general attitude toward the colored man was such as to rob him of his warm human instincts and make him inhuman. (B, 163)

The recollection refers to a comment he made in *Home to Harlem*. (The passage was cited toward the start of this chapter.) There is no sense in the earlier work that this is an especially notable, let alone bitter outburst, and the notion that Ray would recall such a routine formulation from seven years earlier only serves to limit our sense of his consciousness by restricting it to those moments McKay has picked out to narrate.

Across the novel's episodes Ray's reflexivity serves two key functions: he distinguishes degenerate from healthy forms of primitive immediacy and ensures that the latter is not interpreted as the rebelliousness of class *ressentiment*. At the same time, his form of consciousness, and the education that produced it, is the object of painful self-criticism. In *Banjo* this is propelled by the hope that reflexivity might form a new symbiosis with primitive immediacy. In the final pages Ray muses:

> From these black boys he could learn how to live—how to exist as a black boy in a white world and rid his conscience of the used-up hussy of white morality. He could not scrap his intellectual life and be entirely like them. He did not want or feel any urge to "go back" that way. Tolstoy, his great master, had turned his back on the intellect as guide to find himself in Ivan Durak. Ray wanted to hold on to his intellectual acquirements without losing his instinctive gifts. (B, 322–23)

This passage shows that Ray explicitly regards the vagabonds in the terms of nonsynchronicity. To be like them would be to "go back." Banjo serves as remnant, not exemplar. In danger of being paralyzed by his double consciousness, Ray can use the sense of himself activated by the contact with Banjo to dislodge the superego of white normativity. Commenting that "it was not easy for a Negro with an intellect standing watch over his native instincts to take his own way in this white man's civilization," Ray resolves to "bring intellect to the aid of instinct" (B, 164). "Intellect" diverts him from his instincts, but it is also a guide back to them. The proposal to "get down to the roots of the race," we realize, has always been something of a contradiction. If the substance of the roots of the race is something like Banjo's "happy irresponsibility," it should rise into being of its own accord. As a proposal of conscious intent, as primitiv*ism*, it must call on the mediation that has diverted it in order to realize itself.[32]

Ray's belief in his deep racial connection with Banjo and the group seems to be vindicated at the level of the plot. They enjoy a mostly carefree alliance throughout the novel. At the level of narrative voice, however, the fissures that occasionally flash up between them are more apparent, threatening to drive a wedge through the narrative's wish for reconciliation.[33] Once Ray enters the novel, most events are focalized through his consciousness. In the opening part, and this is also true of *Home to Harlem*, the narrator fluctuates between the in situ jazz voice discussed earlier and a detached almost anthropological perspective. In these passages the voice presumes to explain to the reader the cultural mores of black people. For instance: "(a common trait of Negroes in emotional states)" (*HH*, 108); "For the Negro-Negroid population of the town divides sharply into groups" (*B*, 45); and "Negroes are never so beautiful and magical as when they do that gorgeous sublimation of the primitive African sex feeling" (*B*, 105). At times the narrator's descriptions are sanguine if not harsh, such as when the vagabonds are described as "brutes" (*B*, 41, 48). It is a highly flexible voice, though, moving right in close to the characters, even joining in with them as we noted earlier. If the rupture of reflection and immediacy is present in the material of the narration itself, it places ever greater pressure on those attempts at reconciliation attempted at the level of plot and characterization.

It is in this context I would like to come back to that most striking of passages in which the narrator briefly surfaces in the first person:

> The sharp, noisy notes of the banjo belong to the American Negro's loud music of life—an affirmation of his hardy existence in the midst of the biggest, the most tumultuous civilization of modern life.
>
> Sing, Banjo! Play, Banjo! Here I is, Big Boss, keeping step, sure step, right long with you in some sort a ways. He-ho, Banjo! Play that thing. Shake that thing! (*B*, 49).

Each time I read these lines I am struck by the same ambiguity: is "Big Boss" the narrator or Banjo? The grammar suggests the former, the naming of "I" as "Big Boss" interceding between possessive and participle, but the context suggests the latter, Banjo as the "Big Boss" holding the band together. If it were to be treated as an either/or choice, I would assume the latter, but the comma cannot retrospectively be removed from experience. The grammar follows the syntax of self-introduction, and the confusion is not just a local problem of matching the name to the person. Bearing down on this moment is the bifurcation that runs across the novel between modes of cognition, not to mention the larger historical resonances of the opposition of plantation owner and slave. This could be the voice that talks about "Negroes in emotional states," or it could be the voice of abandonment itself. At such moments the novel is suspended between narrative primitivism and philo-primitivist narration.

The Night of the Absolute

Throughout this study I have maintained that literary primitivism's wishful thinking should not be understood merely as a function of the racial terms with which it often expressed itself. If we conclude that Ray's perceptions and desires were corrupted through and through by racial ideology, we disenchant McKay's narrative and are left with only the moral presuppositions of our theoretical apparatus. The primitivist project was carried out with the conviction that nonsynchronous experiences of modernity were not merely a symptom of that modernity.

In this vein we can seize on multiple potentialities latent in a work like *Banjo*, brimming with zeal and contradictions. There is a strand in the narrative that does not place all its chips with biological unity. Rather than insisting on an already achieved communion with Banjo, Ray at times thinks of consciously setting himself the project of transformation. This is made clear in an episode involving a down-and-out character called Lonesome Blue. Twice, Ray successfully persuades immigration officials to give Lonesome the funds he needs to make the passage back to America. Both times he drinks the money away. For Ray this is not healthy spontaneity but a remorseful inability to cope with the world. This leads Ray to question his own sense of charitable duty: "Banjo's back was instinctively turned away from the Lonesome trail that leads you straight along to the Helping-Hand brotherhood of Christian charity with all its sanctimonious cant. And though Ray sometimes had to follow the Lonesome trail a little, he felt deep down in his heart that Banjo's way was the better one and that he would rather lose himself down that road and be happy even to the negation of intellect" (*B*, 242). There is no sense that his form of "intellect," which here amounts to hypocritical moralism, could coexist with Banjo's urge to live life unrepentantly. Ray's first impulse is to help Lonesome, but his deeper desire is to go Banjo's route, and these are not impulses that an insistence on biological filiation could align. He cannot go halfway because Banjo's condition is lived absolutely. At such moments race as biology cannot conveniently solder two conflicting modes of existence. Ray needs to "lose" himself down Banjo's path just as Fanon needed to lose himself in Césaire's negritude. There is no sense that losing himself down Banjo's path would lead him to confront Lonesome's condition. Ray does not find it significant that moments of communal abandon usually turn to violence or that their physical existence is sustained by food often salvaged from unhygienic places and poisonous commodities like alcohol. Though losing himself down Banjo's path appears to him like a positive move, the facts of what has gone before point to a future existence in which an ever impending death is briefly deferred. Banjo may be the real thing, but he lives a life every bit as perilous as Lonesome in present circumstances.

If Fanon allows us to see that Ray's desire to lose himself in Banjo could actually reveal certain truths about the Lonesome condition, we can also say that McKay's novel highlights the affirmative aspect of "The Lived Experience of the Black." It is expedient to posit that the only ontology available in the colonial context is constituted from historical suffering (hence Sartre's "theory" of negritude: black self-consciousness is really consciousness of suffering, and this is what stimulates political consciousness), and it would be easy to see Fanon's idea of plunging into "the repression, the rapes, the discriminations" as making this same point. Fanon's negritude may be an "unhappy romanticism," but this is still romanticism and not masochism.[34]

Fanon states that the leap into the chasm of the past is the condition and source of freedom, and in this vein Ray desires to transform himself on the basis of an imagined primordial connection, what he calls a "common primitive birthright" (B, 321). This is his primitivism, as opposed to a more nebulous neo-African determinism. To speak of this as a "strategic essentialism" would be to rob it of the unconditional quality that makes it a viable wish in the first place. Following Banjo down the path of the absolute is not a decision grounded by a practical weighing of one strategy against another. The essence is not a biological truth but a speculative commonality that enables action. The true reconciliation of Banjo and Ray only makes sense to Ray as a reconsolidation of an ancient bond that has wrested them apart.

It is a big leap, however, from Ray's idealization of Banjo to Fanon's call for the colonized intellectual to enter into the "zone of occult instability where the people dwell" in order to foment a national revolution.[35] McKay's novel was a landmark for young francophone writers because it demonstrated that the transvaluation of racial hierarchies was not a reactive inversion. It is debatable, however, whether anything of the substance of his literary style and approach to form influenced the negritude poets. The awkward shifts of register and style and the passages of didacticism are not to be dismissed as the author's heavy-handedness. McKay would show himself more than capable in his next novel, *Banana Bottom*, of elegantly shaping a consistent narrative voice and a layered narrative with complex characterization. In hindsight the unevenness of the Ray novels perhaps reveals a set of problems that could not be reconciled in the novel form. We have seen similar jarring in Lawrence's novels. The novel promises to provide the primitive with a voice but finds itself overriding it with didacticism. "Cognition" for both writers remains split between immediate and reflexive modes. Both want to provide some kind of experience of immediate consciousness in style and figuration, yet the development of the narrative in each case makes it clear that neither ultimately has faith in the possibility that this could be effectual consciousness in and of itself. This is narrative primitivism's truth content. In *Banana Bottom* there is a clean division between the narrative voice and inset musical excerpts and between creole and noncreole voices. The marriage of English-educated Bita Plant to a peasant who works on her father's farm is an alliance between two separate modes of being but not their unification.

In accepting Ray's task of "getting down to our native roots," the negritude poets did not believe that the "root" necessarily needed a guiding prose consciousness. In surrealism they found an alternative set of notions about literature and knowledge. In his essay "Poetry and Knowledge" Césaire asserts that poetry does not need a supplementary form of consciousness to manifest and know deep being. In a brief survey of French poetry since Baudelaire, he argues that surrealism can restore poetic knowledge in the face of positivism. The poet's act of absolute abandonment is an abandonment to "primal life."[36] In letting go, two things emerge. There is "the individual essence: intimate conflicts, obsessions, phobias, fixations" and, at the same, time "the ancestral essence . . . A buried millenarian knowledge. The cities of Ys of knowledge" (143). The primitivist plunge of negritude will not seek to know itself. The act is itself knowledge.

Conclusion

PRIMITIVISM, DECOLONIZATION, AND WORLD LITERATURE

The purpose of this book has been to reopen the question of primitivism. It has not been to have the final say. If nothing else, a challenge to the consensus view that primitivism is only a *bad thing* might give those who would like to hold on to that consensus a chance to reassess their positions. The aim, however, has not been to challenge the consensus for the sake of doing so. If we are to gain footholds for a critical perspective on our present at a moment when the unified yet constitutively uneven nature of the global capitalist system again is nakedly apparent, we need to be able to call on all the resources of the utopian memory. The insistence that the given world is the only one possible, and that we therefore must accept it, will never be rebutted on empirical grounds. A purely "evidence-based" anticapitalism will only ever achieve minor corrections; it cannot provide the basis for a systemic rebuttal. To reencounter the structure of feeling that gave rise to primitivism is to perceive how fervently was felt the disappearance of social worlds that were not organized according to the imperatives of commodity exchange and the production of surplus value. Across the spectrum of primitivist work this desire was profoundly caught up in the racial mediations of colonialism, mediations that took ideological vengeance when artists tried peremptorily to leap into the immediate mode as though the primitive were there for the taking. We must look to the paradoxical lyric expressions of negritude for a primitivism that proceeds on the basis that authentic immediate experience has been damaged and so makes that condition the grounds for renewal. I do not think, however, that there would be any gain in trying to separate out good from bad primitivism (which is not the same as making the categorical distinction between emphatic primitivism and philo-primitivism). The world-historical wish for the reunification of immediacy and reflection under the sign of the primitive took multiple forms of appearance, and its cumulative force and truth content is only apparent if we register this multiplicity.

In bringing this study to a close, I will state as concisely as possible the understanding of literary primitivism that has been arrived at over its course. I want to highlight again the two major preconditions that gave rise to it and to say a little more about the significance of defining primitivism as an aesthetic *project*, especially in view of the phenomenological connotations that the term carries. In doing so, we will be able better to pinpoint its historical and political significance and tease out the implications that follow from connecting its most exemplary manifestations to the gathering demand for decolonization. There is also an opportunity to reflect on whether primitivism's world-systemic purview might allow us fruitfully to consider it within the terms of "world literature." The concerns that have propelled the recent resurgence of this concept, especially where they have been prompted by the intention to return the concept of *totality* to the theoretical center-ground, have also motivated this study. As we assess the pertinence of reconsidering primitivism in the new millennium, it is interesting to test in what ways the conclusions I have reached align with this broader shift in literary studies.

This study has argued for a limited and historically delineated conception of primitivism considered as an aesthetic phenomenon. Primitivism's epoch of possibility was, in the end, relatively short, spanning the period between the advent of finance-driven imperialism and the global movement of decolonization, after which the capacity to motivate an aesthetics centered on the precolonial (or noncolonial) remnant fell away. Literary primitivism, and cognate modes in other aesthetic media, had two key preconditions: the manifestation of an anguished world-historical consciousness that perceived that the condition of possibility for primitive experience had been eliminated, and a pervasive belief in the capacity of aesthetic practice to revive the remnants of "primitive" social realities. Thus, it is not the fact of the dispersal through colonialism of the practices of European art-making that makes the variety of primitivizing works sufficiently coherent to bear conceptualization. Primitivism testifies to the way in which aesthetic practice under a totalized capitalism necessarily becomes the medium for sustaining the illusion of natural existence. To borrow Adorno's formulation: primitivism was "a fetish against commodity fetishism." Simon Jarvis helpfully glosses this aphorism: "The work of art is an object which makes an illusory claim not merely to be valuable as a for-another but also as something in itself."[1] With the global saturation of the commodity form, the requirement that art preserve the in-itself also became systemic. Césaire did not "appropriate" "Western" primitivism; he more powerfully cast primitivism's counterspell.

For all of these reasons primitivism must be understood as a very different kind of concept from "modernism" and "expressionism," terms with which it has frequently been associated. It is not a school or set of artistic ideas and practices like expressionism; nor, as with modernism, is it a concept that draws attention to a revolution in how artistic practice is conceived and conducted in general. Emphatic primitivism was a mode of aesthetic enactment whose forms and means of expression were diverse. We have analyzed it in terms of its basic morphology: the literary activation of the primitive remnant. Any attempt to expand the discussion of primitivism along the lines of this study would need to proceed from speculative judgments concerning a work's primitivist intensity. This is to say that it is not a matter of identifying a work's objective primitivist features (i.e., an empirical judgment in which "primitivism" is matched to various predicates) but of further developing the concept by bringing attention to other ways in which the phenomenon was manifested.

This book is not comprehensive and has not attempted to be so. I began by noting that a survey of literary primitivism that proceeded according to the scope of current and past usage would be impossibly vast and would necessarily assume a transhistorical and probably essentialist conception of "civilization." My focus therefore has been on establishing the parameters for a historically precise conception of literary primitivism and a slow reading of those literary works that seem to me most forcefully to manifest the primitivist project. Many questions remain at the end of this study, perhaps none more urgent than those relating to gender and sexuality.[2] In each of the studies in Part II we observed that the pursuit of immediacy through narrative undertaken in a damaged social reality pushed stories toward gendered violence (the climactic strangulations of women in *Women in Love* and Richard Wright's *Native Son* and the narrator's intimations of violence with the dancing pair in *Home to Harlem*). The former is especially disturbing in view of the concatenation Rupert Birkin makes between Gerald Crich and the African statue of a female figure. This points to the question of the relation between primitivist utopianism and contemporaneous ideals and ideologies of femininity. The conclusion that the primitive ideal everywhere was gendered female and the primitivist project gendered male, and that its morphology therefore is heteronormative would be hasty, however. The promise of the primitive to come in *Banjo*, for one, rests on a male-male bond between Ray and Banjo, a relation that several queer readings of the novel have delved into.[3] Further research might start with Zora Neale Hurston, whose work has received particular attention under the previous paradigms for understanding primitivism, and there can be no doubt that the primitivist morphology is strongly evident in her work.[4] Above all, this study calls for such questions to be raised in terms of the form and utopian telos of primitivist works.

I   I   I

Throughout this book I have claimed that literary primitivism was a *project*. In lay terms a project refers simply to a series of actions undertaken toward achieving a defined objective. Intrinsic to the notion is the current absence of that which the project seeks to bring into existence. I am not primitive, so I set myself the project of becoming primitive. Primitivism could only become a generalized project in a world where the primitive did not exist—not objectively speaking, but as something evident to consciousness. *Project* is also a verb, something that makes the term appealing to phenomenologists. In undertaking a project, I *project* myself forward to that state into which the project will bring me. To think of primitivism as projection is to draw attention to the projective consciousness and its apprehension of a future condition of selfhood. To fix on and deconstruct a particular representation of the "primitive" thus tends to divert us from the nature of the phenomenon at hand. The principal purpose of this study has been to recover the future toward which primitivism projected itself.

The temporality of "futurity" is a central concern of Jean-Paul Sartre's *Being and Nothingness* (1943). He writes: "the Future is the ideal point where the sudden infinite compression of facticity (Past), of the For-itself (Present), and its possible (a particular Future) will at last cause the *Self* to arise as the existence in-itself of the For-itself."[5] I cite this complex formulation only to demonstrate that the projective structure that we have identified in primitivism was itself a concern for philosophical thought at the time. If we were to replace "facticity" with "the primitive remnant," "For-itself" with "the disenchanted modern subject," "Future" with "primitive," and "in-itself" with "natural," we would have a concise, if convoluted, formulation of primitivism's morphology. Sartre's phenomenology does not explain primitivism; it is historically of a piece with it. His transhistorical claim that the For-itself has an inherent drive toward the condition of the in-itself shares the anguish of inauthenticity that motivated primitivism. It is not unexpected, therefore, that the central debate on primitivism that I discussed in Chapter 5 should have been conducted simultaneously on the terrain of phenomenology and colonial racism. This study could be said to have conducted a historical phenomenology of primitivism and, implicitly, a primitivist historicization of phenomenology.

Sartre's phenomenology highlights the way in which current projections into the future themselves become past, transforming them into what he calls "facticity." To recuperate the primitivist project (that is, the range of primitivist projections in its epoch of possibility) is to recover its "former future" from its now frozen facticity.[6] This brings us to the question of primitivism's political horizon. In general terms, primitivism aimed at a radical negation of the "civilization" that separated its exponents from the forms of social life they perceived to be sedimented in primitive remnants. In more specific terms primitivism necessarily made itself the antithesis to the historical process of imperialist expansion that led to the voiding of the concept of the primitive, as well as to the mentalities and values that attached to colonialism. This is true across the spectrum of primitivist works. There is no such thing as a consciously pro-imperialist primitivism. This is not to suggest, however, that primitivist works held a political *program* in common. To the contrary, primitivism's decolonial political horizon encompasses diverse political ideas, from fascistic to radically communitarian, and sometimes an odd mixture of both. Reflecting on the mood among his fellow black students in the early 1930s, Senghor emphasized the a priori and unstructured nature of their desire for negation: "I confess it, our pride turned quickly into racism. Even Nazism was accepted to reinforce our refusal to cooperate."[7] When I state that the primitivist project has a decolonial horizon, I am not equating it with the struggles for postcolonial sovereignty and Third World internationalism that emerged in the 1940s and 1950s (which we might call historical decolonization). I mean that it is aligned with the *ideal* of decolonization insofar as historical decolonization was motivated by the hope for a social world other than that brought into existence by the worlding of capital. The realization that historical decolonization could not serve as a vehicle for this ideal brought to an end primitivism's epoch of possibility.

To explore primitivism's decolonial horizon a little further, I want to look briefly at two accounts of the Haitian revolution written in the 1930s—one by means of historical fiction, the other by means of historical materialism. In 1934 the American writer Guy Endore published *Babouk*, a fictionalization of the life of the historical figure Dutty Boukman, who led a slave revolt in Northern Saint-Domingue in 1791. Boukman was killed soon after the revolt began, but the uprising would spark the first phase of the Haitian revolution. Endore published the novel on the back of his career-making bestseller *The Werewolf of Paris*. Didactic and highly idiosyncratic, *Babouk* flopped, yet, perhaps owing to the author's confidence following a commercial success, it is unrestrained in its idiosyncrasy. Endore's narrator speaks from the vantage of the author's time with a voice that is at turns sarcastic and earnest. He frequently mocks the presumption of white colonial supremacy yet at other times appears to reproduce exactly those prejudices. (Making clear judgments about the rhetorical register as it slides about can be tricky.) As with Lawrence's and McKay's primitivist narratives, the plot has a primitivizing trajectory. In this case the denouement is rendered in a hyperbolic primitivizing style, to the point of camp.

Beyond further testifying to the breadth of the literary primitivist zeitgeist, the novel is not especially remarkable. It is a weakly executed emphatic primitivism. What is worth drawing attention to is that Endore, a Jewish communist, should have chosen the originary anticolonial revolution as the theme for narrating the upsurge of the primitive. Two sequences in the novel are especially pertinent for thinking about primitivism's decolonial horizon. In the first the freshly branded Babouk escapes from his coastal plantation and wanders into the island's interior. With dramatic irony the narrator notes that Babouk was "unaware that he was three thousand miles from his home, unaware that on all the earth there was not a single spot of ground upon which the ubiquitous white man had not cast his enchantment."[8] Nevertheless, he happens upon a clearing in which stands "the hut of an aboriginal Indian, one of the half dozen or so left on the island, their existence almost unknown to the whites, who supposed them all extinct despite a rare rumor to the contrary" (*Ba*, 107). The family who inhabit this hut live in complete isolation. At first it appears that they are persisting in their traditional form of life just beyond the perimeter of the white man's world. The narrator even slips into speculative ethnology, describing their practices of meal preparation and rituals of smoking. The notion that we are witness to an unmediated indigeneity is countered, though, when the narrator calls attention to a silver medallion hanging around the neck of the Indian man. Now worn smooth, it once held the impression, the narrator informs us, of the Virgin Mary and baby Jesus on one side and the coat of arms of Castile on the other. There follows a historical interlude that relates the history of the island from Columbus to the present. We are encouraged to deduce that this Indian is descended from escaped Indian slaves. Babouk leaves their camp the next morning but soon is seized by Maroons and taken to their village. (Maroons were escaped African slaves who lived in semiautonomous in-land communities.) They can provide no sanctuary, however. After spotting the weals of his proprietorial branding, they hand him over to white soldiers in keeping with the terms of their treaty with the plantations.

The implication of this sequence is clear: there is no escape—not from the plantations and not from the colonial reality from which they have sprung. Subdued, Babouk becomes a docile worker and for several years is entirely mute. His journey to self-reclamation begins when he hears drumming at a nighttime gathering of slaves. Convulsed, he spews forth words, including from the famous creole chant:

> "Eh! Eh!
> Bomba!
> Heu! Heu!
> Canga bafio té!" (*Ba*, 143)

—an oath to kill all the whites. His talent for storytelling revives; he becomes a voodoo priest and leads the revolt of the northern plains. Following his death, the novel ends with a part-didactic, part-onomatopoeic coda that heralds a primal confrontation of the "tom-tom" of the "savage blacks" with the "Dum didi dumdum" snare drums of the "civilized" whites (*Ba*, 293). The narrator prophesies the general revolt of all "Negros":

> Some day the Negro's tomtom [*sic*] will truly be dreadful to hear. It will come out of the forest and beat down the streets of our cities.
>
> TOM-TOM! TOM-TOM! TOM-TOM!
>
> And it will hunt us among the girders of our dying skyscrapers as once we hunted them through their forests.
>
> TOM-TOM! TOM-TOM! TOM-TOM!
>
> And white blood will flow, and it will flow for days. It will flow for years. And yet were it to flow for a thousand years, never would it erase the white path of Negro bones that lines the bottom of the ocean from Africa to America. (*Ba*, 296)

In its narrative arc, prose style, and didacticism the novel charts the process by which primitivist exigency is diverted from seeking out existing primitive sanctuaries toward utopian insurrection. Endore's narrator is full of apocalyptic awe at the primitive to come, welcoming his own annihilation so that the primitive might again live.

I first learned of *Babouk* in a fascinating paper presented by Sascha Morrell in which she compares Endore's largely forgotten novel with *The Black Jacobins*, the celebrated account of the Haitian revolution by the Trinidadian C. L. R. James published four years later. James's protagonist is Toussaint L'Ouverture, who, far from embodying primitivist strivings, is a figure of enlightenment and disciplined self-restraint. James famously concludes that the tragic demise of this student of French revolutionary ideas "was the failure of enlightenment, not of darkness."[9] This verdict has two sides. Historically, Toussaint could not disentangle the ideals of French republicanism from the historical agents, above all Napoleon, who acted in their name. He thus failed to anticipate the full treachery of white republicanism. Philosophically, Toussaint's tendency to rationalize situations meant that he did not always perceive clearly the need to give direct expression to the raw force of discontentment of Haiti's "revolutionary masses" (*BJ*, 279). On this evidence, Endore's and James's accounts would seem opposed. Morrell argues that the two accounts nevertheless overlap in unexpected ways. Both reclaim voodoo from negative representations in French historiography, positively portray the role of drumming in revolutionary organization, and draw connections between the Haitian revolution and the proletarian and anticolonial uprisings of their authors' time.[10] James's work can hardly be called primitivist, but it is striking that both fictional and historical retellings adopt a decidedly presentist perspective. They reconstruct the Haitian revolution's "former future" in order to seize on that movement in their own present toward a decolonial future.

The understanding of historical process that motivates *The Black Jacobins* turns on a dialectic of enlightenment, one more squarely in the tradition of dialectical materialism than that diagnosed by Adorno and Horkheimer. Here the immiserations brought about by capitalist production create the conditions for enlightened counterstruggle: "the French, the half-savage slaves of San Domingo were showing themselves subject to the same historical laws as the advanced workers of revolutionary Paris" (*BJ*, 197). This is not a statement of racial character but a Trotskyist vision of combined and uneven development. The Africans are made "half-savage" by their agrarian slavery, but this also creates the conditions for a leap forward in their revolutionary organization. There are two distinct modes of revolution in James's history: one embodied in

Dessalines's barbarism, the other in Toussaint's enlightenment. When moving dialectically between these poles—the raw desire for revenge and the goal of an equitable postslave society—the revolution follows a positive trajectory. When Toussaint is drawn into Napoleon's trap and Dessalines's more inchoate vengeful drive is unleashed, however, Haiti moves in the direction of postcolonial despotism and insistent class segregation.

Four years separate the efforts of Endore and James. Only one is primitivist, but both are galvanized by the world-historical consciousness that was primitivism's precondition and decolonial horizon: the sense that only a systemic revolt could breach the perimeter of a claustrophobic modernity. On the twenty-fifth anniversary of its publication James added an appendix in which he briefly sketched the history of the Caribbean following the Haitian revolution and reflected on the interwar moment when his own work was composed. In it he aligns *The Black Jacobins* with the broader cultural movement of negritude, and Césaire's *Cahier d'un retour au pays natal* in particular, citing the same anaphoric definitions of negritude to which Fanon gravitates throughout *Black Skin, White Masks*. This is a vision, James writes, of the African "unseparated from the world, from Nature, a living part of all that lives" (*BJ*, 312). Seen from historical decolonization's peak in 1963, it was clear to James that the *Cahier*'s "strictly poetic affinities" (314) decisively had synthesized neo-African utopianism with the political hope for decolonization. This may seem obvious—it's not as though Césaire hides it from view—but the implications that follow from it are easily diminished by a retrospective gaze that understands decolonization to be a matter only of the formal political separation from empire.

I I I

If primitivism was an aesthetic project formed in reaction to the geographical totalization of the capitalist world-system, is there any benefit to thinking about it in the frame of "world literature"? Were we to enlist the materialist definition of world literature proposed by the Warwick Research Collective as "*the literature of the modern capitalist world-system,*" the answer would be an emphatic yes.[11] In its collectively authored *Combined and Uneven Development: Towards a New Theory of World-Literature*, the Collective looks to works in which the "literary registration of modernity" is "dramatically highlighted," especially those in which is found juxtaposed "asynchronous orders and levels of historical experience" (15–16). Literary primitivism fits these criteria squarely, and the conceptualization of primitivism proposed in this study has been helped along by reading the work of the members of the group. However, it is not on the basis of registering the political economy of globalizing capital that I wish to consider literary primitivism in the frame of world literature. Rather than serving as a cue for thinking about literary primitivism's relation to a totalized capitalism (a view that has necessitated a concept of totality but not "world literature"), I want to deploy it in order to think about the kind of countertotalization that literary primitivizations wished to effect, the "worlds" toward which they projected. To explain what I mean by this, I need to discuss briefly the nature of the concept of world literature and its recent resurgence in current research.

World literature's return to theoretical popularity over the last two decades has taken place in similar global conditions to those that gave rise to primitivism, something reflected in the tendency of contemporary economic historians to refer to the period of Imperialism as the "first era of globalization."[12] In both periods of "globalization" the unchecked ascendency of transnational finance and the closure of any alternative spheres of economic and social life led theorists to stress the unitary totality of human society. Accordingly, the methodologies of the world literature revival have been geared toward global systems, whether this be through reflecting on the relations between literature and a globalized capitalist political economy, the global systems of literary dissemination and reception (especially as mediated by translation), the systemic relations between national and regional literary fields, or the overlapping ecologies of different linguistic and cultural spheres. Given these concerns, it is not unexpected that world literary studies should have looked to the social sciences, most notably Pierre Bourdieu's cultural sociology, Immanuel Wallerstein's world-systems theory, the quantitative analyses of the digital humanities, and a variety of linguistically oriented theories of translation systems.

"World literature," however, is a much older concept than "globalization." Before the recent positivist turn, the term was connected not with empirical but highly speculative approaches. To name just three, Alexander Veselovsky's "historical poetics" posited universal morphological structures underlying genres in different epochs and regions;[13] Erich Auerbach recommended starting broad comparative studies with a single aspect of a particular work (an "*Ansatzpunkt*") that possesses "radiating power";[14] and Edward Said practiced what he called "contrapuntal reading"—the comparative interpretation of literary works from center and periphery with an eye to the overall humanist architecture that they mutually constitute.[15] These approaches, and others like them, tended to work from a loose yet fundamental analogy between that which is internal to literary works thought of as acts of human *poiesis* and the external relations that they establish with each other and the human world. "World literature" formed part of a humanist tradition whose precepts we can trace to Giambista Vico's assertion that "the whole world of culture has, for certain, been produced by the physical and mental activity of man, and for this reason one can and, in fact, has to find its principles and regularities within the modes of existence of the spirit of the self-same people."[16] As the result of intensive acts of human making, literary works are especially useful for gaining insight into the values and purposiveness of human society.

In view of its humanist connotations it is not clear why those who led the world literature revival should have wanted to retain the concept of "world literature." I suspect it is due in part to an implicit desire to hold on to the halo of idealism that attaches to the term, something we see reflected in the tendency of studies in the field to recuperate the literary as that which subjects capitalist globalization to fictive critique. What has been left behind is the paradox that was at the core of the critical-humanist notion of world literature (a term I oppose to the rightly scorned canonical-humanist one). Imperialism may have brought languages and literatures together and produced new, transnational literary practices, but this did not take the form of the hoped-for "fruitful intercourse" of literary exchange and creativity. If anything, the substance of the literary was constitutively opposed to that which presaged its globalization: the totalization of exchange value. Auerbach, for one, saw clearly that the convergence of literary cultures in a world-system created by the uneven distribution of power and wealth would at once "realise and destroy" the idea of world literature, the possibility for dialogues between literary ecosystems coming at the cost of their homogenization.[17] In such circumstances, the critical-humanist notion of "world literature" becomes negative—not that which is or will be but that which could have been or ought to be.

It is in this ideal critical-humanist vein that I would like to connect primitivism and world literature. In primitivism's desire to hold on to and reanimate lost social worlds, we see literature's attempt, system-wide in scope, to negate the existing world by projecting itself into alternate ones. It could even be argued that primitivism inaugurated, or at least was coeval with, the transformation of world literature from a positive/anticipatory concept into a negative/utopian one. This is not to suggest that the breadth of primitivist works projected into a single, common "world." Literary primitivism's futurity was decidedly local, pointing to the disaggregation of social realities rather than their unification. At the risk of awkwardness, we might call this "worlds literature": literature that projects into divergent realities, creating a situation in which the universal will consist of "the deepening and coexistence of all particulars."[18]

This last comment comes from none other than Césaire, in a 1956 letter to Maurice Thorez in which he tenders his resignation from the French Communist Party. He is counterposing his vision of a "universal enriched by all that is particular" to what he perceives as the metropolitan party's bureaucratic absolutism. A beautiful notion, it is, nevertheless, delivered as a general prescription and so might easily fall into the habits of the "emaciated universalism" it denounces. If one has decided in advance of any specific content the priority of that content, one easily falls prey to its mediated nature—the kind of thinking that might lead to, say, ethnic nationalism. More than a solution, the formulation points to the conundrum of both particular and universal. In his poetry Césaire is perhaps more concerned with the emaciated particular than he is the falseness of its universalization. Where the universal is false, though, the problem of the particular cannot be addressed only at the local level. Césaire thus is drawn to certain words and images that allow us to imagine how particulars might both be deepened and enabled to coexist.

I want to look finally at passages from two poems from his 1948 collection *Soleil cou coupé* (*Solar Throat Slashed*), "Antipodal Dwelling" and "Noon Knives," with a particular focus on the surrealistic deployment of *dwelling* and *meridian*—two words that recur throughout the collection. In three different poems Césaire makes use of the anaphoric construction "dwelling made of" (demeure faite de), each time to similar effect.[19] His dwellings are not made of "things," at least not the things that one associates with constructing a habitation. What we get, instead, is manically associated noun phrases that push against the expectations of their predication. These compel us to think the associations that dwelling-making brings forth without being able to reconcile these onto a single visual plane. In "Antipodal Dwelling" the following lines succeed two other anaphoric sequences in which astronomical, meteorological, and natural imagery are thrown together:

> dwelling made of water glimpsed upon waking
> dwelling made of rumpled perfumes
> dwelling made of spangled sleep

dwelling made of swelled chests stretched out of benumbed lizards
strength lines me up on the shadowless meridian

pythons crews of catastrophes denatured brothers of my longitude
roads raise themselves to the height of green-eyed female gnomes intersected
    with prayers taking aim at us on the footbridge of the malfunctioning
    compass sky[20]

These lines might well come with the warning "Do not ascribe to me intentions." The poetic method, so typical of Césaire at this time and which he explicitly articulated in his essay "Poetry and Knowledge" (which I discussed in Chapters 5 and 7), aims to confound modes of understanding that would seek to find patterns of conscious intent. Yet the opposite, approaching these lines as having the intention only to intentionlessness, would be equally misguided. Not only do certain classes of objects and experiences recur, at times obsessively, but Césaire's poetic constructions play on the ambiguous interplay of intention and arbitrariness. This is surrealist incantation, in which the lyric subject makes itself the conduit to that which it cannot consciously bring forth in order to be able to wield its power. Breton calls it "objective chance."[21] The rhetoric veers from high-seriousness to absurdity, especially where the predicate stretches to become an autonomous phrase such as with "swelled chests stretched out of benumbed lizards." The incantation is not innocent of the forms of mediation whose spell it wishes to break.

The short dwelling sequence leads to the intentional-seeming utterance: "strength lines me up on the shadowless meridian" (méridien sans ombre). This hints at a causality that links the incantation of dwelling and the strength that draws the speaker into alignment with the shadowless meridian. This sense of an intention is consolidated in the following group of lines, where we have "denatured brothers of my longitude" and "malfunctioning compass sky." Why should dwelling and meridian be decisively linked in this way? There are thirty-three different predications attached to "dwelling made of . . ." across the collection, but none suggest that "dwelling" might be an actual place. Dwelling is made of eroticism, nature, music, animals, fantasy, spices, memories, and actions, but it has no geography. It is "antipodal" to dwelling in a thoroughgoing sense. When antidwelling then brings the speaker into the "meridian," we can only assume that this is an antipodal meridian. It is the antithesis to that vertical alignment of places across the globe that simultaneously experience the high point of the sun. The surrealist register makes definitive judgment impossible, but when, in the next line, the speaker refers to the "denatured brothers of my longitude," significations also start to align. This is a meridian of dwellings without a geography, a meridian of those who have been "denatured." It is a historical and spiritual alignment, not an objective spatial one—hence "malfunctioning compass sky." In a world that has eradicated noncolonial dwelling and the possibility of natural existence, the shadowless meridian encircles another world.

In "Noon Knives" Césaire draws his reader into the light and time of the antipodal meridian. The poem begins:

> When the Blacks make Revolution they begin by uprooting from the Champ de Mars giant trees that they hurl like bayings into the face of the sky and that in the hottest of the air take aim at the pure streams of fresh birds at which they fire blanks [tirent á blanc].[22]

Drawing together the imagery from the two poems, we could say that the "denatured brothers" are denaturing the Eiffel Tower's park and, in a quintessentially negritudist pun, shooting "whites/blanks" at birds. It is a revolt against civilized nature: the negation of the negation. The meridian notionally is a circle, or revolution, of the planet. This gives prescience to the notion of a decolonial revolution taking place at the noon meridian, a moment when outward reality can be seen in the clearest outline. Following the above passage, there comes an anaphoric series in which "Noon," like "dwelling," is surrealistically modulated through a series. The final, culminating utterance in this series makes explicit primitivism's truth content and decolonial horizon. To project toward a primitive world is to disappear in broad daylight:

> Noon? Yes Noon that bears on its scabby glazier's back all the sensitivity toward hatred and ruins that counts. Noon? by god Noon which after pausing on my lips just long enough for a curse and at the cathedral limits of idleness sets on all lines of every hand the trains that repentance kept in reserve in the strong-boxes of severe time. Noon? Yes sumptuous noon that absents me from this world.[23]

NOTES

Preface

1. See György Lukács, *History and Class Consciousness: Studies in Marxist Dialectics*, trans. Rodney Livingstone (Cambridge, MA: MIT Press, 1971), 27; and Warwick Research Collective, *Combined and Uneven Development: Towards a New Theory of World-Literature* (Liverpool: Liverpool University Press, 2015).

2. Aimé Césaire, *Solar Throat Slashed: The Unexpurgated 1948 Edition*, trans. A. James Arnold and Clayton Eshleman (Middletown, CT: Wesleyan University Press, 2011), 160–61.

3. Ibid., 161.

4. Sinéad Garrigan Mattar, *Primitivism, Science, and the Irish Revival* (Oxford: Clarendon, 2004), 3.

5. This appears to be confirmed by a search on Google's Ngram Viewer (https://books.google.com/ngrams), which charts frequencies of yearly uses of search terms across Google's text corpora. A comparative search of *primitive, savage*, and *barbarous/barbarian* restricted to English sources from 1650 to 2008 shows that from 1868 onward *primitive* was the term used most frequently. (Uses of *barbarian* and *barbarous* were added together in view of the dual semantic function of *savage* and *primitive*.) *Barbarous/barbarian* dominated from 1650 to 1800, and *savage* was on top for a brief period from 1849 to 1868. From 1868 to 1930 there was a marked rise in uses of *primitive* and a quite steep decline in uses of *savage* and *barbarian/barbarous*. In 1810, usages of the three terms were roughly equal. By 1930 *primitive* was being used nearly 2.5 times as much as *savage* and more than 4.5 times as much as *barbarous/barbarian*. (Among French sources the ratio of *primitif* to *barbare* was just over 4:1 in the year Césaire published "Barbare.") Usages of all terms have been in steady decline since 1930.

6. See Rory Dufficy, "The Content of the Avant-Garde: Subjectivity, Community, Revolution" (PhD diss., Western Sydney University, 2016), 31–33.

7. Cited by Peter Kirkpatrick in "'Fearful Affinity': Jindyworobak Primitivism," in *Adelaide: A Literary City*, ed. Philip Butterss (Adelaide: Adelaide University Press, 2013), 130.

Chapter 1. Primitivism After Its Poststructural Eclipse

1. Robert Goldwater, *Primitivism in Modern Painting* (New York: Harper and Brothers, 1938); see also Charles Wentinck, *Modern and Primitive Art* (Oxford: Phaidon, 1979); William Rubin, ed., *"Primitivism" in 20th Century Art: Affinity of the Tribal and the Modern* (New York: Museum of Modern Art, 1984); Jack D. Flam and Miriam Deutch, eds., *Primitivism and Twentieth-Century Art: A Documentary History* (Berkeley: University of California Press, 2003); and Colin Rhodes, *Primitivism and Modern Art* (London: Thames and Hudson, 1994).

2. Michael Bell, *Primitivism* (London: Methuen, 1972), 2.

3. Ibid., 1.

4. Michel de Montaigne, *The Essays of Michel de Montaigne*, trans. M. A. Screech (London: Allen Lane, 1991), 236.

5. See Adam Kuper, *The Invention of Primitive Society: Transformations of an Illusion* (London: Routledge, 1988). Perhaps the most succinct summation of the history of primitivism qua philosophical framework that idealizes the idea of the primitive is provided by Armin W. Geertz in "Can We Move Beyond Primitivism? On Recovering the Indigenes of Indigenous Religions in the Academic Study of Religion," in *Beyond Primitivism: Indigenous Religious Traditions and Modernity*, ed. Jacob K. Olupona (New York: Routledge, 2004), 37–70. References in the following survey of scholarship on primitivism are representative. They do not constitute an exhaustive list.

6. See David Ciarlo, *Advertising Empire: Race and Visual Culture in Imperial Germany* (Cambridge, MA: Harvard University Press, 2011); and Annie E. Coombes, "Ethnography of National and Cultural Identities," in *The Myth of Primitivism*, ed. Susan Hiller (London: Routledge, 1991), 156–78.

7. See Raymond Williams, *The Country and the City* (Oxford: Oxford University Press, 1975); and Stephen Horigan, *Nature and Culture in Western Discourses* (London: Routledge, 1988).

8. See Charles Harrison and Gillian Perry, *Primitivism, Cubism, Abstraction: The Early Twentieth Century* (New Haven, CT: Yale University Press, 1993); Daniel Albright, ed., *Modernism and Music: An Anthology of Sources* (Chicago: University of Chicago Press, 2004); Emmanuel Gorge, *Le primitivisme musical: Facteurs et genèse d'un paradigme esthétique* (Paris: L'Harmattan, 2000); and Susan Jones, *Literature, Modernism, and Dance* (Oxford: Oxford University Press, 2013).

9. Jill Lloyd, *German Expressionism: Primitivism and Modernity* (New Haven, CT: Yale University Press, 1991); Vincent Debaene, "Les surréalistes et le musée d'ethnographie," *Labyrinthe*, 12 (2002), 71–94; Iris Därmann, "Primitivismus in den Bildtheorien des 20. Jahrhunderts," in *Literarischer Primitivismus*, ed. Nicola Gess (Berlin: De Gruyter, 2012), 75–91; Joseph Masheck, "Raw Art: 'Primitive' Authenticity and German Expressionism," *RES: Anthropology and Aesthetics*, 4 (1982), 92–117; Lucia Re,

" 'Barbari Civilizzatissimi': Marinetti and the Futurist Myth of Barbarism," *Journal of Modern Italian Studies*, 17 (2012), 350–68; Jeremy Howard, Irēna Bužinska, and Z. S. Strother, *Vladimir Markov and Russian Primitivism: A Charter for the Avant-Garde* (Surrey: Ashgate, 2015).

10. Abigail Solomon-Godeau, "Going Native: Paul Gauguin and the Invention of Modernist Primitivism," *Art in America*, 77 (1989), 118–29; Patricia Leighten, "The White Peril and *L'Art nègre*: Picasso, Primitivism, and Anticolonialism," *Art Bulletin*, 72 (1990), 609–30; Sarah Kennel, "*Le Sacre du Printemps*: Primitivism, Popular Dance, and the Parisian Avant-Garde," *Nottingham French Studies*, 44 (2005), 4–23; Carol McKay, "Modernist Primitivism? The Case of Kandinsky," *Oxford Art Journal*, 16.2 (1993), 21–36.

11. See part 1 of Flam and Deutch; and T. J. Barringer and Tom Flynn, eds., *Colonialism and the Object: Empire, Material Culture, and the Museum* (London: Routledge, 1998).

12. Michael Bell, *D. H. Lawrence: Language and Being* (Cambridge: Cambridge University Press, 1992); Jack Stewart, *The Vital Art of D. H. Lawrence: Vision and Expression* (Carbondale: Southern Illinois University Press, 1999); Dolores LaChapelle, *D. H. Lawrence: Future Primitive* (Denton: University of North Texas Press, 1996); B. Neilson, "D. H. Lawrence's 'Dark Page': Narrative Primitivism in *Women in Love* and *The Plumed Serpent*," *Twentieth Century Literature*, 43.3 (1997), 310–25.

13. Robert Crawford, *The Savage and the City in the Work of T. S. Eliot* (Oxford: Clarendon, 1987); William Harmon, "T. S. Eliot, Anthropologist and Primitive," *American Anthropologist*, 78 (1976), 797–811; Ronald Bush, "The Presence of the Past: Ethnographic Thinking/Literary Politics," in *Prehistories of the Future: The Primitivist Project and the Culture of Modernism*, ed. Elazar Barkan and Ronald Bush (Stanford: Stanford University Press, 1995), 23–41.

14. Sinéad Garrigan Mattar, *Primitivism, Science, and the Irish Revival* (Oxford: Clarendon, 2004); Maria McGarrity and Claire A. Culleton, eds., *Irish Modernism and the Global Primitive* (Basingstoke: Palgrave Macmillan, 2009).

15. Michael North, *The Dialect of Modernism: Race, Language, and Twentieth-Century Literature* (Oxford: Oxford University Press, 1998), 59–76; Susanna Pavloska, *Modern Primitives: Race and Language in Gertrude Stein, Ernest Hemingway, and Zora Neale Hurston* (London: Routledge, 2013), 31–54.

16. Mark Whalan, *Race, Manhood, and Modernism in America: The Short Story Cycles of Sherwood Anderson and Jean Toomer* (Knoxville: University of Tennessee Press, 2007), 73–122; Suzanne Del Gizzo, "Going Home: Hemingway, Primitivism, and Identity," *Modern Fiction Studies*, 49 (2003), 496–523; Dominique Viart, "Faulkner et les paradoxes du primitivisme," *Revue des sciences humaines*, 227 (1992), 196–219; George William Sutton, "Primitivism in the Fiction of William Faulkner" (PhD diss., University of Mississippi, 1967).

17. Edward Manouelian, "Invented Traditions: Primitivist Narrative and Design in the Polish Fin de Siècle," *Slavic Review*, 59.2 (2000), 391–405.

18. Sieglinde Lemke, *Primitivist Modernism: Black Culture and the Origins of Transatlantic Modernism* (Oxford: Oxford University Press, 1998); Carole Sweeney, *From Fetish to Subject: Race, Modernism, and Primitivism, 1919–1935* (Westport, CT: Praeger, 2004).

19. See Chapter 7 for further discussion of the scholarship on McKay and primitivism.

20. Tracy McCabe, "The Multifaceted Politics of Primitivism in Harlem Renaissance Writing," *Soundings*, 80 (1997), 475–97; David Chinitz, "Rejuvenation Through Joy: Langston Hughes, Primitivism, and Jazz," *American Literary History*, 9 (1997), 60–78; Kurt Eisen, "Theatrical Ethnography and Modernist Primitivism in Eugene O'Neill and Zora Neale Hurston," *South Central Review*, 25 (2008), 56–73; Paul Stasi, "A 'Synchronous but More Subtle Migration': Passing and Primitivism in Toomer's 'Cane,'" *Twentieth Century Literature*, 55 (2009), 145–74.

21. A. James Arnold, *Modernism and Negritude: The Poetry and Poetics of Aimé Césaire* (Cambridge, MA: Harvard University Press, 1981); Mara De Gennaro, "Fighting 'Humanism' on Its Own Terms," *differences: A Journal of Feminist Cultural Studies*, 14 (2003), 53–73; Celia Britton, "How to Be Primitive: *Tropiques*, Surrealism and Ethnography," *Paragraph*, 32 (2009), 168–81.

22. Michael Richardson, ed., *Refusal of the Shadow: Surrealism and the Caribbean*, trans. Michael Richardson and Krzysztof Fijałkowski (London: Verso, 1996).

23. Katia Samaltanos, *Apollinaire: Catalyst for Primitivism, Picabia, and Duchamp* (Ann Arbor: UMI Research Press, 1984); Jean-Claude Blachère, *Les totems d'André Breton: Surréalisme et primitivisme littéraire* (Paris: L'Harmattan, 1996); Georges Bataille, *Documents*, ed. Bernard Noël (Paris: Mercure de France, 1968); Rosalind E. Krauss, "No More Play," in *The Originality of the Avant-garde and Other Modernist Myths* (Cambridge, MA: MIT Press, 1986), 42–85; Marie-Denise Shelton, "Primitive Self: Colonial Impulses in Michel Leiris's *L'Afrique Fantôme*," in *Prehistories of the Future: The Primitivist Project and the Culture of Modernism*, ed. Elazar Barkan and Ronald Bush (Stanford: Stanford University Press, 1995), 326–38.

24. Rhys W. Williams, "Primitivism in the Works of Carl Einstein, Carl Sternheim and Gottfried Benn," *Journal of European Studies*, 13 (1983), 247–67; David Pan, *Primitive Renaissance: Rethinking German Expressionism* (Lincoln: University of Nebraska Press, 2001); Andreas Michel, "Formalism to Psychoanalysis: On the Politics of Primitivism in Carl Einstein," in *The Imperialist Imagination: German Colonialism and Its Legacy*, ed. Sara Friedrichsmeyer, Sara Lennox, and Susanne Zantop (Ann Arbor: University of Michigan Press, 1998), 141–61; Nicola Gess, ed., *Literarischer Primitivismus* (Berlin: Walter de Gruyter, 2012).

25. A volume that exemplifies the tendency to tie primitivism to modernism is Elazar Barkan and Ronald Bush, eds., *Prehistories of the Future: The Primitivist Project and the Culture of Modernism* (Stanford: Stanford University Press, 1995).

26. Erik Camayd-Freixas, "Narrative Primitivism: Theory and Practice in Latin America," in *Primitivism and Identity in Latin America: Essays on Art, Literature, and Culture*, ed. Erik Camayd-Freixas and José Eduardo González (Tucson: University of Arizona Press, 2000), 109–34.

27. Peter Kirkpatrick, "'Fearful Affinity': Jindyworobak Primitivism," in *Adelaide: A Literary City*, ed. Philip Butterss (Adelaide: Adelaide University Press, 2013), 125–46.

28. Paul Sherman, *In Search of the Primitive: Rereading David Antin, Jerome Rothen-*

berg, and Gary Snyder (Baton Rouge: Louisiana State University Press, 1986); Jon Panish, "Kerouac's *The Subterraneans*: A Study of 'Romantic Primitivism,'" *MELUS*, 19.3 (1994), 107–23.

29. Peter C. Van Wyck, *Primitives in the Wilderness: Deep Ecology and the Missing Human Subject* (Albany: State University of New York Press, 1997); John Zerzan, *Future Primitive and Other Essays* (Brooklyn, NY: Autonomedia, 1994).

30. Bell, *Primitivism*, 3; James Richard Baird, *Ishmael: A Study of the Symbolic Mode in Primitivism* (New York: Harper and Bros, 1960).

31. Julia Reid, "Robert Louis Stevenson and the 'Romance of Anthropology,'" *Journal of Victorian Culture*, 10.1 (2005), 46–71.

32. Frances S. Connelly, *The Sleep of Reason: Primitivism in Modern European Art and Aesthetics, 1725–1907* (University Park: Penn State Press, 1999). Maximilian Novak also speaks of primitivism "flourishing" in the eighteenth century precisely because the binary of civilized and primitive first became distinct at this time. See "Primitivism," in *The Cambridge History of Literary Criticism*, vol. 4, *The Eighteenth Century*, ed. H. B. Nisbet and Claude Rawson (Cambridge: Cambridge University Press, 2005), 456–69.

33. Irving Babbitt, "The Primitivism of Wordsworth," *Bookman*, 74.1 (1931), 1–10; Anne McWhir, "Purity and Disgust: The Limits of Wordsworth's Primitivism," *Mosaic*, 24.2 (1991), 43–58.

34. Gina M. Rossetti, *Imagining the Primitive in Naturalist and Modernist Literature* (Columbia: University of Missouri Press, 2006).

35. For more on this see Chapter 2.

36. Arthur Lovejoy and George Boas, *Primitivism and Related Ideas in Antiquity*, vol. 1 (Baltimore: Johns Hopkins Press, 1935).

37. Marianna Torgovnick, *Gone Primitive: Savage Intellects, Modern Lives* (Chicago: University of Chicago Press, 1990).

38. Garrigan Mattar, 3.

39. Ernst Bloch, "Nonsynchronism and the Obligation to Its Dialectics," trans. Mark Ritter, *New German Critique*, 11 (1977), 31.

40. Blachère, 233 (my translation).

41. The notion that primitivism is a project is announced by the title of Barkan and Bush's edited volume *Prehistories of the Future: The Primitivist Project and the Culture of Modernism*. The editors do not explain in their introduction in what sense they employ the term *project*, however.

42. *Oxford English Dictionary Online*, www.oed.com, s.v. "-ism."

43. In assuming that primitivism implies the verb, I follow Robert Goldwater. He writes, for instance, of "primitivizing elements," "primitivizing works," and "primitivizing style," and uses the verb form throughout his study. See Robert Goldwater, *Primitivism in Modern Art*, rev. ed. (New York: Vintage, 1967), 139, 243, 213.

44. Daniel J. Sherman, *French Primitivism and the Ends of Empire, 1945–1975* (Chicago: University of Chicago Press, 2011), 3. The distinction with philo-primitivism is not the same as that made by Lovejoy and Boas between "hard" primitivism, which ideal-

izes a savage and brutish condition, and "soft" primitivism, which idealizes a tranquilly Arcadian state—a categorization that seeks a transhistorical axis. Rosalind Krauss's essay "No More Play" has done much to keep this distinction current in the scholarship. Krauss, 42–85. For more on this see the discussion in Chapter 2.

45. Flam and Deutch, 319; herein *PT*. I reference the Flam and Deutch anthology because the responses to the MoMA exhibition that I go on to discuss can also be read in that volume.

46. Thomas McEvilley spoke of "an ethnocentric subjectivity inflated to co-opt such cultures and their objects into itself"; James Clifford of "the restless desire and power of the modern West to collect the world"; Hal Foster of primitivism as "a fetishistic recognition-and-disavowal of difference . . . a (mis)construction of the other." Flam and Deutch, 249, 356, 386.

47. Torgovnick, 9.

48. Ibid., 3, 8.

49. According to Torgovnick, D. H. Lawrence hopes for "systems of thought which might critique Western ones," but he can only think of primitive societies "in Western terms." So "thinkers like Lawrence yearn for, but lack the ground for, radical critique" (173). As with Foster, Torgovnick can only perceive Lawrence's intent in the terms of her own ambitions. The novelist is presumed to be aiming for "critique," even to the point of needing to supply adequate "grounds" for this.

50. Ibid., 247.

51. Rhodes, 195. For Rhodes, "primitivism does not designate an organised group of artists, or even an identifiable style . . . but rather brings together artists' various reactions to ideas of the primitive" (7). He first establishes what these ideas might have been and then runs through an impressive array of movements, artists, and works that were stimulated by them.

52. Ibid., 200.

53. Robert Young, "Postcolonial Remains," *New Literary History*, 43 (2012), 38.

54. Victor Li, *The Neo-primitivist Turn: Critical Reflections on Alterity, Culture, and Modernity* (Toronto: University of Toronto Press, 2006), 32.

55. To be "haunted by the aboriginal," in Gayatri Spivak's righteous words. Quoted in Li, 32.

56. Li, 38.

57. Having decisively shown that you cannot subtract domination from concepts by trimming off their ideological component or finding new ones, Li finds his own study at an impasse. He has argued that the deconstruction of the primitive requires the standpoint of an unknowable alterity but then admits that he himself has relied on this structure of critique. What Li has forgotten by the end of his study is the importance of the historical content that deconstruction hollowed out—what I am calling primitivism's nonsynchronous remnant.

58. Three signal collections within this research paradigm are David Palumbo-Liu, Bruce Robbins, and Nirvana Tanoukhi, eds., *Immanuel Wallerstein and the Problem of the World: System, Scale, Culture* (Durham, NC: Duke University Press, 2011); Jed Esty

and Colleen Lye, eds., with Joe Cleary, "Peripheral Realisms," special issue, *Modern Language Quarterly*, 73.3 (2012); and Warwick Research Collective, *Combined and Uneven Development: Towards a New Theory of World-Literature* (Liverpool: Liverpool University Press, 2015).

59. Keya Ganguly, *Cinema, Emergence, and the Films of Satyajit Ray* (Berkeley: University of California Press, 2010), 2.

60. Nicholas Brown, *Utopian Generations: The Political Horizon of Twentieth-Century Literature* (Princeton, NJ: Princeton University Press, 2005), 3.

Chapter 2. Primitivism and Philo-primitivism

1. Brennan includes in posthumanism's "empire" the following: "object-oriented criticism, cognitive hermeneutics, machine cultures, surface reading, thing theory, deep ecology, systems theory, some variants of animal studies, autopoiesis, and the theory of hybrid natural/human environments." Timothy Brennan, *Borrowed Light: Vico, Hegel, and the Colonies* (Stanford: Stanford University Press, 2014), 225.

2. Sheldon Pollock, "Philology in Three Dimensions," *Postmedieval: A Journal of Medieval Cultural Studies*, 5.4 (2014), 399.

3. Marjorie Perloff has pointed out the pitfalls of taking a "puritanic yardstick" to primitivism. See "Tolerance and Taboo: Modernist Primitivisms and Postmodernist Pieties," in *Prehistories of the Future: The Primitivist Project and the Culture of Modernism*, ed. Elazar Barkan and Ronald Bush (Stanford: Stanford University Press, 1995), 339–54.

4. Theodor W. Adorno, *Aesthetic Theory*, ed. Gretel Adorno and Rolf Tiedemann, trans. Robert Hullot-Kentor (London: Continuum, 2004), 251.

5. Robert Goldwater, *Primitivism in Modern Art*, rev. ed. (New York: Vintage, 1967), 257.

6. Ibid., 252.

7. Ibid., 266–67 (my emphasis).

8. Gaile McGregor, *Noble Savage in the New World Garden: Notes Toward a Syntactics of Place* (Toronto: University of Toronto Press, 1988), 12.

9. Arthur Lovejoy and George Boas, *Primitivism and Related Ideas in Antiquity*, vol. 1 (Baltimore: Johns Hopkins Press, 1935), 8.

10. Ibid., 1–14.

11. See Tony C. Brown, *The Primitive, the Aesthetic, and the Savage: An Enlightenment Problematic* (Minneapolis: University of Minnesota Press, 2012), 25–43.

12. John Dryden, *The Works of John Dryden*, vol. 11 (Berkeley: University of California Press, 1978), 30.

13. Quoted in Maximillian E. Novak, "Primitivism," in *The Cambridge History of Literary Criticism*, vol. 4, *The Eighteenth Century*, ed. H. B. Nisbet and Claude Rawson (Cambridge: Cambridge University Press, 2005), 458.

14. He also considers the writings of George Chapman, Diderot, Voltaire, Baron de Lahonton, and others. Anthony Pagden, "The Savage Critic: Some European Images of the Primitive," *The Yearbook of English Studies*, 13 (1983), 32–45. Ian Almond recently

has tracked broader patterns in this impulse to leverage the "Other" when conducting self-criticism. *The New Orientalists: Postmodern Representations of Islam from Foucault to Baudrillard* (London: I. B. Tauris, 2007).

15. As Ter Ellingson puts it: "European ideas of the 'savage' grew out of an imaginative fusion of classical mythology with the new descriptions that were beginning to be conceived by scientifically minded writers as 'observations' of foreign peoples by Renaissance travel-ethnographic writers." Ter Ellingson, *The Myth of the Noble Savage* (Berkeley: University of California Press, 2001), 11.

16. See especially Joseph-François's *Mœurs des sauvage amériquains*. William H. Truettner, *Painting Indians and Building Empires in North America, 1710–1840* (Berkeley: University of California Press, 2010), 40. We might also look to Lafitau's comparison of the oratorical style of Indians with Spartans, on which see Novak, 460.

17. Andrew Hadfield, *Literature, Travel, and Colonial Writing in the English Renaissance, 1545–1625* (Oxford: Clarendon, 1998); Chloë Houston, ed., *New Worlds Reflected: Travel and Utopia in the Early Modern Period* (Farnham: Ashgate, 2010).

18. This was especially prevalent in northern America, where the identification of settlers with their colonized "primitives" was impelled by the notion of "the American Adam." See R. W. B. Lewis, *The American Adam: Innocence, Tragedy, and Tradition in the Nineteenth Century* (Chicago: University of Chicago Press, 1955).

19. George Catlin, *Letters and Notes on the Manners, Customs and Condition of the North American Indians* (London: self-published, 1841), 15.

20. "My enthusiastic admiration of man in the honest and elegant simplicity of nature . . . together with the desire to study my art, independently of the embarrassments which the ridiculous fashions of civilized society have thrown in its way, has led me to the wilderness for a while, as the true school of the arts" (ibid.).

21. Ibid., 16.

22. Steven Conn has discussed this tension between artistry, history, and ethnography in *History's Shadow: Native Americans and Historical Consciousness in the Nineteenth Century* (Chicago: University of Chicago Press, 2004), 54–63.

23. Charles Darwin, *The Voyage of the Beagle* (Ware, Herts.: Wordsworth Editions, 1997), 412. See also Richard H. Grove, *Green Imperialism: Colonial Expansion, Tropical Island Edens and the Origins of Environmentalism, 1600–1860* (Cambridge: Cambridge University Press, 1995), 355–79.

24. Claude Lévi-Strauss, *Tristes tropiques*, trans. John and Doreen Weightman (New York: Penguin, 1992), 49.

25. Catlin, frontispiece.

26. See, e.g., Hoxie Neale Fairchild, *The Noble Savage: A Study in Romantic Naturalism* (New York: Columbia University Press, 1928); and Tzvetan Todorov, *On Human Diversity: Nationalism, Racism and Exoticism in French Thought*, trans. Catherine Porter (Cambridge, MA: Harvard University Press, 1994).

27. Ellingson, 7.

28. Jean-Jacques Rousseau, *The First and Second Discourses*, trans. Roger D. Masters and Judith R. Masters (New York: St Martin's, 1964), 92. Consequently, we find that

Rousseau's grammar is deductive: "Alone, idle, and always near danger, savage man *must* like to sleep." Rousseau, 112 (my emphasis).

29. Ellingson, 83–85.

30. Rousseau, 110.

31. In a long footnote, he observes that "it is an extremely remarkable thing, for all the years that Europeans have been tormenting themselves to bring the savages of various countries in the world to their way of life, that they have not yet been able to win over a single one" (223). He relates the story of one "Hottentot" who, having been raised a Christian with European customs, immediately renounced those ways after visiting his relatives. Rousseau does not regard this to be the manifestation of, say, a racial essence but this man's rational preference. It is the European that is the more likely to convert to "savage" ways: "one reads in a thousand places that Frenchmen and other Europeans have voluntarily taken refuge among these nations" (223).

32. R. L. Stevenson, *The Collected Poems of Robert Louis Stevenson*, ed. Roger Lewis (Edinburgh: Edinburgh University Press, 2003), 128. Of these lines Sean Pryor lucidly comments: "This is a distinctly nineteenth-century classical aesthetic. The scene is less like Homer, or even Theocritus, than Thomas Moore's *Evenings in Greece* (1825)." Sean Pryor, "Stevenson Among the Balladeers," *Victorian Studies*, 57 (2014), 44–45.

33. It overlays "the break between Greek and Roman onto the geographical separation of the Pacific and 'home,' and onto the historical division between 'antiquity' and 'modernity.'" Pryor, 44–45.

34. Ibid., 37–38.

35. Vanessa Smith, *Literary Culture and the Pacific: Nineteenth-Century Textual Encounters* (Cambridge: Cambridge University Press, 1998), 15.

36. Neil Lazarus, "The Fetish of 'the West' in Postcolonial Theory," in *Marxism, Modernity, and Postcolonial Studies* (Cambridge: Cambridge University Press, 2002), 43–64.

37. Vivek Chibber's recent critique of the Subaltern Studies project, *Postcolonial Theory and the Specter of Capital* (London: Verso, 2013), elaborates on this aspect of Lazarus's position. He argues that the subalternists mistook Marx's theory of the logic of capital (the accumulation of capital through appropriated surplus value, which most typically is stolen by means of the labor contract) for the historically diverse means by which this logic has been established and maintained, in Europe and elsewhere. This process always requires coercive antiliberal practices. A more detailed and comprehensive view of the way in which the fields of subaltern and postcolonial studies formed and evolved in such a way as to circumvent political economy can be found in Vasant Kaiwar's *The Postcolonial Orient: The Politics of Difference and the Project of Provincialising Europe* (Leiden: Brill, 2014).

38. Norman Etherington outlines both the breadth of the concept's entrance into economic and political discourse and its historical novelty at this time in *Theories of Imperialism: War, Conquest and Capital* (London: Croom Helm, 1984).

39. Hobson defined *imperialism* as "the desire of strong organized industrial and financial interests to secure and develop at the public expense and by the public force private markets for their surplus goods and their surplus capital." J. A. Hobson, *Imperialism: A Study*, 3rd ed. (London: Allen and Unwin, 1938), 106.

40. Both cited in Etherington, 77 and 152, respectively.

41. So, for example, Robert Harvey replaces the notion of "primitive accumulation" with "accumulation by dispossession" to signal that it is a continual strategy of accumulation. See Robert Harvey, *The New Imperialism* (Oxford: Oxford University Press, 2003), 144–45.

42. Leon Trotsky, *Results and Prospects and the Permanent Revolution*, trans. Brian Pearce (London: Union Books, 2006).

43. Karl Marx, *Capital: A Critique of Political Economy*, vol. 1, trans. Ben Fowkes (Harmondsworth: Penguin, 1976), 929.

44. Rosa Luxemburg, *The Accumulation of Capital*, trans. Agnes Schwarzschild (London: Routledge, 2003), 397.

45. Ibid., 426.

46. Ibid., 349. Trotsky makes a similar point in *Results and Prospects* when arguing against the narrow perspective of the Mensheviks: "Today they fail to see the unified process of world capitalist development which swallows up all the countries that lie in its path and which creates, out of the national and general exigencies of capitalism, an amalgam whose nature cannot be understood by the application of historical clichés, but only by materialist analysis." Quoted in Michael Löwy, *The Politics of Combined and Uneven Development: The Theory of Permanent Revolution*, abr. ed. (Chicago: Haymarket, 2010), 52.

47. Goldwater, 266–67.

48. Walter Benjamin, *Illuminations*, ed. Hannah Arendt, trans. by Harry Zorn (London: Pimlico, 1999), 248.

49. The original phrase reads: "myth is already enlightenment; and enlightenment reverts to mythology." Theodor W. Adorno and Max Horkheimer, *Dialectic of Enlightenment*, trans. John Cumming (London: Verso, 1997), xvi.

50. Sigmund Freud, *Totem and Taboo: Some Points of Agreement Between the Mental Lives of Savages and Neurotics*, trans. James Strachey (London: Routledge, 2001), 26.

51. David Pan, *Primitive Renaissance: Rethinking German Expressionism* (Lincoln: University of Nebraska Press, 2001), 16.

52. Raymond Geuss, introduction to Friedrich Nietzsche, *Nietzsche: The Birth of Tragedy and Other Writings* (Cambridge: Cambridge University Press, 1999), xxx.

53. Friedrich Nietzsche, *"On the Genealogy of Morality" and Other Writings*, trans. Carol Diethe (Cambridge: Cambridge University Press, 2006), 23–24.

54. Ibid., 54. "We modern men are the heirs of the conscience-vivisection and self-torture of millennia" (95).

55. Ibid., 15.

56. See "Unofficial Versions," in *The Myth of Primitivism*, ed. Susan Hiller and Guy Brett (London: Routledge, 2006), 102.

57. Nietzsche, *"On the Genealogy of Morality,"* 66.

58. Cited in Brennan, 173.

59. See ibid., 178.

Chapter 3. Primitivism and Negritude

1. Carl Einstein, "On Primitive Art," trans. Charles W. Haxthausen, *October*, 105 (2003), 124.

2. Charles W. Haxthausen, "Bloody Serious: Two Texts by Carl Einstein," *October*, 105 (2003), 112–13.

3. Carl Einstein, "African Sculpture," in *Primitivism and Twentieth-Century Art: A Documentary History*, ed. Jack D. Flam and Miriam Deutch (Berkeley: University of California Press, 2003), 89. The essay appears in full in this volume.

4. Haxthausen, 112.

5. A nearly identical sentiment can be found in Hermann Bahr's 1916 work *Expressionismus*: "People little know how near the truth they are when they jeer at these pictures and say they might be painted by savages. The bourgeois rule has turned us into savages. . . . The Savage discovered in himself the courage to become greater than the threat of nature, and in honour of this mysterious inner redeeming power of his . . . brought very near the edge of destruction by 'civilisation,' we discover in ourselves powers which cannot be destroyed. With the fear of death upon us, we muster these and use them as spells against 'civilisation'" (Flam and Deutch, 101). Again the contact point between the primitivist and the primitive is the rebellion against the broader situation of bourgeois rule. He does not seek a set of guiding principles from primitive art as it pursues its own ends but is openly projective, in the sense of projecting his wishes in the general direction from which he perceives the "primitive" expression to be emanating.

6. Theodor W. Adorno, *Notes to Literature*, ed. Rolf Tiedemann, trans. Shierry Weber Nicholson (New York: Columbia University Press, 1991), 20.

7. The generational transitions of German expressionism are well documented in Rose-Carol Washton Long's anthology *German Expressionism: Documents from the End of the Wilhelmine Empire to the Rise of National Socialism* (Berkeley: University of California Press, 1995).

8. Ernst Bloch et. al, *Aesthetics and Politics*, ed. Ronald Taylor, trans. Anya Bostock et. al (London: Verso, 2010), 17.

9. Ibid., 22.

10. Ibid., 24.

11. Ernst Bloch, "Nonsynchronism and the Obligation to Its Dialectics," trans. Mark Ritter, *New German Critique*, 11 (1977), 26.

12. See Robbie Aitken and Eve Rosenhaft, *Black Germany: The Making and Unmaking of a Diaspora Community, 1884–1960* (Cambridge: Cambridge University Press, 2013).

13. T. E. Lawrence, *Seven Pillars of Wisdom* (London: Vintage, 2008), 355.

14. Michael Richardson, ed., *Refusal of the Shadow: Surrealism and the Caribbean*, trans. Michael Richardson and Krzysztof Fijałkowski (London: Verso, 1996), 42.

15. Aimé Césaire, "Conscience raciale et révolution sociale," *L'étudiant noir: Journal mensuel de l'Association des Étudiants Martiniquais en France*, 3 (1935), 1–2; repr. in Christian Filostrat, *Negritude Agonistes: Assimilation Against Nationalism in the French-Speaking Caribbean and Guyane* (Cherry Hill: Africana Homestead Legacy, 2008),

123–26. My translation is the same as Christopher L. Miller's save one word. Miller translates "immédiat" as "immanent" (the corresponding words are the same in the two languages), perhaps displaying the sort of misguided sensitivities that this study hopes to correct. See Christopher L. Miller, "The (Revised) Birth of Negritude: Communist Revolution and 'The Immanent Negro' in 1935," *PMLA*, 125.3 (2010), 747.

16. Richardson, 97.

17. Ibid., 98.

18. Ibid., 99–100.

19. Flam and Deutch, 192.

20. Ibid., 191.

21. René Ménil, *Antilles déjà jadis, précédé de "Tracées"* (Paris: Jean-Michel Place, 1999), 90 (Ménil's emphasis; my translation).

22. Aimé Césaire, *Solar Throat Slashed: The Unexpurgated 1948 Edition*, trans. A. James Arnold and Clayton Eshleman (Middletown, CT: Wesleyan University Press, 2011), 49.

23. Jacques Louis Hymans, *Léopold Sédar Senghor: An Intellectual Biography* (Edinburgh: Edinburgh University Press, 1971), 71–72.

24. Aimé Césaire, *Notebook of a Return to My Native Land*, trans. Mireille Rosello and Annie Pritchard (Newcastle: Bloodaxe, 1995), 121.

25. The divergence of my argument from received postcolonial common sense can be seen by contrasting it with Victor Li's recent essay "Primitivism and Postcolonial Literature," which is the most rigorously argued postcolonial critique of primitivism. Anchoring his discussion with a short history of Western ideas of the primitive in the nineteenth and early twentieth centuries, Li understands the primitivism practiced by the West's "Others" to be, after Spivak, "strategic" (983), performing an "appropriation and resignification" (988) in the course of subverting "Western epistemic regimes" (983). Accordingly, negritude is understood to be a strategic inversion of the terms of Western primitivism, yet it is an inversion that succeeds only in deepening the binary opposition. In concluding, Li pushes against the initial terms of his essay, conceding at the end that the notion of "strategic essentialism" suffers from bad faith and that, rather than offering up compensatory postcolonial identities, primitivist works might have attempted "determined negations": "a proleptic search for alternatives to the inadequacies and immiserations of the present" (1002). On this latter point we are in agreement. See Victor Li, "Primitivism and Postcolonial Literature," in *The Cambridge History of Postcolonial Literature*, vol. 2, ed. Ato Quayson (Cambridge: Cambridge University Press, 2012), 982–1005.

Chapter 4. The Question of Representation

1. Robert Goldwater, *Primitivism in Modern Art*, rev. ed. (New York: Vintage, 1967), 259.

2. Jill Lloyd, *German Expressionism: Primitivism and Modernity* (New Haven, CT: Yale University Press, 1991), 170.

3. Quoted in ibid., 173.

4. Ibid., 181.

5. Ibid., 175.

6. Ibid., 181.

7. See ibid., 182–83.

8. Ibid., 184.

9. See Nicholas Thomas and Diane Losche, eds., *Double Vision: Art Histories and Colonial Histories in the Pacific* (Cambridge: Cambridge University Press, 1999).

10. Quoted in Lloyd, 225.

11. "An original segment of being is lost with the disappearance of the original state of these children of nature." Quoted in Lloyd, 230.

12. See Andrew Zimmerman, "Primitive Art, Primitive Accumulation, and the Origin of the Work of Art in German New Guinea," *History of the Present*, 1 (2011), 17.

13. Lloyd, 220.

14. Zimmerman detects a certain emphasis on skin tone in these depictions when mounting the argument that these depictions are deliberately racialized. I do not find the argument convincing. As Zimmerman himself notes, these are quickly executed and gestural works, and there is no sense that the selection of color has been premeditated to the extent that pigment is precisely captured.

15. This fissure on the question of expressionism is perhaps most famously on show in the debate between Ernst Bloch and György Lukács touched on in Chapter 3. Lloyd refers to this debate several times.

16. Lloyd, 187.

17. Accordingly, that which many art historians have identified as the beginnings of modernism (i.e., the move to abstract composition via the example of African art) would be an impulse that either departs from or has a different aesthetic potentiality from primitivism. When subject gives way entirely to geometry, to paraphrase Goldwater, it wants to leave behind the remnant. The manifestoes of plasticism would be one place to look. The following comment of Josef Čapek's captures the nonprimitivist standpoint of certain modernists in relation to the "ethnographic" objects that gave them impetus: "They did not look here for a model to study, but rather for some sort of stimulation; it was only an episode in the development of young French art, which then went its own way, following its own problems." Josef Čapek, "Negro Sculpture," in *Primitivism and Twentieth-Century Art: A Documentary History*, ed. Jack D. Flam and Miriam Deutch (Berkeley: University of California Press, 2003), 116.

18. Picasso's own comments about the role that African sources played in the evolution of his métier are tantalizing: "I kept looking at the fetishes. I understood: I too am against everything. I understood what the purpose of the sculpture was for the Negroes. . . . They [the fetishes] were used for the same thing. They were weapons. To help people stop being dominated by spirits, to become independent. . . . *Les Demoiselles d'Avignon* must have come to me that day, but not at all because of the forms: but because it was my first canvas of exorcism—yes, absolutely!" (Flam and Deutch, 33). This comment suggests that he perceived himself to be much more in alignment with the primitivist project than familiar narratives of modernism allow.

19. Erhard Schüttpelz, "Zur Definition des literarischen Primitivismus," in *Literarischer Primitivismus*, ed. Nicola Gess (Berlin: Walter de Gruyter, 2012), 13–27.

20. D. H. Lawrence, *The Rainbow* (London: Penguin, 2007), 9; herein *R*.

21. M. M. Bakhtin, "The Bildungsroman and Its Significance in the History of Realism (Toward a Historical Typology of the Novel)," in *Speech Genres and Other Late Essays*, ed. Caryl Emerson and Michael Holquist, trans. Vern W. McGee (Austin: University of Texas Press, 1986), 10–59.

22. Joshua Esty, *Unseasonable Youth: Modernism, Colonialism, and the Fiction of Development* (New York: Oxford University Press, 2012), 7.

23. Not that I want to imply that a given medium or genre will have its own set of primitivizing processes. For instance, in his reading of E. M. Forster's *Howard's End* Fredric Jameson discusses aspects of representation and finitude in Forster's novel that correlate to some of the observations I have made about *The Rainbow*. Jameson likewise discovers that the sensation of vertigo felt by one of Forster's characters when looking at England's transport infrastructure (here it is the Great Northern Road) is in fact the apprehension of an empire without limit. Jameson argues that this is connected to the novel's indictment of the homogenizing effects of a totalizing imperialism, citing comments from Forster's narrator about the all-encompassing grayness of empire that could easily be found in a Lawrence narrative. Jameson concludes that the sensation of total immanence that suffuses the novel points toward a narrative logic in which the limits of knowledge and representation would need to be drawn "back into system." The impulse to "cognitive mapping" using the novel form, Jameson argues, would henceforth be forced to represent "the unrepresentable totality." We might think to make the claim that *Howard's End* and *The Rainbow* are novels that stand at the precipice of a certain tradition of novelistic realism, identifying in them a tendency that would lead others beyond this mode. We could even speculate that this tendency is guided by an emergent consciousness, in Raymond Williams's sense, of a now totalized world-system. This may be true, but it would be absurd to claim, as a corollary, that the movement toward abstraction (or the unrepresentable) is or is not "primitivist"; one must attend to specific materials and contents of the narrative at hand. See Fredric Jameson, "Modernism and Imperialism," in Terry Eagleton, Fredric Jameson, and Edward W. Said, *Nationalism, Colonialism, and Literature* (Minneapolis: University of Minnesota Press, 1988), 43–66, esp. 58.

24. For a synoptic account of French *negrophilie* of the 1920s see Petrine Archer Straw, *Negrophilia: Avant-Garde Paris and Black Culture in the 1920s* (London: Thames and Hudson, 2000).

25. Langston Hughes, *The Ways of White Folks* (New York: Vintage, 1971), 19; herein *WW*.

26. David Chinitz, "Rejuvenation Through Joy: Langston Hughes, Primitivism, and Jazz," *American Literary History*, 9 (1997), 74.

27. For example: "In the blues she made the bass notes throb like tom-toms, the trebles cry like little flutes, so deep in the earth and so high in the sky that they understood everything" (110).

28. Langston Hughes, *The Collected Works of Langston Hughes*, vol. 1, *The Poems: 1921–1940*, ed. Arnold Rampersand (Columbia: University of Missouri Press, 2001), 57.

29. Hughes, *The Poems*, 59.

30. Ibid., 122.

31. Ibid., 122–23.

32. Langston Hughes, *The Collected Works of Langston Hughes*, vol. 9, *Essays on Art, Race, Politics, and World Affairs*, ed. Christopher C. De Santis (Columbia: University of Missouri Press, 2002), 470.

33. Jacques Roumain, *When the Tom-Tom Beats: Selected Prose and Poems*, trans. Joanne Fungaroli and Ronald Sauer (Washington, DC: Azul Editions, 1995), 25 (translation modified).

34. Ibid., 88.

35. Ibid., 93 (translation modified).

36. Ibid., 97, 95.

Chapter 5. Césaire, Fanon, and Immediacy as a Project

1. Theodor W. Adorno, *Aesthetic Theory*, ed. Rolf Tiedemann and Gretel Adorno, trans. Robert Hullot-Kentor (London: Continuum, 2004), 194.

2. I discuss matters of material and materialism in greater depth in Ben Etherington, "What Is Materialism's Material? Thoughts Toward (Actually Against) a Materialism for 'World Literature,'" *Journal of Postcolonial Writing*, 48.5 (2012), 539–51.

3. Frantz Fanon, *Black Skin, White Masks*, trans. Charles Lam Markmann (London: Pluto, 1986), 99 (my emphasis; herein *BS*). Charles Markmann paid no heed to Fanon's intertexts when translating *Black Skin, White Masks*, obscuring the conceptual resources he draws from psychoanalysis, phenomenology, dialectics, and other fields. At the same time, the long life this translation has had in Anglophone scholarship makes it a difficult text to ignore. Rather than provide my own translations, or use Richard Philcox's more recent one, I have retained Markmann's and indicated my modifications with underlining. This will enable readers familiar with his translation to see where the intertexts have been obscured. This procedure has been extended to other translated texts so that the relations between them can be seen clearly. Markmann's translations of literary citations are particularly inadequate. I have translated these myself or have inserted translations from other sources as indicated.

4. I have replaced Markmann's at times lamentable translations of Fanon's citations of Césaire's *Cahier* with the relevant passages from Mireille Rosello and Annie Pritchard's powerful translation of the work. Page numbers supplied in the body of my text are to *Black Skin, White Masks*; endnotes indicate the page number in the Bloodaxe edition of the *Cahier*. Aimé Césaire, *Notebook of a Return to My Native Land*, trans. Mireille Rosello and Annie Pritchard (Newcastle: Bloodaxe, 1995), 111. Rosello and Pritchard translate from the 1956 *Présence Africaine* edition of the *Cahier*, which postdates Fanon's essay. All the passages cited in "The Lived Experience" are common to both editions, however. (Markmann consulted the 1956 edition when conducting his translation.) A. James Arnold has argued that Césaire's revisions to the 1956 edition

brought to the fore the work's socialist politics and diluted the surrealist aesthetics of the 1947 edition (from which Fanon cites). Where Arnold understands this to have diminished the aesthetic force of the work, the argument of this chapter, and indeed this book, is that Césaire's decolonial politics are the expression of that which is latent in the aesthetic project of negritude. What I will identify later in this chapter as Césaire's "passionate sarcasm" is undiminished in the later edition, veering as it does between earnest commitment and abandonment to sarcastic metaphorization. See A. James Arnold, "Beyond Postcolonial Césaire: Reading *Cahier d'un retour au pays natal* Historically," *Forum for Modern Language Studies*, 44.3, 258–75.

5. Frantz Fanon, "L'expérience vécue du noir," *Esprit*, 1951, 657–79. For further details see David Macey, *Frantz Fanon: A Life* (London: Granta, 2000), 154–61.

6. See Césaire, *Notebook of a Return to My Native Land*, 115.

7. Neither translation of *Black Skin* translates with fidelity the compound verb *faire passer* (make pass), so each loses the specifically Hegelian notion of a dialectical movement of consciousness "passing" by negation to a new state. (See *Black Skin, White Masks*, trans. Richard Philcox [New York: Grove, 2008], 161.) It should be kept in mind that in Hegel's conception of dialectical negation the process of "sublation" carries forward the impress of that which has been negated.

8. Jean-Paul Sartre, *What Is Literature?*, trans. Bernard Frechtman (London: Routledge, 2001), 57 (translation modified; herein *WL*).

9. See Sartre, 72, 77, 122, 193. The most resonant instance reads: "concrete literature will be a synthesis of Negativity, as a power of uprooting from the given, and a Project, as an outline of a future order; it will be the Festival, the flaming mirror which burns everything reflected in it" (122).

10. Ato Sekyi-Otu's excellent and sometimes neglected *Fanon's Dialectic of Experience* (Cambridge, MA: Harvard University Press, 1996) is a notable exception. Where Sekyi-Otu reads Fanon's oeuvre as a larger dialectical narrative involving various coordinated speech acts spanning his career, my focus is on Fanon's literary influences and his attempt to dramatize the passage of consciousness within this particular essay.

11. "I have no doubt charity or anger can produce other objects, but they will likewise be swallowed up [in flesh]; they will lose their name; there will remain only things haunted by a mysterious soul (âme obscure). One does not paint meanings; one does not put them to music. Under these conditions, who would dare require that the painter or musician commit himself?" (*WL*, 4–5). Note the connection to Sartre's invocation of *âme noir* in "Black Orpheus," discussed in the next section. Correlations between the figurations of musical and black ontology are discussed in Chapter 7.

12. See Benjamin Suhl, *Jean-Paul Sartre: The Philosopher as a Literary Critic* (New York: Columbia University Press, 1970), 20–22.

13. In an essay on "commitment" Adorno criticizes Sartre's conception of freedom as abstract. He claims Sartre posits freedom of choice in advance of anything concrete in an actual situation that might be chosen. Adorno believes that this effectively reifies freedom, making the concept an end in itself rather than serving as a means toward realizing a free social reality: "What remains is merely the abstract authority of a choice

enjoined, with no regard for the fact that the very possibility of choosing depends on what can be chosen" (180). This disregards Sartre's claims that freedom is not experienced as an open-ended choice but as a demand to make a decision within a particular circumstance. See Theodor W. Adorno, "Commitment," trans. Francis McDonagh, in Ernst Bloch et. al, *Aesthetics and Politics*, ed. Ronald Taylor, trans. Anya Bostock et. al (London: Verso, 2010), 177–95.

14. Sartre explicitly makes the connection between Wright and French Enlightenment writers, particularly Rousseau (*WL*, 83).

15. Jean-Paul Sartre, "Black Orpheus," in *Race*, ed. Robert Bernasconi, trans. John MacCombie, with revisions by Robert Bernasconi (Oxford: Blackwell, 2001), 115–42 (translation modified; herein *BO*). I have modified MacCombie and Bernasconi's translation to demonstrate those points at which Sartre's and Fanon's conceptual vocabularies overlap. Again, modifications have been underscored.

16. Interestingly, in an earlier and shorter article published in *Présence Africaine* that sets out in embryo the argument of "Black Orpheus," Sartre did not use the classical analogue. See Belinda Elizabeth Jack, *Negritude and Literary Criticism: The History and Theory of "Negro-African" Literature in French* (Westport, CT: Greenwood, 1996), 61.

17. He goes on to comment that "any attempt to conceptualize its [negritude's] various aspects would necessarily end up showing its relativity, *whereas it is lived in the absolute through sovereign consciences*, and because the poem is an absolute, it is poetry alone that will allow the unconditional aspect of this attitude to be fixed" (*BO*, 139).

18. Sartre attempts at the end of his essay to reprise the thesis from *What Is Literature?* that literary freedom is enacted in its reception, stating that negritude calls to the "spectator's liberty and absolute generosity" (139), but it is a cut-and-paste job. The "pact of human freedoms" between writer and reader has been inverted: the reader does not offer the freedom of her consciousness as the gift of mediation but receives the writer's self-negating negritude as an already enacted freedom: "it is in the bottom of his heart that the negro finds race, and he must tear out his heart" (*BO*, 138).

19. Léopold Sédar Senghor, ed., *Anthologie de la nouvelle poésie nègre et malgache de langue française*, 2nd ed. (Paris: Presses universitaires de France, 1969), 116 (my translation).

20. James Penney, "Passing into the Universal: Fanon, Sartre, and the Colonial Dialectic," *Paragraph*, 27.3 (2004), 49–67. Kathryn T. Gines treads the theoretical terrain in much the same way as the other essays discussed here in her essay "Fanon and Sartre 50 Years Later: To Retain or Reject the Concept of Race," *Sartre Studies International*, 9 (2003), 55–67.

21. Robert Bernasconi, "The European Knows and Does Not Know: Fanon's Response to Sartre," in *Frantz Fanon's "Black Skin, White Masks": New Interdisciplinary Essays*, ed. Max Silverman (Manchester: Manchester University Press, 2005), 100–111; "On Needing Not to Know and Forgetting What One Never Knew: The Epistemology of Ignorance in Fanon's Critique of Sartre," in *Race and Epistemologies of Ignorance*, ed. Shannon Sullivan and Nancy Tuana (New York: SUNY Press, 2007), 231–40.

22. "Fanon learns about his race, his blackness, from experience as he negotiates for himself the contradiction of his own existence" ("On Needing," 236).

23. Not surprisingly, Bernasconi does not hear Fanon's ironies. He comments, for example, that "Fanon underwrites the view that Whites cannot understand Louis Armstrong" ("The European," 101). In the passage in question Fanon quite obviously is lampooning Mayotte Capécia for espousing precisely this view (*BS*, 44–45).

24. Azzedine Haddour, "Sartre and Fanon: On Negritude and Political Participation," *Sartre Studies International*, 11.1–2 (2005), 286–301.

25. Frantz Fanon, *Toward the African Revolution*, trans. Haakon Chevalier (New York: Monthly Review Press, 1967), 43.

26. Ibid., 42–43.

27. Janheinz Jahn, *A History of Neo-African Literature: Writing in Two Continents*, trans. Oliver Coburn and Ursula Lehrburger (London: Faber and Faber, 1968), 265.

28. Fanon continued to show deep concern for his authorial voice. In correspondence with Daniel Guérin several years later he would write: "I want my voice to be brutal, I do not want it to be beautiful, I do not want it to be pure. I want it to be completely strangled. I do not want my voice to enjoy this." Quoted in Macey, 159 and 273.

29. The following lines from Césaire's *Cahier* may well have been at the back of his mind: "words which are tidal waves and erysipelas and malarias and lavas and bushfires, blazes of flesh, and blazes of cities" (Césaire, *Notebook of a Return to My Native Land*, 99). Macey comments on the Césairean resonances when he too cites Jeanson; see Macey, 157.

30. Quoted in Macey, 210.

31. Peter Geismar, *Fanon: The Revolutionary as Prophet* (New York: Dial, 1971), 23.

32. The following comment from Keston Sutherland's essay on the cognitive content of Marx's style is apposite: "risks and failures of style are arguments in themselves, irreducible to theoretical propositions." "Marx in Jargon," *World Picture*, 1 (2008), 5.

33. Césaire published *Discourse on Colonialism* with Éditions Reclamé in 1950. See David Alliot, *Aimé Césaire: Le nègre universel* (Gollion: Infolio, 2008), 118–19. Fanon cites the work in chapter 4 of *Black Skin* (91–92) and uses an excerpt from it as an epigraph to the introduction (9).

34. Aimé Césaire, *Discourse on Colonialism*, trans. Joan Pinkham (New York: Monthly Review Press, 1972), 38–39.

35. Césaire, *Notebook of a Return to My Native Land*, 98–99 (translation modified).

36. Cited in Lilyan Kesteloot, *Black Writers in French: A Literary History of Negritude*, trans. Ellen Conroy Kennedy (Washington, DC: Howard University Press, 1991), 35.

37. Carrie Noland, "Red Front/Black Front: Aimé Césaire and the Affaire Aragon," *Diacritics*, 36 (2006), 80.

38. Of the polemics in *Black Skin*, this is perhaps the riskiest. Diop was a founding member of *Présence Africaine* and influential in black intellectual circles in France. The significance of using Césaire's voice to discredit Diop would not have been missed among francophone intellectuals.

39. Césaire, *Notebook of a Return to My Native Land*, 115 (translation modified).

40. René Ménil, *Antilles déjà jadis, précédé de "Tracées"* (Paris: Jean-Michel Place, 1999), 90 (Ménil's emphasis; my translation).

41. Theodor W. Adorno, *Aesthetic Theory*, ed. Gretel Adorno and Rolf Tiedemann, trans. Robert Hullot-Kentor (London: Continuum, 2004), 25.

42. Jean-Paul Sartre, *Being and Nothingness: An Essay on Phenomenological Ontology*, trans. Hazel E. Barnes (London: Routledge, 2003), 282–88.

43. Jean-Paul Sartre, *Nausea*, trans. Robert Baldick (London: Penguin, 2000), 123–24, 125.

44. David Trotter, "Fanon's Nausea," *Parallax*, 5 (1999), 40.

45. Fanon was well aware of this passage, and he comments on it in chapter 6 of *Black Skin*. Again, it is to the effect that racial mediations can only be broken by being passed through:

> While he was in France, studying for his degree in literature, Césaire "*recovered* his cowardice." He knew that it was cowardice, but he could never say why. He felt that it was ridiculous, idiotic, I might say even unhealthy, but in none of his writings can one trace the mechanism of that cowardice. That is because what was necessary was to shatter the current situation and to try [to] apprehend reality with the soul of the child. *The tram nigger was comical and ugly. For sure, Césaire amused himself* [*Le nègre du tramway était comique et laid. Pour sûr, Césaire s'amusa*]. That was because there was nothing in common between himself and this authentic Negro. (193)

46. Trotter, 39–40.

47. Césaire, *Notebook of a Return to My Native Land*, 115.

48. Gary Wilder, "Here/Hear Now Aimé Césaire," *South Atlantic Quarterly*, 115.3 (2016), 585–604.

49. Michael Richardson, ed., *Refusal of the Shadow: Surrealism and the Caribbean*, trans. Michael Richardson and Krzysztof Fijałkowski (London: Verso, 1996).

50. In several respects my reading of *Cahier*'s rhetoric as anti-ironic, passionate sarcasm is indebted to Timothy Brennan's essay "The Case Against Irony," *Journal of Commonwealth Literature*, 49.3 (2014), 379–94.

51. Antonio Gramsci, *Prison Notebooks*, vol. 1, ed. and trans. Joseph Buttigieg (New York: Columbia University Press, 2011), 117–18.

52. Christopher L. Miller, "The (Revised) Birth of Negritude: Communist Revolution and 'the Immanent Negro' in 1935," *PMLA*, 125.3 (2010), 745–46; Natalie Melas, "Poetry's Circumstance and Racial Time: Aimé Césaire, 1935–1945," *South Atlantic Quarterly*, 115.3 (2016), 479–80. I have used Miller's translation of the passage from Césaire's "Conscience raciale et révolution sociale."

53. Melas, 480.

54. In saying this, I do not mean that the poem has only one rhetoric and voice. Rather, the moments of passionate sarcasm are enabled by the work's rhetorical dexterity and rapid stylistic shifts. Gregson Davis has written a perceptive essay on the *Cahier*'s mixture of registers, which also cites some excellent passages of commentary from an unpublished paper delivered by Derek Walcott. See Gregson Davis, "Forging a Caribbean Literary Style: 'Vulgar Eloquence' and the Language of Césaire's *Cahier d'un retour au pays natal*," *South Atlantic Quarterly*, 115.3 (2016), 457–67.

55. Césaire, *Notebook of a Return to My Native Land*, 113–15 (translation modified).

56. Richard Wright, *Native Son* (London: Vintage, 2000), 136.

57. Ibid., 159–60.

58. Ibid., 179.

59. This marks the difference between my approach and Benita Parry's in her essay "Resistance Theory/Theorizing Resistance or Two Cheers for Nativism," in her *Postcolonial Studies: A Materialist Critique* (London: Routledge, 2004), 37–54, in which she brings together many of the passages that I also have considered. She, however, sees the "drama of consciousness" in Fanon's essay as setting the pattern for an ongoing attempt to articulate the transition from negritude to universal solidarity and the "radical hope of a realized humanism" (54). Unlike the critics on the "Black Orpheus" debate considered earlier, Parry does see that Fanon's notion of decolonization "as the agency of a transfigured social condition" sublates (and does not reject) negritude. By examining Fanon's style within the essay form, I have supplemented and augmented Parry's description by showing with greater specificity the aesthetic materials through which Fanon grounds his political convictions. This has meant moving away from the notion that Fanon writes "resistance theory." The aim has been to bring out the dialectic of aesthetics and politics rather than to conflate them.

60. Fanon, *Toward the African Revolution*, 23–24.

61. Ibid., 37.

Chapter 6. D. H. Lawrence's Narrative Primitivism

1. See Peter J. Beurton, Raphael Falk, and Hans-Jörg Rheinberger, eds., *The Concept of the Gene in Development and Evolution: Historical and Epistemological Perspectives* (Cambridge: Cambridge University Press, 2000), 337.

2. Of course, many eugenicists claimed that belonging to certain racial groups precludes specialized cognitive activity. For a detailed account of one context in which eugenics was used to argue that different races have stronger or weaker cognitive faculties, see Chloe Campbell, *Race and Empire: Eugenics in Colonial Kenya* (Manchester: Manchester University Press, 2007).

3. D. H. Lawrence, *Fantasia of the Unconscious* (London: Heinemann, 1961), 163.

4. Ibid., 112.

5. D. H. Lawrence, *Studies in Classic American Literature* (London: Penguin, 1971), 91.

6. Lawrence, *Fantasia of the Unconscious*, 9.

7. Ibid.

8. Lawrence, *Studies in Classic American Literature*, 31.

9. See Vincent Sherry, "Wyndham Lewis," in *The Cambridge History of Literary Criticism*, vol. 7, *Modernism and the New Criticism*, ed. George Alexander Kennedy and A. Walton Litz (Cambridge: Cambridge University Press, 2000), 138–50.

10. Wyndham Lewis, *Paleface* (London: Chatto and Windus, 1929), 6; herein *P*.

11. "This absolute valorization almost in defiance of reality, objectively indefensible, assumes an incomparable and subjective importance." Frantz Fanon, *Toward the African Revolution*, trans. Haakon Chevalier (New York: Monthly Review Press, 1967), 43.

12. Fredric Jameson, *Fables of Aggression: Wyndham Lewis, the Modernist as Fascist* (Berkeley: University of California Press, 1979), 21.

13. Frantz Fanon, *Black Skin, White Masks*, trans. Charles Lam Markmann (London: Pluto, 1986), 186.

14. "It has been my intention to stress that the fiery ethics of the Melting-pot are conjunctly european and protestant in origin more than anything else" (*P*, 281).

15. In a similar vein he comments earlier: "my position is that I am ready and most anxious to assist all those who suffer from *paleness* of complexion and all those under a cloud because their grandfathers exterminated the Redskins, or bought and sold cargos of Blacks" (*P*, 3).

16. Wyndham Lewis, *Time and Western Man* (London: Chatto and Windus, 1927), 209.

17. Ibid., 480. Almost immediately Lewis admits that this neo-Berkeleyanism is inadequate:

> we think, for instance, that the mind, *in its unconscious part*, could be said to maintain the mountains, tables and chairs in imaginative sub-existence, when not directly objects of perception: and I think we should be justified in saying that by some analogical process the inside of an elm or a cedar, for example, could be said to be there, although it has never been perceived. When the food goes into the body we can *feel* it, of course, so that gives us back our own insides, even on the berkeleyan basis. It has not been with a view to promoting any theory of my own, however, that I undertook the writing of this essay. (480–81; my emphasis)

Again, Lewis is happy to admit to the inconsistencies in his argument.

18. Ibid., 271.

19. Lewis argues that philosophers like Spengler and Bergson call on art to convey the temporality of a cognition that reaches beyond the correctness of discrete propositions; artists like Stein and Lawrence call on time philosophy to justify their artistic rejection of spatiality and representation.

20. "Mr. Lawrence is beneath the spell of this evolutionist, emotional, non-human, 'mindless' philosophy" (*P*, 176–77).

21. Lawrence, *Fantasia of the Unconscious*, 72.

22. I would like to acknowledge Michael Bell's excellent monograph *D. H. Lawrence: Language and Being* (Cambridge: Cambridge University Press, 1992), which covers similar ground to that which follows, though from a different vantage. My argument situates Lawrence's primitivism in the context of the imperialist world-system rather than with respect to modernism and the development of the novel form in Europe only. So, while I agree with claims such as "conscious primitivism is by definition incompatible with the mode of being it is seeking to recover," I do not think this can be accounted for in terms of the limits of the novel form within the European tradition alone (see 192) or that it "grows with a fatal logic from his personal and artistic difficulties" (206).

23. D. H. Lawrence, *Women in Love* (London: Penguin, 2000), 250; herein *WL*. Emphases in the second paragraph are mine; the remainder are Lawrence's.

24. Wyndham Lewis, *The Apes of God* (London: Nash and Grayson, 1931), 39.

25. For instance: "This pivotal scene illustrates the way that the image of black female flesh as the embodiment of such an extreme female sensual primitivism that it is beyond the known, serves as an instrument of Lawrence's attempt to affect the resurrection of the white male body." Stephane Dunn, "'I Thought There Was No "Real" Sex Left': D. H. Lawrence and the Sexed Vision of Black Femininity," in *Like a Black and White Kaleidoscope Tossed at Random*, ed. Philippe Romanski and Jean-Paul Pichardie (Rouen: Publication de l'université de Rouen, 2001), 66.

26. Joseph Schumpeter, *Capitalism, Socialism and Democracy* (London: Routledge, 1976), 83.

27. D. H. Lawrence, *New Poems* (New York: B. W. Huebsch, 1920), vi, ix.

28. Halliday reads aloud the following from a letter Birkin writes: "Surely there will come an end in us to this desire . . . [for] going back to the savages for our sensations, always seeking to *lose* ourselves in some ultimate Black sensation, mindless and infinite—burning only with destructive fires, raging on with the hope of being burnt out utterly" (*WL*, 384).

29. Bell, 170.

30. D. H. Lawrence, *The Plumed Serpent* (London: Wordsworth Editions, 2009), 208; herein *PS*.

31. See Jed Esty and Colleen Lye, "Peripheral Realisms Now," *Modern Language Quarterly*, 73.3 (2012), 269–88.

32. For example, see the overlapping repetitions of "dark," "phallic," "cloud," "zenith," "twilight," and "blood" at pp. 280–81.

33. Bell comments that *The Plumed Serpent* "asserts doctrinally the importance of the pre-conscious while its actual narrative language, in keeping with its principal personae, is highly self-conscious and explicit" (Bell, 168).

34. J. M. Coetzee, *White Writing: On the Culture of Letters in South Africa* (Braamfontein: Pentz, 2007), 143.

35. For example, Rupert asks: "Is every man's life subject to pure accident, is it only the race, the genus, the species, that has a universal reference? Or is this not true, is there no such thing as pure accident?" (*WL*, 26).

36. Coetzee, 144.

37. Ibid., 156.

38. This anticipates Fanon's comments on the Manichean antagonism of peasants in *The Wretched of the Earth*: "The pride of the peasant, his reluctance to go down into the towns and rub shoulders with the world built by the foreigner, and the way he constantly shrank back every time an agent of the colonial regime approached, served as a permanent reminder that he was pitting his own dichotomy against that of the colonist." Frantz Fanon, *The Wretched of the Earth*, trans. Constance Farrington (Harmondsworth: Penguin, 1967), 88–89.

39. D. H. Lawrence, *Studies in Classic American Literature*, 40.

40. Lawrence's novels of the 1920s are often referred to as his "leadership novels," with *The Plumed Serpent* routinely cited as the worst offender.

41. See, for example, Cedric Watt's introduction to the Wordsworth Classics edi-

tion to which I have been referring (*PS*, xv–xix). My discussion is by no means the only attempt to read *The Plumed Serpent* in its colonial context. Euyung Oh has written an interesting account of the novel as a "rewriting of the colonized history of Mexico" (123), interpreting Lawrence's overt anticolonialism in terms of gender politics. She also considers the few other critics who have pointed in this direction. See Euyung Oh, *D. H. Lawrence's Border Crossing: Colonialism in His Travel Writings and "Leadership" Novels* (London: Routledge, 2007), 123–65.

Chapter 7. Claude McKay's Primitivist Narration

1. Léopold Sédar Senghor, *Liberté I: Négritude et humanisme* (Paris: Seuil, 1964), 19. The paragraph is cited in Jacques Louis Hymans, *Léopold Sédar Senghor: An Intellectual Biography* (Edinburgh: Edinburgh University Press, 1971), 90.

2. Senghor, 19.

3. Senghor, 21. The translation is Brent Hayes Edwards's from *The Practice of Diaspora: Literature, Translation, and the Rise of Black Internationalism* (Cambridge, MA: Harvard University Press, 2003), 188. I have made one modification, "plunging," for "diving," in view of the importance this word has in the negritude lexicon.

4. Claude McKay, *Banjo*, trans. Ida Treat and Paul Vaillant-Couturier (Paris: Rieder, 1931). As Edwards notes, Senghor's citation of the translation is not exact. See Edwards, 361–62n8. The original passage in English is: " 'Getting down to our native roots and building up from our own people,' said Ray, 'is not savagery. It is culture.' " Claude McKay, *Banjo: A Story Without a Plot* (New York: Harvest, 1957), 200; herein *B*. Both the translation and Senghor's misquotation replace "native" with "race."

5. Senghor, 116. The following citations, along with comments of a similar nature, have been rehearsed in different combinations in a variety of publications over the last thirty years. The most rigorous discussions can be found in Edwards, *The Practice of Diaspora*; Gary Wilder, *The French Imperial Nation-State: Negritude and Colonial Humanism Between the Two World Wars* (Chicago: University of Chicago Press, 2005); and Michel Fabre, *From Harlem to Paris: Black American Writers in France, 1840–1980* (Urbana: University of Illinois Press, 1991).

6. "An Interview with Aimé Césaire," in Aimé Césaire, *Discourse on Colonialism*, trans. Joan Pinkham (New York: Monthly Review Press, 1972), 71.

7. Cited in Chidi Ikonné, *Links and Bridges: A Comparative Study of the Writings of the New Negro and Negritude Movements* (Ibadan: University Press, 2005), 158.

8. For an account of *Banjo*'s dissemination see Fabre, 154. The excerpt in *Revue du monde noir* was translated separately before the full French translation appeared.

9. The latter, along with the Césaire and Léro led *L'Étudiant noir*, has gained seminal status in the history of black francophone radicalism, whether justified or not. In French scholarship see Lilyan Kesteloot, *Les écrivains noirs de langue française: Naissance d'une littérature* (Bruxelles: Université de Bruxelles, Institut of Sociologie, 1977); in English see Michael Richardson's introduction to *Refusal of the Shadow: Surrealism and the Caribbean*, ed. Michael Richardson, trans. Michael Richardson and Krzysztof Fijałkowski (London: Verso, 1996). Edwards argues that the journal was only a minor voice within a

blooming black print culture: "*Légitime Défense* looks much less like a radical break and much more like the loud but rather hasty student journal that it was" (Edwards, 191). A full account of this intellectual moment can be found in Wilder, 149–200.

10. The popularity of this area of research since Paul Gilroy's *The Black Atlantic: Modernity and Double Consciousness* (Cambridge, MA: Harvard University Press, 1993) has seen McKay's reputation greatly augmented. See also Michelle Ann Stephens, *Black Empire: The Masculine Global Imaginary of Caribbean Intellectuals in the United States, 1914–1962* (Durham, NC: Duke University Press, 2005).

11. Léon Damas commented, "We read *Banjo* and found it wonderful. Why? Because all the same it had chosen Marseille; it had chosen the black-French problem which concerned us in particular. And it had clearly understood our problems." Cited in Ikonné, 158–59.

12. This is evident in the following passage from "An Interview with Aimé Césaire" (Césaire, 68), a conversation between René Depestre and Césaire:

R.D. That's how surrealism has manifested itself in your work: as an effort to reclaim your authentic character, and in a way as an effort to reclaim the African heritage.

A.C. Absolutely.

R.D. And as a process of detoxification.

A.C. A plunge into the depths. It was a plunge into Africa for me.

13. Though their arguments follow different paths, the following critics share the tendency to approach McKay's literary work as the container of a cultural critique that the critic must extract: Leah Rosenberg: "*Banjo* links an explicit critique of European modernist aesthetics with a critique of European and U.S. modernity." Leah Rosenberg, "Caribbean Models for Modernism in the Work of Claude McKay and Jean Rhys," *Modernism/Modernity*, 11.2 (2004), 223; Michael Maiwald: "I will demonstrate how McKay in *Home to Harlem* engages a critique of capitalism and its role in maintaining racial hierarchies." Michael Maiwald, "Race, Capitalism, and the Third-Sex Ideal: Claude McKay's *Home to Harlem* and the Legacy of Edward Carpenter," *MFS Modern Fiction Studies*, 48.4 (2002), 826; Gary Edward Holcomb: "McKay's three key novels collectively articulate a post-nationalist critique of state nationalist hegemony and imperialist ideology." Gary Edward Holcomb, *Claude McKay, Code Name Sasha: Queer Black Marxism and the Harlem Renaissance* (Gainesville: University Press of Florida, 2007), 16.

14. Claude McKay, *A Long Way from Home* (London: Pluto, 1985), 247–48.

15. Claude McKay, *Home to Harlem* (Boston: Northeastern University Press, 1987), 227; herein *HH*.

16. Claude McKay, *The Passion of Claude McKay: Selected Poetry and Prose, 1912–1948*, ed. Wayne F. Cooper (New York: Schocken, 1973), 31.

17. Cultural studies scholars have tended to opt for the latter: "Like [Judith] Butler, he [McKay] challenges the conception of a 'natural' self who exists a priori to the construction of cultural identity" (Holcomb, 10). "I would also suggest that within this vision of 'ancient black life rooted' are multiple racial significations that, like mercury, flow both toward and away from ideas of blackness as an essentialist physiological basis to racial identity" (Stephens, 153).

18. "A Negro Writer to His Critics," in McKay, *The Passion of Claude McKay*, 137.

19. McKay, *The Passion of Claude McKay*, 137.

20. Edwards, 203–5.

21. This possibility is also entertained by Leo Hamalian in "D. H. Lawrence and Black Writers," *Journal of Modern Literature*, 16.4 (1990), 584.

22. Wyndham Lewis has as much scorn for Lawrence's musical biases as he does his sanctification of "primitives": "the Mexican Indian is purely emotional—'musical,' in a word." Wyndham Lewis, *Paleface: The Philosophy of the "Melting-Pot"* (London: Chatto and Windus, 1929), 176. This comment comes before a section titled "Spengler and the 'Musical' Consciousness," in which Lewis lays out the "musical" ethos that he claims drives Lawrence's primitivism.

23. D. H. Lawrence, *Aaron's Rod* (London: Penguin, 1950), 345; herein *AR*.

24. See, e.g., *AR*, 36, 51, 59, 108, 182, 238, 333.

25. McKay, *A Long Way from Home*, 254.

26. See Alan Lomax, *Mister Jelly Roll: The Fortunes of Jelly Roll Morton, New Orleans Creole and "Inventor of Jazz"* (London: Cassell, 1952), 147–54.

27. See also *Banjo*, 54.

28. McKay insisted that he had not read Van Vechten's novel until he had almost completed *Home to Harlem*. McKay, *A Long Way from Home*, 282–83.

29. Carl Van Vechten, *Nigger Heaven* (New York: Knopf, 1926), 281.

30. Elsewhere in *Banjo* a white sailor is killed by a pimp (*B*, 99–100); we hear a story of American sailors brawling with Senegalese (*B*, 197–98), and the former lover of a chauffeur enters a bar and empties a revolver into him (*B*, 300).

31. See Wayne F. Cooper, "Foreword to 1987 Edition," in McKay, *Home to Harlem*, xvii.

32. Michael North also comments on the importance of the relation between unreflective immediacy and conscious reflection in McKay's treatment of character in *Banjo*: "there is so much discussion of earthy primitivism in the novel, in fact, that it is easy to miss how much of it remains pure discussion and how the unreflective activities of the international cast of *Banjo* are raised time and again to consciousness. As McKay defended what seemed to some critics primitivist stereotypes, he defined a peculiarly reflective spontaneity, avidly dissected and evaluated even as it was enjoyed." North understands as resolved what in fact stimulates many of the conflicts and tensions in the narrative. Ray idealizes the primitive precisely because it does not dissect and evaluate itself. When Ray gives Banjo a short lecture on the difference between the romance of their vagabond condition and the "instinct of civilization," Banjo responds: "I can't make out nothing, pardner, about that instinking thing that youse talking about. But I know one thing and that is if I ain't got the stink of life in me, I got the juice" (289). Banjo unwittingly confirms Ray's point: it does not matter what you call it because I already am it. See Michael North, *The Dialect of Modernism: Race, Language and Twentieth-Century Literature* (Oxford: Oxford University Press, 1998), 121.

33. The most overt fissure within the group is between Ray and Goosey, who have an ongoing argument over whether a racial renaissance should take the form of attain-

ing respectability according to white middle-class standards or of embracing the hard living of the black proletariat and drifters. When, in one such encounter, Goosey criticizes Ray for using the word *nigger*, Ray is "swept by a brainstorm" and accuses Goosey of being "half baked, half educated, full of false ideas about Negroes," furiously ending, "sometimes you get me so worked up with your niggery bull, I feel like giving you a poke in your stupid yaller jaw" (*B*, 183). Sensing an opportunity, Goosey responds by attacking Ray for having "no race pride": "You can't go back to Haiti. You feel there is no place for you in Africa, after you've hung around here, trying to get down into the guts of the life of the Senegalese. . . . You pretend you'd like to be a vagabond like Malty and Banjo here, but you know you're a liar and the truth is not in you" (183–84). This is the only point that the difference between Ray and the others is so openly expressed and is perhaps the novel's tensest moment. Ray knows that he cannot claim an equivalent status to the others, and none of them comes to his defense.

34. Frantz Fanon, *Black Skin, White Masks*, trans. Charles Lam Markmann (London: Pluto, 1986), 186–87, 135.

35. Frantz Fanon, *The Wretched of the Earth*, trans. Constance Farrington (Harmondsworth: Penguin, 1967), 183.

36. Aimé Césaire, "Poetry and Knowledge," in Richardson, 140.

Conclusion

1. Simon Jarvis, *Adorno: A Critical Introduction* (Oxford: Polity, 1998), 117.

2. I am referring to questions that arise when reconceiving of primitivism as an aesthetic project specific to the moment of Imperialism. There has been a lively discussion of primitivism and gender and sexuality within the poststructuralist paradigm. Citing just the most prominent example, Robin Hackett considers the gendered nature of primitivism in her book-length study *Sapphic Primitivism: Productions of Race, Class, and Sexuality in Key Works of Modern Fiction* (New Brunswick, NJ: Rutgers University Press, 2004).

3. See in particular Gary Edward Holcomb, *Claude McKay, Code Name Sasha: Queer Black Marxism and the Harlem Renaissance* (Gainesville: University Press of Florida, 2007).

4. Take the following passage from Hurston's short essay "How It Feels to Be Colored Me." In it the relationship between the remnant and the lost social reality to which it testifies is perhaps more direct than in any of the works I have discussed:

This orchestra grows rambunctious, rears on its hind legs and attacks the tonal veil with primitive fury, rending it, clawing it until it breaks through to the jungle beyond. I follow those heathen—follow them exultingly. I dance wildly inside myself; I yell within, I whoop; I shake my assegai above my head, I hurl it true to the mark *yeeeeooww*! I am in the jungle and living in the jungle way. My face is painted red and yellow and my body is painted blue. My pulse is throbbing like a war drum. I want to slaughter something—give pain, give death to what, I do not know. But the piece ends. The men of the orchestra wipe their lips and rest their fingers. I creep back slowly to the veneer we call civilization with the last tone and find the white friend sitting motionless in his seat, smoking calmly.

The details of the world beyond civilization's veil are sketchy and nonspecific—she uses the Latinate term for African spear, for instance—and Hurston only vaguely intuits its social codes, yet its illusory presence nevertheless consumes her. The register is playful, perhaps bordering on satiric, but, as with Hughes and Césaire, we risk anachronism if we want to cast this passage as only an ironic comment on stereotypes. Zora Neale Hurston, *I Love Myself When I Am Laughing . . . and Then Again When I Am Looking Mean and Impressive: A Zora Neale Hurston Reader*, ed. Alice Walker (Old Westbury, NY: Feminist Press, 1979), 154. The essay was first published in *World Tomorrow* in 1928. For a survey of critical responses to this passage see Brian Carr and Tova Cooper, "Zora Neale Hurston and Modernism at the Critical Limit," *MFS Modern Fiction Studies*, 48.2 (2002), 285–313. Susanna Pavloska has discussed Hurston's primitivism according to the conception of primitivism that this study has critiqued in *Modern Primitives: Race and Language in Gertrude Stein, Ernest Hemingway and Zora Neale Hurston* (London: Routledge, 2013), 75–98.

5. Jean-Paul Sartre, *Being and Nothingness: An Essay on Phenomenological Ontology*, trans. Hazel E. Barnes (London: Routledge, 2003), 151.

6. Ibid.

7. Quoted in Jacques Louis Hymans, *Léopold Sédar Senghor: An Intellectual Biography* (Edinburgh: Edinburgh University Press, 1971), 71.

8. Guy Endore, *Babouk* (New York: Vanguard, 1934), 107; herein *Ba*.

9. C. L. R. James, *The Black Jacobins: Toussaint L'Ouverture and the San Domingo Revolution* (London: Penguin, 2001), 234; herein *BJ*.

10. Sascha Morrell, "Percussion and Repercussion: The Rhythms of Revolution in Guy Endore's *Babouk* (1934) and C. L. R. James's *Black Jacobins* (1938)," presented at the Australian Association for Caribbean Studies Conference 2015, University of Wollongong.

11. Warwick Research Collective, *Combined and Uneven Development: Towards a New Theory of World-Literature* (Liverpool: Liverpool University Press, 2015), 15.

12. See, e.g., Michael D. Bordo, Alan M. Taylor, and Jeffrey G. Williamson, eds., *Globalization in Historical Perspective* (Chicago: University of Chicago Press, 2007).

13. Alexander Veselovsky, "Envisioning World Literature in 1863: From the Reports on a Mission Abroad," trans. Jennifer Flaherty and Boris Maslov, *PMLA*, 128.2 (2013), 439–51.

14. Erich Auerbach, "Philology and *Weltliteratur*," trans. Maire Said and Edward Said, *Centennial Review*, 13.1 (1969), 1–17.

15. Edward Said, *Culture and Imperialism* (London: Chatto and Windus, 1993).

16. Quoted by Emilio Betti in "Hermeneutics as the General Methodology of the *Geistewissenschaften*," trans. Josef Bleicher, in *The Hermeneutic Tradition: From Ast to Ricouer*, ed. Gayle L. Ormiston and Alan D. Schrift (Albany: State University of New York Press, 1990), 189.

17. Auerbach, 3.

18. Aimé Césaire, "Letter to Maurice Thorez," trans. Chike Jeffers, *Social Text*, 28.2 103 (2010), 152.

19. See also "Making and Remaking the Sun" (75–77) and "Dwelling I" (37). Aimé Césaire, *Solar Throat Slashed: The Unexpurgated 1948 Edition*, trans. A. James Arnold and Clayton Eshleman (Middletown, CT: Wesleyan University Press, 2011).

20. Césaire, *Solar Throat Slashed*, 151. I have modified one word of Arnold and Eshleman's translation: "denatured" for "unnatural" in view of the temporality implied in "frères dénaturés."

21. André Breton, *Mad Love*, trans. Mary Ann Caws (Lincoln: University of Nebraska Press, 1988), 87.

22. Césaire, *Solar Throat Slashed*, 113.

23. Ibid.

INDEX

Note: page numbers followed by n refer to notes, with note number.